The Mystery of
GEORGES SIMENON

The Mystery of
GEORGES SIMENON

A Biography

Fenton Bresler

BEAUFORT BOOKS, INC.
NEW YORK

For
Graham Tarrant

Published in the United States by Beaufort Books, Inc., New York
Published in Canada by General Publishing Co. Limited
Published in Great Britain by William Heinemann Ltd

Library of Congress Cataloging in Publication Data

Bresler, Fenton S.
    The mystery of Georges Simenon: a biography
    1. Simenon, Georges, 1903–   —Biography
2. Novelist, French—20th century—Biography
I. Title.
PQ2637.I53Z59 1983 843'.912   82–24302
ISBN 0–8253–0145–9

Printed in Great Britain

Contents

Illustrations

vii

ILLUSTRATIONS

Between pages 150 and 151 (contd)

Annette de Bretagne in 1939 (*Annette de Bretagne*)

The village of Cerizay, set fire to by the Germans in August, 1945 (*Constant Vaillant*)

Members of the FFI, French resistance fighters (*Keystone Press Agency*)

Charcoal drawing of G. S. by Régine Renchon, the first Mme Simenon (*Simenon Foundation, University of Liège*)

Régine at Lakeville, Spring 1953 (*Maxine Mallach*)

The Simenon home at Lakeville, Connecticut (*Fenton Bresler*)

G. S. and two-year-old John, March 1952 (*Keystone Press Agency*)

At the Venice Film Festival with Denise, August 1958 (*Keystone Press Agency*)

Between pages 214 and 215

Denise Simenon (*née* Ouimet) (*Denise Simenon*)

Henriette Simenon, mother of G. S. (*Simenon Foundation, University of Liège*)

The empty house at Epalinges, 1979 (*Ben Lee*)

G. S. with the young Marie-Jo (*François Gonet*)

Marie-Jo a year or two before her death in 1978; and in 1968, aged 15 (*Georges Simenon*)

Pierre Renoir in *La Nuit du carrefour*, 1932 (*Simenon Foundation, University of Liège*)

Jean Gabin with Annie Girardot in *Maigret tend un piège*, 1957 (*Simenon Foundation, University of Liège*)

Charles Laughton as Maigret in *The Man on the Eiffel Tower*, 1948 (*Simenon Foundation, University of Liège*)

Michel Simon in *Brelan d'as*, 1952 (*Simenon Foundation, University of Liège*)

Simone Signoret and Jean Gabin in *Le Chat*, 1970 (*Simenon Foundation, University of Liège*)

Unveiling the statue of Maigret at Delfzijl, September 1966 (*Maria Austria*)

Maigret's 'home' at 130 Blvd. Richard-Lenoir, Paris (*Fenton Bresler*)

John Simenon (*John Simenon*)

Régine Simenon at La Richardière, 1980 (*Fenton Bresler*)

A rare photograph of Teresa taken in April 1979 (*Ben Lee*)

G. S. at home in the 'little pink house' in Lausanne, April 1979 (*Ben Lee*)

Acknowledgements

This book would not have been possible without the kindness and co-operation of Georges Simenon, who has been more than generous with the time that he has put at my disposal, with his permission for me to quote at will from his works and with the readiness that he has displayed to answer my questions. I can only hope that my awareness of the debt of gratitude that I owe him has not affected my objectivity or blurred my judgment.

My thanks are also due to Mme. Régine Simenon, Mme. Denise Simenon, Mme. Teresa, and to Mm. Marc and John Simenon, all of whom have given freely of their time to talk to me.

I owe a special debt to Professor Maurice Piron of the *Centre d'études Georges Simenon* of Liège University for his continuing interest and help and for his kind permission to reprint so many of the photographs in this book.

A lot of people have been of the greatest assistance to me, too many to mention them all by name, but I would like to give particular thanks to the following persons:

France: Mlle. Henriette Liberge, Mme. Mylene Simenon, Mme. Annette de Bretagne, M. Claude Nielsen, Mme. Daisy Paraud and the Library staff at *Presses de la Cité* in Paris, Mr. Sam White, Dr. and Mme. Jean Martinon, Mm. Constant Vaillant, Jim Dindurand and Pierre Chaigneau, M. Gilbert Sigaux, Professor Bernard Alavoine of Amiens University, and Commissaire Marcel Leclerc and M. Philippe de Lagune of the *Police Judiciare* in Paris.

Switzerland: Mme. Joyce (Aitken) Hache, Dr. Pierre Rentchnick.

Belgium: M. Michel Lemoine.

The Netherlands: Professor Hendrik Veldman of Leusden University.

The United States: Mr. and Mrs. Campbell Becket and their daughter, Mrs. Elise Smith, Miss Maxine Mallach, Mr. and Mrs. Ralph McAllister Ingersoll, Mrs. Dorothy James, Mr. William Doolittle, Dr. Robert L. Fisher, Mrs. Orpha Robertson, Mr. Harry Torczyner,

ACKNOWLEDGEMENTS

Mrs. Helen Woolf, Mr. Herbert A. Klein, Mr. Brendan Gill and the Library staff of *Newsweek* magazine in New York.

I would also like to thank the following for giving me permission to quote from published material in copyright: Hamish Hamilton Ltd., for extracts from the English translations of the following works by Georges Simenon: *Pedigree, Maigret's Memoirs, Chez Krull, Maigret in Society, The Patient, The Neighbours, Maigret and the Enigmatic Lett;* William Collins & Co. Ltd., for extracts from *My Life and My Films* by Jean Renoir and from *Paris in the Third Reich* by David Pryce-Jones; Faber and Faber for an extract from *Bloody Murder from the Detective Story to the Crime Novel: A History* by Julian Symons; Routledge & Kegan Paul Ltd., for an extract from the English translation of *Banana Tourist* by Georges Simenon, published by George Routledge & Sons; Robson Books Ltd., for extracts from *Naked at the Feast* by Lynn Haney, published in 1981 (£7.50); for extracts from *Georges Simenon* by Lucille F. Becker, reprinted by permission of Twayne Publishers, a division of G. K. Hall & Co. of Boston, Mass.; for extracts from Brendan Gill's profile of Georges Simenon "Out of the Dark" (January 24, 1953), reprinted by permission: © 1953, 1981 *The New Yorker* magazine; for an extract from Lis Harris' book review "Maigret le Flaneur" (April 2, 1979), reprinted by permission: © 1979 *The New Yorker* magazine; the *Sunday Times* and John Mortimer for an extract from the latter's profile of Georges Simenon (May 16, 1982); the *Observer* for extracts from an interview with Georges Simenon (September 30, 1962); the *New York Times* for an extract from the interview between Georges Simenon and Federico Fellini that appeared in *L'Express* (February 21–27, 1977).

While every effort has been made to contact all copyright holders, I apologise for any errors or omissions that may have occurred.

Fenton Bresler

CHAPTER 1

The Mystery of Georges Simenon

He denies that he is "a phenomenon". "Every time I read in the newspapers about 'the phenomenon of Georges Simenon'," he says, "I remember again how just before the War the London *Daily Mail* published a study on me on the front page with 'The Simenon Phenomenon' in big letters across the whole page. It made me very angry. Why 'a phenomenon'?"

He prefers to call himself "a man like any other" because he does not consider himself an exception. "But that is, of course, exactly what he is," says Claude Nielsen, head of the French publishing house, *Les Presses de la Cité*, that has published him since 1947.

He is, in fact, the most prolific major novelist the world has ever known. He has written so many books that even he does not know the precise number, and in interviews over the years he has constantly quoted a different figure. The nearest assessment is around 220 written under his own name, plus another 200 shorter novels – novellas – written under a total of seventeen pseudonyms back in the twenties when he was "learning his trade".

Both Dashiell Hammett and Raymond Chandler rated him their favourite mystery writer, but he is much more than just that. His most famous character, Inspector Maigret, the Parisian policeman who, with only his pipe and his instinctive knowledge of human nature to help him, solves the most complex crimes, is, as Julian Symons has said, "the archetypal fictional detective of the twentieth century." The Maigret stories have been turned into highly successful television series in countries as different as Britain and Italy, Germany and Japan. Millions of people throughout the world who have never read one of the books know and love Maigret from seeing him on their television screens.

But the Maigret books – eighty-four of them – are much less than half his total output. The rest are psychological thrillers – "hard novels", Simenon calls them – in which he explores the darkest

1

corners of the human mind and, in tautly written prose, creates an atmosphere that is both sinister and entirely his own. André Gide has called him "perhaps the greatest" novelist of contemporary France and François Mauriac, himself no novice, has written, "I am afraid I may not have the courage to descend right to the depths of this nightmare which Simenon describes with such endurable art."

According to a UNESCO survey published in 1972, he is the most translated writer in the world after Lenin, read by an estimated – and staggering – 350 to 500 million people. Indeed he has always, in the years of his maturity, written with the deliberate aim of being translated into the largest possible number of languages and being understood by the greatest number of people.

"I have since the age of eighteen tried to have a style as simple as possible," he told a French interviewer* in February 1978 on the eve of his seventy-fifth birthday. "And that was for a reason: I once read a statistic that revealed that over half the people in France used no more than a total of 600 words. So what was the good of my using abstract words? An abstract word will always have different shades of meaning in the head of two readers: they will never interpret it in the same way. So I always endeavoured to use only 'material' words: a table, a chair, the wind, the rain.

"If it rains, I write, 'It rains': you will not find in my books drops of water that transform themselves into pearls, or I don't know what. I want nothing that resembles literature. I have a horror of literature. For me, Literature with a capital 'L' is rubbish."

Other writers have employed simple words but few with the deliberate universality of Simenon. "It is precisely the lack of adornment in my writing," he told the same interviewer, "that, I think, makes my books read in so many countries that have nothing in common, such as Saudi Arabia, China, Japan or Russia.

"I believe that all men are alike but, in order to perceive that, one has to avoid the picturesque in one's writing. I have twice made a tour of the world and I have never felt myself out of my own country, I have never felt myself 'abroad', never felt myself 'a foreigner'.

"I believe in the universality of human life where everything is the same. Nationalities are a see-saw that pick you up and drop you down by chance, without any basis in reality. I always go to the most general, the most common. I talk of 'my tree' that stands here in the garden of my house, never of 'my cedar'."

His books are not happy, carefree affairs. You are unlikely to burst

*Jean-Louise Egine

2

out laughing when reading them. And they do not contain much spine-chilling suspense, to use the old cliché of the thriller-writer. They are dark, taut studies of human beings pushed to the limit of their characters, explored with such deep instinctive knowledge of human nature that they have become part of the syllabus of university examinations and post-graduate students write learned theses devoted to them.

Yet, for all their sombre value and consummate craftsmanship, they have nearly all been written at breakneck speed in not much more than a week – with, at the end, a compulsive need to indulge in a veritable orgy of sexual activity as "a necessary hygienic measure". It is here, with sex, that we have our first inkling that the "phenomenon" is also a mystery and that the story of Simenon's own life is as dark and compelling as any of his novels – if only we can get at the truth.

Apart possibly from Christopher Isherwood, Simenon would seem to have put more of himself into his writing – whether in his novels or his memoirs on which he embarked when he gave up writing fiction – than any other contemporary novelist; but he is a dangerous guide to follow on a trail into his personal reality. Partly, he genuinely does not know himself all that there is to know about the mainsprings of his own character. When asked during a television interview whether he liked the painter Van Gogh, he replied: "I see maybe there is a kind of comparison with him because Van Gogh was completely unconscious of what he was doing and it is the same with me. We are about the same. Maybe I am not completely crazy, but I am a psychopath."

Partly, he tends, like his favourite American author, William Faulkner, to say in an interview what he thinks the person to whom he is talking would like to hear – or perhaps what he, Simenon, would like them to hear. In a rare moment of unguarded honesty, he has once admitted as much himself. Writing to André Gide in 1939, in a serious and detailed answer to a thoughtful letter about his style and source of working methods, he said: "I prefer to put these things into a letter – face to face, *it would be false*. Automatically, face to face with the person to whom I am talking, I play a role and I become a character in a novel. *Sincerely* I lie [Simenon's own italics]."

Partly, he *insincerely* lies when he feels the truth is too revelatory or he deliberately wishes to erect a false façade behind which he can keep himself intact. Even as astute a critic as Julian Symons, for instance, writing in *The New York Review*,* can say of *Quand j'étais vieux* ("When I Was Old"), a supposedly intimate journal covering the years

*October 12, 1978.

3

1960–2, that it is "disturbingly honest. Nobody reading it could doubt Simenon's love for his wife and children." Whereas the truth is that Simenon was starting to loathe Denise, his wife at that time, with a rare and desperate intensity. "Of course, I wrote well about her," he says now. "She read the journal every day. I *had* to say those things – but they were false." But although he was long since separated from Denise when the book was published in 1970, no corrections were made to the text.

According to Dr. Pierre Rentchnick, a Swiss psychiatrist who with four colleagues once spent a whole day questioning him for a special study that appeared in a Swiss medical journal and was later published as a book under the appropriate title, *Simenon sur le gril*,* he is a fantasist and will not always himself know what is true and what is false.

Given such a complex personality and such a prodigious output, there is plenty of scope for a true-life mystery in the tale of this creator of mysteries.

The first element in the story concerns Simenon's sexuality. He has been twice married – first, for thirty-three years, to a Belgian woman named Régine Renchon, three years his senior; then to the much-younger Denise Ouimet, a French-Canadian from whom he has been bitterly estranged for well over ten years – but at the age of seventy-four, in April 1977, he suddenly chose to enliven a routine interview with a Swiss journalist by making the proud claim that he had had sex with 10,000 women. That awesome piece of news promptly appeared in practically every newspaper in the world. Many commentators scoffed, but undaunted he later enlarged the claim to "tens of thousands of women."

Asked for her views of Simenon's boast, which has now gone into the reference books, Régine says: "All I can say is that in all the time we lived together, I knew nothing about it – but I suppose, if you chase after it like a rabbit, anything is possible. . . ." Denise's comment is more succinct: "Georges always exaggerates. We worked it out ourselves once and it came to no more than 1,200 women. Ten thousand really is too much."

But is it true and, even if it is, why make the claim at all? On the one hand, he writes with great tenderness and yearning about the delicacy of women: in *La Femme Endormie* ("The Sleeping Woman"), a volume

*("Simenon on the grill"), Presses de la Cité, 1968.

4

of dictated memoirs published in 1981, for instance, he rhapsodizes about "this kind of adoration that all my life I have reserved for women. Between man and woman, there has been since their birth a fundamental difference that I have always sought to explain to myself." Whereas, in reality, he treats sexual satisfaction as virtually an emetic release. His one-time secretary, Annette de Bretagne, uses the expression *"les femmes-récréations de Georges Simenon"*, and when explaining the "10,000 women" claim to a *Newsweek* journalist, he himself says: "It's quite a normal number – even banal. I know a lot of friends who are in the same situation. Why did I do it? When you are hungry, you eat. When you are thirsty, you drink. I would say it is essential."

He then tries to put a more sophisticated gloss on his basic urges and adds, "I am curious about all women and you can't know a woman unless you make love to her. I don't know why everyone is getting so excited about this business. It seems to me just a banal aspect of normal behaviour." Even though he admits that 8,000 of his 10,000 women were prostitutes, he still seeks to put a lofty tone on it all and five years later is assuring John Mortimer in an interview in the London *Sunday Times*: "I tell you, I have found many 'real' women among prostitutes. I treated them with consideration and like a gentleman. I always let them have their pleasure first. And of course I was enough of a connoisseur to know if their pleasure was faked."

But this is only one aspect of the enigma involving this remarkable man. He has become a multi-millionaire for whom money, as such, has long lost all practical significance. As he laconically puts it, "Since I thought of Maigret, I have never been poor." But although he still negotiates all his own contracts and shrewdly only sells the rights for ten years at a time to guard against inflation and the added value of his works, he refuses to invest his wealth and, as he told the five Swiss psychiatrists, he finds it "revolting" to think of his money making more money for him. "I find it completely normal that I should amass wealth by my own efforts," he told them, "but not that my money should do it for me. I am not a capitalist."

His last few years have been spent in almost bare simplicity in a "little pink house", consisting mainly of a single large bedroom/living room, in one of the inner suburbs of Lausanne on the banks of Lake Geneva; while a vast 26-roomed house, that cost millions of Swiss francs to build, stands empty at Epalinges on the hills above the town. He has not even bothered to sell it. His five cars have been sold. His twenty-four Buffets, his Picassos, his Légers, his Soutine and his numerous Vlamincks are in store.

5

And even when he did live at Epalinges, it doesn't seem that he was truly happy there. "When I last saw Georges in that big white house," one American visitor says, "I felt so sorry for him. I wanted to go away and knit him a sweater or something – something that he could have for his very own – as a present. The house was so huge, so impersonal, so cold."

Further examples of the mystery of Georges Simenon, the inconsistencies and the contradictions, abound. More than any other living writer, he is identified with France and, above all, with Paris. Yet he is a Belgian, without a drop of French blood in his veins, who has made his home in Switzerland for the last quarter of a century and who lived in Paris for less than ten years nearly half a century ago.

He announces to the world on his seventieth birthday, in February 1973, that he is giving up writing novels and starting his "retirement". He puts away his IBM electric typewriter, with which he hurled on to paper the words that came thrusting from his mind at the almost computer-like rate of ninety-two a minute, and prints "without profession" on his visiting cards instead of "novelist". He then promptly starts dictating over twenty volumes of memoirs, including one, *Lettre à ma mère* ("Letter to My Mother") – a summing up of his unhappy relationship with his mother viewed from the calm of three years after her death at the age of ninety-one – that is without doubt one of the finest things he has written.

Then, when the dictated memoirs are finished, at the beginning of 1980, he goes back to writing in longhand and takes nearly two years to complete and revise a massive tome of some quarter-of-a-million words, called *Mémoires intimes* ("Intimate Memoirs"), that covers some of the same material again but in much greater detail. Published towards the end of 1981, it is by far the longest work he has ever written: verbose and heavy-handed, it is in a totally different style from any of the novels.

He adores his children and has been a doting father to the point of over-indulgence – only to find that the three older ones could not, for all their love for him, bear living with him and left home as soon as they possibly could. The result in one case was tragedy.

He is fond of proclaiming his belief, inherited, so he says, from his father, in "the little joys of life" – such as "the smell of the first cup of coffee in the morning . . . the fruit and the vegetables in the market, the flowers, the girls on the street, the birds singing in the trees, everything!" But his own son, John, now an executive for an American film company in London, gives a harsher, more realistic assessment: "My grandfather was the ideal father Dad would like to be – but cannot! Calm and happy. My father *has* that theory of 'the little joys of life' and one of the reasons probably that he cherishes this (and by the way it is one of the first things he ever talked to me about) is that it is so difficult for him to get them, to savour them, *because he is so unquiet a man*."

Simenon admits to his "unquiet" inner life. He says that the characters of his novels entered under his skin, that he was only ready to write when he felt they had taken him over, that at times he was driven to vomit by the pressure within him, that in the highly charged two hours a day that he spent actually writing he *became* his characters. He wrote his novels almost as a sleepwalker (which in his youth he was) in what he has always called "a state of grace." He entered "into a novel as one enters into a religion." But to get himself into this near-mystic condition, and operate within it, he had to resort to the most painstaking, highly detailed routine, with everything laid out on his desk in exactly the same way, even as to the number of sharpened pencils waiting to be used and pipes ready primed with tobacco.

In a rare public lecture on his craft, at the World Fair in Brussels in October 1958, he defined the novel as "a passion that completely possesses and enslaves the writer and permits him to exorcize his demons by giving them a form and casting them out into the world."

What are the demons that lurk within Simenon? He has sought all along, he claims, to present in his novels "the naked man, the one who looks at himself in the mirror while shaving and has no illusions about himself." To seek the naked man in Georges Simenon, one has to embark on an investigation as daunting as any he ever set Inspector Maigret.

CHAPTER 2

Roots, Parents and Birth

Belgium is hardly a country pre-eminent on the international literary scene. Apart from Simenon and possibly Maurice Maeterlinck, author of *The Blue Bird* and Nobel Prize-winner for literature in the earlier years of this century, the best-known Belgian literary figure is probably the fictitious one of Hercule Poirot, Agatha Christie's moustachioed and idiosyncratic detective.

The nation's ten million people, jammed into a space not much more than a third the size of Scotland, have a reputation for being industrious, hard working, good businessmen and marvellous pastry cooks, but for the most part its writers have achieved little fame outside their own borders.

Perhaps one reason is that, despite its small size, Belgium is, in a very real sense, two countries in one. Two quite distinct cultures coexist side by side. Just over half the population are Flemings, living in Flanders in the north, ethnically little different from their Dutch neighbours and speaking a language, Flemish, which is very similar to Dutch. The rest are Walloons, living in the south and ethnically little different from *their* neighbours, the French, whose language they speak with only a slight variation of accent.

Ever since the modern state of Belgium was formed, by insurrection in 1830, when the country threw off the yoke of Dutch rule, this basic dichotomy of language and race has been a major cause of unrest, at times provoking almost civil war. The official language for the whole country used to be French, the Walloon-dominated south being the richer and more industrialised part of Belgium. But in 1962, with Flanders becoming ever wealthier and Flemish nationalism more powerful, a compromise was reached. Flemish was accepted as the official language in the four northern provinces, French in the four southern provinces, with the central province of Brabant, containing Brussels, the capital, officially made bilingual.

The tensions of contending race, language and blood, implicit in the

Belgian national character, find their microcosm in the family background of Georges Simenon. He himself used to claim, based upon
what his French-speaking paternal grandfather had told him, that he
was descended from a Breton soldier in the army of Napoleon who,
having broken his leg in the retreat from Moscow, stopped for the
night in a village near Liège, Belgium's third largest city in the southeast of the country, and then did not bother to hobble on home to
Nantes. He married a local girl, and that was it.

The truth is different. There was no wounded Breton soldier returning from the Napoleonic Wars. Recent research into Belgian
church records has revealed that the earliest traceable ancestor on his
father's side was a Fleming named Lambert Simenon, who was born
in a small village near the Albert Canal in 1732. He eventually moved
to Vlyjtingen in the province of Limburg, where he married and had
children.

Simenon now accepts that his grandfather's tale was charming but
false. "I don't have a drop of French blood in me," he says. "There is
not a drop of Latin blood in my veins. I am a man of the North, purely
from the North. And, even though I shall live in Switzerland till the
end of my days, I am still a man of the North." His paternal ancestors
were, for the most part, all Flemings, and presumably Flemish-speaking
but at some stage someone moved down to the predominantly French-
speaking Liège in the south of the country, and the strain became
admixed with the local Walloons. Some became millers, others small
shopkeepers and one, still living when Simenon was born, entered the
Church and rose to be a bishop. With the exception of the worthy lord
bishop, they were all undoubtedly what Simenon calls *les petits gens*,
members of the lower middle classes; and that is still how he chooses to
regard himself today.

His background on his mother's side is totally different and he
has never made any claim that it was anything other than what it
was. Indeed, throughout his writings there seems to be a love-hate
relationship with the disparate, contending elements that went into his
mother's family and origins. They had no Belgian blood in them at all.
They were neither Flemings nor Walloon but a mixture of Dutch, the
race that formerly ruled Belgium, and German, the race that twice
invaded it. His mother's mother was pure Dutch and her father pure
German.

Désiré Simenon, Georges's father, was tall, erect and handsome like
a soldier with his waxed moustache. When, at the age of twenty-three,
he brought home for the first time to the family kitchen behind his

father's hat shop on the bustling rue Puits-en-Sock in Liège the girl he wanted to marry, his parents looked at petite, twenty-one-year-old Henriette Brull, with her pale grey eyes and light blonde hair, as if she were almost a foreigner. The impact must have been something like that of a Jewish young man bringing home to his parents, in traditional times, a potential bride who was Christian; or (although both Simenons and Brulls were Roman Catholics) like a Roman Catholic Irishman bringing home a Protestant girl in contemporary Northern Ireland.

Throughout her long life, Henriette remained something of a foreigner in the French-speaking Walloon city of Liège. She never spoke the language well, but always with a heavy Dutch accent, and was much happier in her own *patois* of mixed Flemish and German. She was not a natural Liègeoise.

Chrétien Simenon, the Walloon hatmaker, and Marie his wife, the daughter of two generations of Liège mine-workers, never really accepted her. When every Sunday morning after their marriage, Désiré would go round to his parents' house to collect the week's bread that his mother always baked for him (and for her twelve other children, married or not), Henriette would never accompany him; even before she had children of her own and therefore some kind of an excuse not to go.

Socially, too, she and her family were different from the Simenons. By the time of the marriage, she was as lower middle class as they were but she had arrived at that level from a different direction. Désiré's family had worked themselves up to that status from peasant origins. She had fallen to it from a higher social and financial plane.

Henriette's father, Wilhelm Brull, had been a successful businessman, owning barges that plied the canals and rivers of the Low Countries. At one time he had held the important post of dyke master at Herstal, where a vital canal met the River Meuse north above Liège. In an economy so dependent on rivers and waterways, that was almost like being a member of the aristocracy.

But there was in Brull the seed of mental instability and hypertension that was later to show itself in several of his children, two of whom drank themselves to death, another ending her days in a lunatic asylum – literally being dragged off screaming in front of the terrified young Georges.

When Brull was about fifty, in the late eighteen-seventies, he began drinking to excess. One night, when he was drunk, he countersigned some promissory notes for a friend. The friend went bankrupt and

10

Brull was ruined. With the weakness of the coward, unable to face reality, he sank into alcoholism and by 1885, at the age of fifty-seven, he was dead.

His widow, Maria, and the five-year-old Henriette had to leave their splendid large house by the river at Herstal and come to live in a shabby little apartment in the lower middle class district of Outre-Meuse at Liège, in a street even more humble than rue Puits-en-Sock, where hatmaker Chrétien Simenon lived. Times were so bad and Maria Brull so proud that, if she heard someone knock at the door, she would run and put saucepans of water on the stove to boil so that the visitor would think she was cooking a fine stew for her child and herself.

Her twelve other children – all much older than Henriette who had come along when everyone thought Maria was past child-bearing age – did little to help her. One son, a rich farmer's merchant with a château in the country, came to see her and told her that the few worthwhile pieces of furniture she had salvaged from her former home were "rickety and no good" and that he would get her some new things instead. Whereupon, he carted away the family antiques and generously replaced them with valueless items bought in a cheap furniture store.

Maria Brull remained hard-eyed, haughty and defiant until she died, worn out at the age of sixty-five, in 1901. By then, her daughter had learned to face poverty in her own different, though equally uncompromising, way. "You tended to bow your head," Simenon wrote in *Lettre à ma mère*. "You humbled yourself. You said, 'thank you'. You said, 'Thank you' to everyone and everything, to the woman who sold you milk and even to your sisters."

The Brulls' last born – "a canary for the cat", as Simenon has called her – decided early on that she could only save herself by her own resources. She was proud to be poor and never to ask for anything. She pretended throughout her life to be poorer than she really was, as if poverty itself was a virtue. "We manage with the strict minimum" became her standard expression, the words grating on her son's ears.

When her mother died, Henriette went to live for a brief while with a married sister (who later died from drink); but not as a member of the family. She acted as nursemaid to her niece and nephew and ate in the kitchen with the other servants. With rare courage for a girl of twenty-one in those days, she walked out and got herself a job as sales assistant at Innovation, Liège's leading department store.

It was shortly after starting work at Innovation that she first saw the tall, handsome figure of Désiré Simenon striding past on his way to work. "What a lovely walk!" she said to a fellow shop-girl.

Désiré's way of walking was almost the key to his character. "He walked in long strides, with the regularity of a metronome," says Simenon. In *Pedigree*, he relates how he always left home at the same time so that "his neighbours could tell what time it was without looking at their alarm clocks. Shopkeepers taking down their shutters knew whether they were early or late; big Désiré went by, swinging his legs along at such a regular pace that you might have thought they had been given the task of measuring the passage of time." This is not a novelist son's poetic licence. Professor Maurice Piron of Liège University remembers how his mother, who knew Désiré and Henriette very well as youngsters, would describe the way that Désiré walked: never taking one step bigger than the other, always exactly the same.

Poetic licence *does* come into it when Simenon enthuses that Désiré seemed "to be accompanied always by music which he alone heard and with which his regular steps kept time. Beneath his moustache, his avid lips half opened in a vague smile, which expressed complete inner contentment." He told the Swiss psychiatrists, interrogating him for *Simenon sur le gril*, that his father went to his office exactly as he would have gone to heaven!

Be that as it may, he *was* a handsome man. He held down a good, safe job. He had encouraging prospects. His parents were respectable, stolid and secure. He did not drink, except for one glass of beer on a Sunday. He did not play cards, except for one session a week with his friends, also on a Sunday. He did not gamble. He did not womanise. When he joined a local amateur dramatic society, he chose not to be one of the actors on stage but the club's prompter, sitting in the wings.

What more could a worried young woman, anxious about her future, with nerves inside her taut like violin strings, want from a prospective husband?

She did not know then that he was totally devoid of materialist ambition. That when later he would be asked by his employer to choose between fire and life insurance as a sales career, Désiré would choose fire because life insurance was very new and uncertain; although life insurance was to prove far and away the more lucrative, with the result that a junior colleague, who had chosen the reverse, ended up earning much more money than he did. She did not know then, nor maybe even stop to think, that there was possibly something far deeper lacking between them. In later years, she was to complain to

him: "When I think that I've never heard you once say, 'I love you'."
And he was to reply, almost uncomprehendingly: "But you're here!"
Deep in her heart, the frightened young woman, whom even her own
brother had cheated, wanted more than Désiré, or perhaps any man,
could give her.

In the year 1901 none of that was apparent. No one now knows who
made the first contact between them. Whether it was Désiré doffing
his hat to the pert sales girl, a foot shorter than he, peering out at him
from Innovation's ornate façade, or whether Henriette managed to
contrive a first meeting.

At all events, it was a very brief courtship. Within a few months,
this disparate – some might say, totally inappropriate – couple were
joined together in holy wedlock. They went to live in a small two-
roomed apartment, with water drawn from a communal tap on the
half-landing below, situated over a hat shop on the rue Leopold near
the cobblestoned heart of the city.

It was there early on the morning of Friday, February 13, 1903, that
their first son, Georges, was born. With typical neurosis, his mother
was terrified of the date. She persuaded the family doctor to register
the birth as having taken place a few minutes before midnight on
Thursday, the 12th. Simenon began life with a lie.

Liège, the fat, prosperous bourgeois city of today, with its fleet of
Mercedes taxis, has not in essence changed since that day in February
eighty years ago. Even now, where road-widening schemes, the
effects of two world wars and the anonymous steamroller of late
twentieth-century architecture have done so much to make the city
bland, universal, just like so many others, the River Meuse, with its
barges, tankers and freighters, still puts its stamp on the central areas of
the town as it cuts through the streets like a glacier through rock. One
can well understand why Simenon, from a child, has been obsessed by
boats, the water, canals and rivers.

In Lettre à ma mère, written three years after her death, Simenon tells
her that he is trying to imagine the little girl she once was, "for you
never really know a person unless you've known their childhood." So
it is with him as well. To a French radio interviewer in 1955, he said: "I
think that man only adds to his nature, only grows until he is about
eighteen years old. What you have not absorbed at eighteen, you will
no longer absorb. It's over. You will be able to develop what you have

absorbed. You will be able to make something of it or nothing at all. You have finished the period of absorption and, the rest of your life, you will remain, in consequence, the slave of your childhood and early adolescence.''

Liège, where he spent the first twenty years of his life, is, in a sense, to haunt him for the rest of it. It was a colourful, exciting place in which to spend one's early, formative years: the rich in their carriages; the *petits gens* striding, like his father, top-hatted to work; the miners from the surrounding coal mines, on whom the city's prosperity was in large part based, walking home through the streets, in the days before pithead baths, with their white eyes blinking in their black, grimy faces under the unaccustomed sun; the squads of mounted police charging into mobs of striking workers with their sabres flashing in the air.

There was another, more peaceful, side. In Simenon's own words: "The bluish paving-stones, the tram rattling past, the baker across the street who had come out for a breather, covered in flour and with laughter in his eyes, and the shop assistant who was washing her windows with a chamois leather." And there were the pubs with "sun on the sidewalk. Inside, a bluish shadow, and the waiter, not yet dressed for the day, sweeping up the sawdust or spreading it afresh. Smell of beer. Barrels of beer rolled on the sidewalk, and enormous brewery horses which wait, sometimes striking the pavement with their hooves."

In the autobiographical *Je me souviens* ("I Remember"), Simenon says that among the happiest memories of his childhood were his early morning visits with his mother to the open market, among the baskets and crates of vegetables and fruits. Henriette, deliberately not wearing a hat "because then one paid more," dragging her small child along with her, was heedless of "the most beautiful spectacle in the world in the symphony of muted colours, of blue and of gold, of the early morning."

Then there was the remarkable clan of twenty-four uncles and aunts, their spouses and the sixty first-cousins with whom he grew up. The Simenons were city-dwellers, rooted in their home district of Outre-Meuse (to which Désiré, his wife and baby son moved back six months after Georges's birth), set in their ways and firmly under the thumb of their matriarch, the bread-making miner's daughter, Marie Simenon.

There was little laughter or spontaneous joy on *that* side of young Georges's family. Perhaps the only one whom the child really loved

14

was his great-grandfather, the old miner, Guillaume Moers, called "Vieux-Papa", who, blind and in his eighties, lived with his grand-daughter, Marie, and who every Sunday morning, when Simenon accompanied his father to collect the week's freshly baked bread, would slip a coin into the little boy's hand. One critic has suggested that the silhouette of Maigret, as it first appeared in the early stories of the nineteen-thirties, large, impassive and powerful in his dark over-coat with its black velvet collar, has its origin in the vast figure, "monstrous in size and with hands like a gorilla", sitting in his own special corner of the kitchen with a bear's skin spread over his shoulders.

"Vieux-Papa", who must have been a tough old dog, having his first tooth extracted – and without gas – at the age of eighty-six, was forbidden by his doctor to eat onions, even though they were his favourite. Nearly fifty years later, Simenon was to tell the American writer Brendan Gill, for a profile in *The New Yorker* magazine, how he could still remember his great-grandfather wandering through town stealing off carts. Because he was blind, he assumed that no one could see him.

But with the exception of "Vieux-Papa", the true "characters" were all on Henriette's side; the restless, maladjusted, anguished children of the dead alcoholic, Wilhelm Brull, all seeking in their own way, like Henriette herself, to escape from – or conform to – their destiny.

One brother, Albert, went hunting with nobles and hardly had anything to do with his sister in her "fallen" social position; when she wrote to him, asking to borrow some money to open a small dairy shop – one of several potential money-earning schemes when Simenon was a baby – he did not answer her letter. Another brother, Leopold, was a handsome young man who dropped out of university to become a soldier (and then shocked the family by marrying the regiment's canteen girl), whereafter he dropped out of ordinary life almost entirely by taking odd jobs as a waiter or barman before disappearing for six months or a year at a time when no one, including Eugénie, his wife, would hear from him. She would quietly get a job, and when he returned he would put an advertisement in the newspaper to find her. She never reproached him and they would take up life together again until once more he went off.

He became a drunk and an anarchist, and when Henriette saw him staggering along the streets of Liège she would turn her head and look the other way. Désiré, as might be expected, simply accepted him for what he was and, according to Simenon, was mildly amused to have someone like that in the family.

15

One day, Leopold disappeared for ever – to die, alone, of cancer of the tongue. A few weeks later, Eugénie's body was found in her room; she had starved herself to death. In 1954, Simenon was to tell the story of this great love, transformed into fiction, in *Le Grand Bob* ("Big Bob") one of his few novels that can truly be described as "romantic" and, although tragic, is untouched by the darker side of the moon. The image of his uncle, a man who scorned all normal social life and normally acceptable behaviour by "taking off" whenever he wanted to in search of freedom without responsibility or care, has stayed with him throughout his long life.

The theme of flight is one of the most important in his work and more than once has he sung the praises of the tramp or vagabond. In the early summer of 1968, amid the sterile, millionaire's splendour of the house at Epalinges, he was to tell his five visiting Swiss psychiatrists that Leopold Brull was the favourite of all his uncles. "He was non-conformist. . . . The tramp is the man who lives without concessions of any kind, who can live in the knowledge of his own truth. . . . If it were not for my children, I would not be unhappy to find myself now in the streets of Lausanne without a sou."

His aunts were a motley lot. Most Sunday afternoons were spent visiting one or other of Henriette's sisters. Aunt Marie had a grocery store combined with bar on the Quai de Coronmeuse, where she would supply the boatmen and their families who lived on the waters of the canal. Life on the water and on the water's edge has always fascinated Simenon and he has painted this vivid word-picture, etched into his mind in childhood, of the store and its environs:

> The Quai de Coronmeuse, and with it the canal and the port in which a hundred or two hundred barges, perhaps more, lay side by side, sometimes ten abreast, with washing, drying, children playing, dogs dozing, an invigorating smell of tar and resin. . . . Here was the shop window, an old-fashioned window cluttered up with starch, candles, packets of chicory and bottles of vinegar. Here was the glazed door and its transparent advertisements; the white lion of Remy starch, the zebra of a grate polish, the other lion, the black one, of a brand of wax. And the doorbell, which you would recognize among a thousand others.

> Finally, the unique and wonderful smell of that house where there was nothing commonplace, where everything had a rare, exceptional quality, as if years had been spent on it.

> Was it the smell of gin that predominated? Or was it the more insipid smell of the groceries? For the shop sold everything, barrels oozing American lamp-oil, rope, stable lanterns, whips and tar for boats. There

were jars containing sweets of a doubtful pink and glazed drawers stuffed
with sticks of cinnamon and cloves. . . . And there was another smell too,
the smell of wicker, which came from the end of the corridor, for (Aunt
Marie's) husband was a basket-maker and worked with a hunchbacked
assistant in the back room overlooking the yard.

There was Aunt Marthe, for whom Henriette had briefly worked as
nursemaid for her children. She was the wife of a wealthy wholesale
grocer and lived in an impressive large house opposite the meat
market, which did not prevent her being deeply unhappy and de-
generating into drunken despair. And there was Aunt Félicie – "the
most unfortunate, also the prettiest, the most moving of my aunts,
whom I still see leaning her elbows on the counter of her café in a pose
full of romantic nostalgia." Félicie, too, became an alcoholic and it was
she who was carried off, screaming, to a lunatic asylum. Simenon,
aged only eight or nine, was there when the cab called for her. He
remembers her husband sobbing, with his back braced against the wall
and his head between his hands, and wondering to himself: "What if
some day a cab came and took my mother away?"

For Henriette was not happy. She gave vent to blind rages. She
reacted intensely to the slightest setbacks, the slightest pinpricks. Her
hair being wayward and continually falling down when she was trying
to roll it up into a bun would be enough to make her throw herself on
the bed, sobbing in anguish. It would happen a hundred, two hundred
times – and always Désiré, calm and patient, would counsel Georges
and his young brother, Christian, born three years after him: "Don't
worry, children. Your mother isn't feeling well."

In fact, it was the impending birth of Christian, in September 1906,
that prompted the single disagreement between Désiré and Henriette
which – even at that early stage in their marriage – soured Henriette's
regard for her husband and led to a change in the family's lifestyle. A
change that was to have a profound effect upon Simenon personally
and upon his future development as a writer.

CHAPTER 3

Childhood and Early Sexual Discovery

As in most countries of Western Europe in the early nineteen-hundreds, there was no social security in Belgium, no old age pensions provided by the state. If you fell on hard times, you had to sink or swim by your own efforts; as Henriette had learned only too well. Although Désiré had a good job, it carried no pension. What if anything were to happen to him? What safeguard did she have if once again tragedy struck and she was deprived of her sole breadwinner? For, as was usual at that time, she had given up her own job at Innovation when Georges had been born and the family totally depended on Désiré financially.

Early in 1906, Henriette fell pregnant again and her naturally neurotic, highly-strung temperament became even more overwrought. Soon she would have *two* small children to worry about, if anything happened to their father. There was only one obvious remedy. Désiré worked in an insurance office: why did he not take out an insurance policy on his life? In that way, she would have security. It would be as good as a pension.

So she asked him, and he sidestepped the question. She asked him again, and again he gave her no direct answer. Henriette kept up the pressure and eventually it became clear, even to her persistent nature, that Désiré was not going to do it; he was not going to insure his life. She raged, she stormed, but it made no difference. He bore her insults, her taunts of selfishness, with his customary calm, and remained unmoved. In future years, the young Simenon was to hear his mother's repeated refrain: "When I think that you never even took out life insurance!"

There was only one thing to be done; as before, Henriette would have to save herself by her own efforts. She bundled Georges, then just three, off to a convent nursery school to give herself more free time and persuaded Désiré that they should leave their small apartment on the rue Pasteur (now the rue Georges Simenon) for a rented house around the corner, in the rue de la Loi. There she hung out a modest

18

sign, "Furnished Rooms to Let". From then on, throughout Georges's childhood and that of his brother, Christian, there were always foreign students in the house. "I held it against you," Simenon told Henriette over half a century later in *Lettre à ma mère*. "Child as I was, I had a feeling that the household was out of kilter, that no one mattered but you. You worked hard from morning to night, you wore your fingers to the bone doing huge piles of laundry. . . . Now I know that it wasn't malice or even selfishness on your part. You followed your bent, and no sentiment could stop you."

Yet ironically this decision of Henriette's was to have the most profound, and beneficial, effect upon her son's future life and literary career. This was in two ways. First, his early, one might say too early, thrusting into school made him virtually an infant prodigy so far as reading and writing were concerned. With the secret assistance of Soeur Adonie (who was forbidden by the Mother Superior to encourage precocity and made Georges swear not to give her away) he mastered the rudiments of reading and writing at the age of three. Later, when children of his own age were playing games and having fun (although he did that too), he would sit in his small bedroom beneath the rafters in the house on the rue de la Loi writing poetry and drawing maps, which was another early passion.

The second effect upon Simenon of his mother taking in students was that it opened his eyes, at a very young age, to a whole new world outside the restricted area where he lived. The students, three or four at a time, some staying for only a year, others for three to four years, all attended Liège University. They mainly came from Eastern Europe, Russians and Poles for the greater part, drawn to Liège because it was the least expensive of the French-speaking universities. Some were there also to pursue their revolutionary activities, and they filled the young Georges's ears with tales of their remote homeland and of their exciting lives. Their counterparts are later to appear in many of his novels, especially the earlier ones. Maigret's adversary in the very first Maigret story to be written is "Pietr, the Lett", an international villain of indeterminate nationality, from Latvia or Estonia, who has "for years been clocked across the European frontiers by Interpol".

Georges quickly learned to speak Russian. He devoured the students' books; by the time he was twelve he had read Chekhov, Gogol, Dostoevski, Pushkin and Gorki. For him, Gogol remains to this day the greatest writer of the nineteenth century (with William Faulkner the greatest writer of the present century). The young, impressionable Simenon was reading the great works of Russian literature before those of his native tongue; he conversed with the mind of Gorki before that of Balzac or Flaubert.

There was another advantage: Simenon (and later Christian, following his example) was to sleep with several of the women students. It was very convenient for the two young men to have such a fascinating range of sexual companions available right there in their own home in a narrow, tightly-packed street in a lower middle-class district of a Belgian provincial town.

Many of the students were studying medicine and this, too, was to have an important effect upon Simenon. He read their medical books as well as their "ordinary" books and early on mastered Testut's *Treatise on Anatomy*, which was to give him a biological knowledge of man that is one of the keys to his work. It went even further than that. He told the Swiss psychiatrists in 1968: "If I had not been a novelist, the only other thing I could have been was a doctor"; and it is clearly no coincidence that Maigret was a medical student for two years before the death of his aunt, who was supporting him through college, forced him to join the police instead. All in all, the influence of his mother's students on Simenon can hardly be overstated.

As for his ordinary schooling, it was a continual success story. In 1909, at the age of six, Soeur Adonie's prize pupil entered primary school at the Institut St. André, a Roman Catholic school run by friars near his home on the rue de la Loi. In his adolescence, Simenon was to be an anarchist and to rebel against the conformity around him, but as a small child he was almost mystically religious – "trembling," as he has said, "before a vulgar plaster statue of the Virgin."

He was his teachers' favourite, always given the best tasks, doing well in all his subjects and eventually, in July 1914, passing out with 293.5 points out of a possible total of 315. One anecdote, from about the year 1912, gives the flavour of the worthy friars and the very respectable school that they ran for the very respectable children of the correct, hard-working, God-fearing lower bourgeoisie of Outre-Meuse:

Georges and Christian were playing one day on the banks of the Meuse, on a piece of land that the army used for its manoeuvres. They were throwing pebbles into the river, seeing how far they could go, as children have been doing almost from the beginning of time. In his excitement, little Christian fell into the water. Georges did not hesitate; he dived in and managed to grab hold of his brother. The current was strong and twice it seemed that he would not be able to regain the land; but in the end he succeeded. Undoubtedly, he saved his brother's life.

A fine story, reflecting considerable credit on the young Simenon, one would have thought. But the Friar Superior of the Institut St. André did not see it like that.

Georges had told the police the truth about the incident, but the Friar Superior insisted that it had not happened in that way at all. He made Georges write out a totally different version which he then submitted to the authorities. No, the children were not playing games or idly throwing stones into the river, like the vulgar working-class children who went to the free schools run by the state. They had gone along to watch the soldiers at their manoeuvres and it was one of the army horses that had jostled against Christian and sent the little fellow flying into the water; whereupon his brave elder brother had plunged in and rescued him, at risk of his own life!

The lie that Simenon had to support entered deep into him. He resented it. He loathed, and still does at any conscious level, anything other than the absolute truth, yet here he was being taught to lie as a schoolboy by a learned cleric, steeped in the teaching of the Church.

Even so, he remained firmly a believer, bending low before the Cross. From the age of eight, back in 1911, he had started as an altar-boy at the church that formed part of the vast brick-built mass of the Hôpital de Bavière, whose high walls dominated the district of Outre-Meuse. He used to wake up every morning, the first in the house, at 5.30 and run breathless through the deserted streets to church, keeping to the middle of the road because he was afraid of unknown, unseen figures chasing after him.

Even as a small child, Simenon had an intense inner life. The early religious mysticism was only one manifestation of it. Another was the dreams that came to crowd his sleeping hours (today, in his late seventies, he still dreams every time he sleeps – even during his afternoon siesta – and always now in English!). Yet another was his sleep-walking.

Once his parents found him, sound asleep, walking in the street outside his house, having somehow managed to navigate three difficult flights of stairs in his long flannelette nightshirt. On another occasion, Désiré, awoken in the night, came downstairs to find him doing his homework in a sleep-like trance, oblivious of the fact that he had done it once already while awake on his return from school.

The doctor advised Henriette and Désiré to put iron bars on his window to prevent the boy doing himself serious harm. And so the young Simenon spent the nights of his childhood and early adolescence in a room beneath the rooftops of Liège with bars on the window like a prison cell.

Simenon's religiosity had a morbid side, for at a very early stage in his life it brought him into frequent close contact with death. Two or three times a week, at the hospital where many years later his own mother was to die, he would cross the courtyard a few steps in front of the priest, holding in one hand a long, black wooden pole topped with a silver cross, and in the other a bell. All the patients they passed knew what that meant: Georges, the altar-boy, and the priest were on their way to give extreme unction to one of their number, who was perhaps only a short while ahead of them. The patients in bed in the ward would prop themselves up on one elbow and make the sign of the cross.

"Those were the moments I liked least," says Simenon in *Lettre à ma mère*. "They got me down." Yet he professes that death in itself did not upset him. It simply meant that he would be paid fifty centimes extra for each Requiem Mass that he attended on top of the meagre two francs a month that he received for the usual weekday morning Mass, plus two on Sunday; in between which he was at least given a decent breakfast of two soft-boiled eggs, bread and butter, and coffee. Over fifty years later, dictating *Lettre à ma mère*, the seventy-one-year-old Simenon could still remember "the smell and even the taste" of those childhood breakfasts. Whatever the circumstances, the younger Simenon was always a hearty eater.

On August 4, 1914, while the eleven-year-old Simenon was enjoying his summer holidays before going on as a scholarship boy to enter the Belgian equivalent of grammar school at the Jesuit-run College St. Louis, Kaiser Wilhelm II's German army smashed its way across the frontier. The Belgians fought bravely and well, and there were twelve days of hard battle before the ring of forts defending Liège was finally silenced and four long years of alien occupation began.

At his young age, the First World War made little direct impact on Simenon's life. But he still remembers the German officers in the streets of Liège, with their helmets with tall points, grey capes, and many of them with a monocle in their eye or a scar on the cheek. "You know, we had to step off the pavement when an officer passed and, if we didn't, we were sent straight to the Commandant. You could always tell a senior officer by his collar – and because they all wore corsets."

In fact, the summer of 1915 was to prove of far greater importance to Simenon than the summer of 1914, and to understand that one has to consider the early, precocious sexuality of Simenon.

Most of us manifest an interest in sex long before we are prepared to admit. "Doctors and patients" is a game, involving much undressing and exploring of each other's bodies, that many of us learn to play very early on in our childhood. What young boy or girl has not felt a satisfying tingle of reassurance that "there is nothing wrong with them" when they discover that other young boys and girls go through the same early sexual trauma as they do? Yet Simenon's childhood involvement with sex seems much more intense than normal. One might almost say more serious.

He certainly documents it with almost clinical precision. In *Un homme comme un autre* ("A man like any other"), his first volume of dictated memoirs, he tells how one night, at the age of about five and a half, he and Christian, then aged two and a half, were sleeping in the same bed in the attic room that they then shared. In his half-sleep he became conscious of his sex lying against his brother's thigh and he deliberately pushed closer to Christian, moving himself up and down. After a few seconds, Christian realised that something was happening but he just lay there and let Georges continue. "I have to admit that I was seized with pleasure," Simenon recalls. "It didn't last more than five minutes, probably only about three. Nevertheless, that stamped my childhood and took away its innocence."

Needless to say, he did not tell his confessor nor his parents.

At the age of seventy-six, dictating *La Femme Endormie*, the "retired" novelist feels the need to relate the story of his first sexual contact, solely visual, with a member of the opposite sex. He was six and she was about seven, or eight. She was the daughter of the man from whom Henriette bought the family's vegetables and Simenon had met her by chance in the rue Pasteur at a time when it was deserted. There was no one around to see what was going on.

It was the eve of his first private communion and the highly religious little boy was coming home from confession, having put himself into a state of grace for the important ceremony that was to take place the following day. However, for all his state of grace and his deep regard for the almost mystic significance of the event ahead of him, he put a proposition to this little girl. It was entirely typical of a man who was later to admit that 8,000 of his famous "10,000 women" had been prostitutes, paid for their services. For he offered the vegetable-seller's daughter ten centimes if she would lift her skirt and show him her sex.

Millions of little boys before and since have asked little girls to expose to them their hidden delights but very few, one would have thought, have done so in terms more appropriate to a tired businessman and a whore; but that, at the age of six, was already Simenon's way.

He records that the girl accepted his offer and complied with his request "as if it were the most natural thing in the world, although for me it was a capital discovery." In the years that followed, pursuing his own dedicated inquiry into what he calls "the mystery of women", he "risked even more daring gestures, in particular with my girl cousins when we were in the country."

It was in the country, at a little village called Embourg just outside Liège, that he had his first full sexual experience with a girl. He was by no means a late-starter, for he was only twelve and his partner was sixteen. He still remembers her name. Simenon has never disclosed the details before, but this is how he now describes the incident:

> It was a very amusing story. We went to the country on holiday that summer – you called it country then but now it's nearly the suburbs of Liège – a little place called Embourg, with lots of wood, some streams, etc.
>
> My mother left Christian and myself alone in the little *auberge*, as she had to get back to Liège because of the students. There were only two rooms in the place let out as a "pension" and into the other bedroom, next door to mine, came a young girl with lovely brown hair . . . I think she was Jewish, she had their satin skin . . . and we became pals.
>
> One day we went into the wood, which was really thick, and she looked up at a holly-tree and high up there were big branches with lots of red berries. "Oh," she said, "will you cut me a bunch?" I said, "Of course!" The lower branches hardly had any, you know, it's always the higher ones that have the red berries, and I was wearing shorts with a bare chest – it was the middle of August – and I climbed up getting scratched everywhere.
>
> I cut her some branches with berries and then climbed down again. She said, "You are bleeding everywhere" and I said "Naturally, climbing up there into a holly tree!" So she said, "Lie down there" – and so I lay down and she started to wipe my legs, then to lick them, then my chest, and then she said, "Turn over." I did so and she licked my back. Then she took off my knickers and I found her on top of me. She hurt me a lot, because I wasn't fully "decapped". That's when it happened. She virtually circumcised me!

Besides the physical pain, the schoolboy's introduction to what a British bestselling writer has called "the joy of sex" did not go well. Young Georges very soon learnt the fickleness of women. After an idyllic time at Embourg, during the rest of their month there, he went back to Liège determined to see as much as he could of the pretty young Jewess with the satin skin.

She was a pupil at the most expensive private school in Liège, which happened to be close to the only other Roman Catholic "grammar school" for boys in the city. It was called College St. Servais and specialised in modern languages and science, as against the school to which Simenon went – the College St. Louis – which concentrated on the classics; and where, until then, he had been perfectly happy.

> When I got back home, I told my parents that I wanted to give up classics and go to St. Servais. So they sent me there. The first day I went to the gate of the school where the girl was and waited for her to come out. I waited and I waited. Finally I saw her come out – and she ran to the street corner, where waiting for her was a man. I call him a man but he could only have been twenty-one. Anyway, he took her by the arm – and I went home.
>
> I had changed colleges for *that*! If only I hadn't, I would have done classics rather than modern studies because I adored classics. That's what love does. . . .

At least, there was one good result from this somewhat bitter-sweet story; it determined what his future career would *not* be.

Early on, at the age of eleven, Simenon had decided that he wanted to write: "I realised that it was a need. Something I had to do. There was no question about it." But at that stage he never supposed that he could earn his living by doing so. He was naturally attracted to the Church, with the Army as a possible, rather remote, alternative. As he was later to say, "I had noticed the priests walking in their gardens with their breviaries. It followed that they must have a lot of free time, in which I could do my writing. As for the officers, I had also seen them, at whatever time of the day, with their spurs, strolling around in the streets near the cavalry barracks, where later I was to do my military service. They too seemed to have a lot of spare time on their hands."

Now, at least, one thing was certain; having had sexual intercourse with a girl at the tender age of twelve and savoured the experience with a joy that transcended all previous pleasures, he realised at once that there was no way that he could live the life of a celibate priest. Sex and his pursuit of "the mystery of woman" was going to play far too great a role in his life. The satin-skinned young Jewess had helped open his eyes to an essential part of his personality.

CHAPTER 4

Turning-point and Adolescence

A major theme in the works of Georges Simenon is, as he told the Swiss psychiatrists, that in everyone's life there is a "turning point", which changes the course of that life for good. One may cavil at the universality of this allegation. Surely it does not happen in *every* life? Even so, there is no doubt that it did occur in Simenon's life, and at the almost pathetically young age of fifteen.

It took place in June 1918, just five months before the end of the war. Life had gone on for Georges at a fairly even pace after the excitement and then disappointment of the summer of 1915. His true love really was the classics; he did not do so well at College St. Servais, with its emphasis on modern studies, as he had done at his earlier school. But at least his boredom with his formal education meant that he spent more time on his juvenile efforts as a writer.

His Jesuit teachers were not fools. They appreciated that here was a talent they should encourage. Unlike the other pupils in his class, he was soon accorded the right to set his own subjects for his homework in French language and literature. He signed his efforts "Georges Sim" rather than "Georges Simenon", for even then he had taken the decision to put his real name to something he had written only if it was worthy of it. The teachers accepted this caprice without laughing at it. Nor did they complain when occasionally his essays would be submitted in verse, one with the typically mournful title for a sensitive, introspective youth of "Melancholy of the Tall Bell-Tower".

At home, too, the war years unfolded themselves with dull, monotonous tread. Henriette's tantrums got no fewer. "She suffers through habit, almost through a sense of vocation," he later wrote in *Je me souviens*. "I have nothing to reproach you with, and I don't reproach you," he tells her in *Lettre à ma mère*. "You had your aim in life and you pursued it with rare perseverance." By contrast, his father was a saint. "Despite the mediocrity of our lives, he was at peace with himself and with others," Simenon told the Swiss psychiatrists.

26

The bitterness of his words, describing his father's lot, screams out at one from the printed page. He admits to feeling "a sort of rebellion against my mother. I considered that she was wrong to have insisted on taking in her student lodgers despite my father's objections. He used to come home from work at 6.30 in the evening. His armchair (there was only one in the house) would be taken by one of the students. Another student would be reading his newspaper. He would have to wait.

"The meals were no longer served at a time that suited his convenience but that of the students. They would have to be served first before we could sit down to our meal, and even the menus would be more to their liking than to his.

"That my mother imposed this on my father, I found totally indecent and I wanted him to see it that way too – but he didn't. And in addition to all that, there were her constant complaints that he did not concern himself for her or for her welfare and, above all, the perpetual moan that he had not even taken out life insurance for himself, even though he worked in an insurance office."

What then was Simenon's "turning point"? It came when a message arrived at the College St. Servais from Doctor Fischer, the family physician, asking the fifteen-year-old lad to call in and see him on his way home. "Georges, I have bad news for you," he told him. "You must give up your studies and go out into the world and earn your living." "But why?" asked Simenon. "Because I examined your father a few days ago and I don't believe that he has more than two or three years to live at the most."

It was Désiré's heart. He was suffering from angina. Georges was later to discover that his father had known about it for a very long time – ever since, at Henriette's insistence, he had tried to take out life insurance when young Christian was born and been refused on medical grounds. Indeed, the man *was* a saint never once to have replied with the truth when his wife nagged him about not having insurance.

But for now Doctor Fischer insisted that Désiré should not be told how badly his condition had deteriorated. Life must seem to go on as normal, with Georges all the while preparing himself for the burden that may all too soon fall upon him.

Simenon did not cry. He did not shout or beat the walls of his room at home. But the injustice of his father's fate, and, to a less extent, the sadness of his own plight in having to give up school and take on at once the responsibility of potential breadwinner, left him with a feeling of outrage that still rankles beneath the surface. As he himself says, "Since the age of fifteen I have been a rebel."

At that moment, he ceased to be a Believer and the teachings of the Church became a mockery. He no longer went to Mass. From then on, too, he began to dream one particular dream that has continued to recur throughout his life: the scene is a great lake. It is night. The lake is flat like a vast skating-rink. It reflects the moon and all around it stand large black mountains. He arrives between two of these mountains. He looks at the lake and at the mountains and at the moon – and that is all! Nothing happens. Absolutely nothing. It is a sterile, forbidding landscape.

Only someone who has known true grief for himself can appreciate how the young Simenon must have felt, how empty and cruel life must have seemed, as he left Doctor Fischer's house that evening and walked back pensively through the streets of Outre-Meuse. The family now lived on the rue de l'Enseignement, in a bigger house which Henriette had insisted on Désiré renting so that she could take in more students. "Good evening, son," said Désiré as the boy entered – he never called him by his name but always "son" – and Georges had to look away and run straight up to his room.

He told his parents that he wanted to leave school, that he had lost interest in his studies, that he wanted "to grow up" and earn his own living. We do not know how Désiré took the news, but Henriette accepted it happily enough. She had always dreamed of owning a pastry shop with herself serving behind the counter and her son cooking marvellous *patisseries* in the back kitchen. Now her dream could come true.

Incredible though it may seem, the young Georges actually agreed to become apprenticed to a local pastrycook. One can only assume that he must still have been shell-shocked by the news about his father, or that he had lost temporarily the will to resist. He was, after all, still only fifteen.

But he soon recovered his resolve. After two weeks, he walked out of the pastry shop; he could stand it no longer. Henriette no doubt had one more thing to complain about, but Georges was quite certain that cooking pastries all day was not going to be his lifestyle.

But what else to do? Through a friend of his father's, he got a job as junior assistant in a bookshop on the rue de la Cathedrale, one of the main shopping streets in the heart of Liège. That was more to his taste, nevertheless he lasted only six weeks, being sacked on the spot when he contradicted his aged employer on the correct authorship of a novel by Alexandre Dumas in front of a customer. Such things were not done by polite young lads who knew their place.

By now it was February 1919. The war was four months over. Georges, aged sixteen, was wearing his first pair of long trousers and wandering disconsolately through the streets looking for work. On impulse, he walked into the offices of the *Gazette de Liège*, a leading local newspaper, and asked for a job as a reporter. He knew nothing about newspapers, never read them at home, had no idea that this particular one – ultra-Conservative, ultra-Catholic – was of all the local papers the one most opposed to his own views.

But the editor, a formidable bearded man with a great red nose lighting up the middle of his face, called Joseph Demarteau, was so impressed with the young man's courage (plus the fact that he was related to a former Bishop of Liège!) that he gave him a job on the spot. At last, Simenon had found his true apprenticeship. He became a cub reporter, scouring round Liège looking for news, going to police headquarters every morning for daily briefings, attending the law courts, covering every kind of story from dog shows to funerals; he was in his element. His parents had always been too poor to buy him a bicycle – unlike most of his friends, who already had one – but with his first few weeks' wages he now bought his own.

Life was marvellous, life was exciting. One day he picked up a lawyer's confidential file, lying around forgotten in a hallway at the local Law Courts, and took it home, only to report in the newspaper the next day on its sensational disappearance – and a few days later to describe, in an exclusive, its amazing reappearance. He quickly acquired the journalist's typical enthusiasm for drink; he consumed vast amounts of beer and was often drunk. One afternoon, after lunch, he staggered back to the office and accosted his editor: "You're a hypocrite!" he said. "Is that nose really yours – or is it a filthy big strawberry stuck in the middle of your face?" Miraculously, he was not fired.

Nor was he sacked when, after attending too well a banquet on behalf of his newspaper, he tried to pick up a young dancer in the street as she was hurrying to work and followed her on to the stage of the theatre where she was performing. The kindly Demarteau merely said: "No more banquets!"

For "*mon petit Sim*", as the editor affectionately called him, was good at his job. As a journalist Simenon was a natural, and after six months Demarteau promoted him. As well as his ordinary news stories, often with his own by-line, "Georges Sim", he was given a daily gossip column. It was called *Hors du Poulailler* ("Out of the Barnyard") and, under the pen name *Monsieur le Coq*, Simenon was given almost free rein to write what he liked about the comings and goings of Liège society and the behind-the-scenes stories in his native town.

His three and a half years on the *Gazette de Liège* were a perfect training ground for the future novelist. With a pipe stuck constantly in his mouth (he had started with pipes at the age of thirteen but now it was no longer an early-adolescent pretension), his youthful, stocky figure, clad in the traditional young journalist's "uniform" for that time of raincoat and soft felt hat pulled down over the brim, became a familiar figure around the city. If a famous foreign dignitary such as Marshal Foch, the ex-French President Raymond Poincaré or Winston Churchill visited Liège, it was "*le petit Sim*" who was sent to interview him.

Through his daily contact with the police and the courts, he learned early, and at close quarters, about crime and the sordid side of life. He covered the debates in the Municipal and Provincial Councils and, in his own words, "soon learned about their little plots and intrigues in the corridors." If there was an explosion below ground in one of the coal mines that encircled the town, it would be Simenon who would tear off on his motor cycle—he had quickly gone beyond a mere bicycle—and stand among the crowds of anxious women waiting to see if their loved ones would be brought up safely to the surface.

Already he had started on his search for "the naked man". When he went to interview Foch, the most famous French soldier of World War One, he was not looking for "a statue of Marshal Foch seated astride his horse" – as over fifty years later he told his friend, the French literary critic, Francis Lacassin – "but Foch in his bedroom where he received me in his nightshirt".

He was also gathering experience of life at a more personal level, and not merely as an interviewer or observer of other people's lives. Seeing himself as an embryonic man of the world, his sexuality exploded into a virtuoso performance of teenage vigour. "At sixteen," he says, "I already had a very pretty little mistress and I rented a furnished room for her about half a kilometre from my home.

"To begin with, I saw her until about eleven o'clock, then it became half-past eleven and eventually I finished by spending whole nights with her, getting back home on tiptoe at about half-past five or six. But sometimes it happened that my mother would get up early, come into my room – and I wasn't there! Invariably, on those occasions, my father would have got up in the night, gone into my room, unmade my bed and when my mother came in to complain that I hadn't come home yet, he would say, 'But I heard him go out. I heard his motor bike. He must have had an early story to do for the newspaper.' So there was nothing she could do about it.

"My mother was very, very religious, you know. She would literally pray to God that I should still be a virgin when I got married – but I wasn't!"

The "very pretty little mistress" had no monopoly of the young Simenon's sexual favours. In *Quand j'étais vieux*, he gives a graphic description of those years:

> At the time of the *Gazette de Liège*, when I was sixteen and a half to nineteen years old, I had two women available to me each day, almost every day, at one moment or another. I would be like a dog on heat.
>
> An example. A case that comes back to me. In Belgium at that time, as in Amsterdam to this day, there were strange houses: a dimly lit ground floor: half-open curtains behind which could be seen one or two women knitting or reading, raising their heads when they heard the step of a passer-by.
>
> These houses, the same as in Amsterdam, were not necessarily in deserted or disreputable streets. There was one on the Boulevard de la Constitution, just opposite the largest secondary school, and I had to pass in front of it each time I came back from the centre of town through the Passerelle (one of the bridges linking Outre-Meuse to the city).
>
> I was passing this way one night at about ten o'clock. I did not see the familiar silhouette, but a splendid Negress and suddenly I felt that it was absolutely necessary for me to enter and make love with her. I had never known a Negress.
>
> I had only a small sum in my pocket. I hesitated. My father was already sick, dying. A little while before, he had given me his watch, a silver watch with the arms of Belgium on it, which he had won in a shooting match, for my father was an enthusiastic marksman.
>
> Shamefacedly, I paid with the watch, and it was one of the acts that I regret most, not for moral reasons, but because it would mean so much to me to have this souvenir of my father. At home, I was obliged to lie about it. Then to declare the loss of the watch to the police. And if it had been found it might have had far-reaching consequences.
>
> It is only a small example. At the same time, I spent evening after evening all by myself in the most disreputable streets, where I risked being beaten up at every corner.

In his *Mémoires intimes*, written at the age of seventy-seven, he can still recall how in those years the mere sight of an attractive bottom, as its owner wiggled her way through the streets, could give him an erection that was "almost painful".

He has always been fascinated by prostitutes. He claims now that some of his finest moments with women have been with those he calls "professionals". He says that even half an hour with a whore can teach him something about the eternal truth of woman, his perpetual quest. With such a complex character, he probably believes that himself, and certainly wants to believe it; but at least as strong a motivation was that which nearly forty years later he was to put into the mouth of one of his characters, Mâitre Gobillet, a successful Parisian criminal lawyer, who, in the novel *En cas de malheur* ("In Case of Emergency"), tries to explain the reasons for his sensual bondage to a no-good young girl named Yvette whom he defends and with whom he becomes hopelessly entangled: "My strongest impulse was probably a craving for pure sex . . . without any consideration of emotion or passion. Let's say sex in its raw state, the need to behave like an animal."

Everything was good for Simenon in those years. He was literally as well as figuratively a young man in a hurry. He considered himself a good athlete and late one night got to disputing his track skill with a stranger in a bar. He challenged the stranger to a hundred-metres dash, led him out into the deserted street, measured off the distance between lamp-posts – and was dismayed to be raced to a tie.

Afterwards, he learned that his opponent was an Olympic champion.

After less than a year on the *Gazette de Liège* Simenon felt himself ready to write his first novel. So, not yet seventeen, he sat down at his typewriter and, in his spare time, knocked out *Au Pont des Arches* in a mere ten days.

Named after the principal bridge linking the city with Outre-Meuse, the book has never been translated and was only privately published by a friend, who was a printer, and illustrated by another friend, who was a painter. Even so, the book opens with characteristic Simenon directness and contempt for middle-class life: "On that particular Sunday morning, Joseph Planquet, who ran the chemist's shop at the sign of the *Pont des Arches*, was not allowed to lounge about in bed. Promptly at eight, he was aroused by his wife on her return from Mass. Her nose was red and moist, her voice slightly hoarse. 'Hurry up, now!' she said. 'You know what a job we have to do today.' " One is immediately involved in the action, with a thumb-nail picture of the main characters. Simenon at sixteen had already acquired a quite remarkable precision and deftness of touch.

What will surprise most readers of Simenon, regarded by many, rightly or wrongly, as the arch-writer of "black" novels, searing and at times depressing in their exploration of the human soul, is that his very first book was a humorous one; more in the style of a Belgian Jerome K. Jerome than anything else. Its main theme was the plight of the unfortunate Joseph Planquet who, of all things, ran a chemist's shop specialising in purgative pills for pigeons. It does not sound too promising a subject, but to this day Simenon insists that he had been much maligned by the critics, especially the French, who he says ignore the humour that he maintains exists even in his darkest novels.

In fact the young author persisted in this lighthearted vein. "*Le petit Sim*" – for *Au Pont des Arches* appeared with the name "Georges Sim" on the jacket – followed up his first teenage novel with two others, both deliberately humorous. The first one, written the next year in collaboration with a fellow cub reporter, was, in his own words, "a detective-thriller, so-called comic or at least ironic". Its title was *Le Bouton de col* ("The Collar-stud") and when some fifty years later his one-time collaborator sent him the original manuscript to re-read, he could not get beyond the fourth page. "If, among the manuscripts that they send me to read, there appeared one so bad," he says, "I would advise the author to take up any occupation, no matter what it might be, rather than attempt to be a writer, even of a humorous work."

His third "comic" novel, *Jeban Pinaquet*, all about a young man of that name, "more or less ridiculous", with a long, trumpet-like nose who walked around town sniffing at the odours of street corners and shop windows, was, like *Le Bouton de col*, never published. As Simenon recalls in his memoirs, a woman friend who ran a printer's business did offer to publish it for him free of charge but "happily, I took the precaution of giving it to M. Demarteau to read, and he said, 'If you publish that, you will no longer be a member of the staff of the *Gazette de Liège*.'"

Enough was enough. "Le petit Sim" gave up writing books for a while and, for all the self-claimed humour in some of his hundreds of subsequently published novels, he has never again written a book specifically intended to be funny.

The damp squib of his books was the only major disappointment in Simenon's life at that time. Everything else was excitement and panache, and "all stations go!"

With resilience – and maybe the selfishness – of youth, he pushed all conscious thoughts of his father's impending death safely to the back of his mind.

He spent little time at home. His evenings, when he was not roaming the town looking for girls or danger – or both – were spent in an attic in one of the tall, crumbling old houses by the St. Pholien church in Outre Meuse. Here, with some friends of the same age, most of them painters or students at the Academie des Beaux-Arts, he would talk into the night, endlessly discussing the great questions of life: the nature of God, the meaning of philosophy, the true significance of art, and so on.

They called themselves La Caque ("The Barrel") after the barrel of herrings around which, traditionally, Belgians would sit and talk, while dipping into the contents to pick out a snack. But these young-sters had stronger refreshment. To their garret, lit by a paraffin lamp and with only a couple of broken-down armchairs and an old mattress for furniture, each one would bring a bottle of wine or spirit – or some raw ether.

It was in such a setting, passions and tempers enflamed by strong, undiluted alcohol, that Simenon was later, in his second Maigret novel, Le Pendu de Saint Pholien ("Maigret and the Hundred Gibbets"), to place the meetings of "The Companions of the Apocalypse": a group of young Liègeoise artists and students who similarly met to discuss life, with a capital "L", and whose high-powered sessions one night ended in murder – with one of their number stabbed to death and the culprit hanging himself from the main door of the St. Pholien church the next morning.

This early Maigret is, incidentally, a fascinating example of how Simenon could take a fact from life and weave around it a story of pure imagination and ingenuity of plot. There was a member of La Caque who hanged himself on the main door of St. Pholien; but he had committed no murder. He was a twenty-year-old artist, "very blond, almost white-haired, very thin, with feverish eyes," who on the night of Christmas Day, 1919, had drunk so much, along with two fellow members of the group, that he was unable to walk. He lived, like Ratso in Midnight Cowboy, in a derelict building awaiting demolition. Simenon and his friends carried the young man "home" and left him on a straw mattress on the floor, in a state of abject poverty. The next morning he hanged himself. And from that pathetic little tale Simenon, twelve years later, spun a detective story that took Maigret to three different countries, with the former members of the group conspiring to cover up the story of the guilty suicide's "murder".)

Yet *La Caque* has a greater significance in Simenon's life than merely to provide the factual setting of one of his stories. It was directly as a result of another drunken session by the same group on Christmas Night of the following year, 1920, that Simenon met the girl who was to be his first wife. Staggering around in the heart of Liège at between three and four o'clock in the morning, having spent all the previous hours of the night in their gaunt little attic, the young bohemians – for that is how they regarded themselves – ran into another young man, who many of them knew: an architect, recently graduated from the Academie des Beaux-Arts. In the alcoholic bonhomie of the hour and the occasion, he invited them – "for what reason, I do not know," says Simenon – to spend New Year's Eve with him at the studio of his sister, an art student at the Academie.

So at about nine o'clock on New Year's Eve, Simenon presented himself at the door of an imposing, rather splendid house on the rue Louvreux. He had spent most of the afternoon in a café, welcoming in the New Year with his friends on the *Gazette de Liège*. He was hopelessly drunk. He could not climb the stairs in normal fashion but had to clamber up the last few steps on all fours. It was in that condition, grunting like a big, husky dog, that he entered what he expected to be a studio, full of his young friends, and found, to his horror, was a large elegant drawing room, where his friends *and all the architect's family* were solemnly awaiting him! M. Renchon, the architect's father, had insisted that the youngsters should stay down with the family until midnight when they could all then ascend to his daughter's studio on the top floor and carry on celebrating the New Year in their own fashion.

Simenon slumped into a chair, the others went on talking and drinking. He drank no more and by the time midnight came and the younger folk staggered upstairs to the studio, they were all drunk and he was the only one sober – save for the young architect's sister, Régine. Not pretty, three years older than Simenon but with an active and intelligent mind, he found her the only sympathetic person to talk to.

What was the attraction? In appearance, she was the exact opposite of the sort of women who excited him sexually. Plain, with hair pulled back severely and secured by a headband, she was of less than medium height and somewhat mannish in her ways. Yet, says Simenon, "she was extremely intelligent and cultivated, and all the girls I met then

35

lacked conversation. I couldn't discuss with them Schopenhauer or Rembrandt or Leonardo da Vinci or Renoir – but with her I could."

The two agreed to meet once a week in the studio: to talk. But with the seventeen-year-old Simenon talking was not enough; even with a plain young woman, whose mind intrigued him more than her body. Within just over two weeks, they were lovers. Nearly sixty years later, in *La Femme Endormie*, he reveals that Régine Renchon was the first of only three virgins that he has known in his life and that, "as I did not want to rush her, I took more than a fortnight, habituating her by caresses, awaking her sexuality, before she would accept the true pleasure of sex. Then I was able to penetrate her."

There is no doubt that Régine was very much in love. This was her first love and to this day Simenon remains the only man she has loved. For his part, he did what he was always to do with a woman who plays a major role in his life: he took her over. He changed her into his image of what he wanted. He detested the name Régine, so he invented a new one for her that she still keeps, even though they have been divorced since 1950: "Tigy".

Was it a first love for Simenon as well? In *Un homme comme un autre*, he gives the answer: "I don't think so. I don't think I ever really loved her. I am almost sure of that." A few weeks before meeting Régine, he had thought seriously of getting married "as a refuge against all the accidents of life." With that in mind, he had gone out with "a plump, pretty little girl with a fresh open smile", who was the sister of a friend; but nothing had come of it. Now, "playing at love", as he says, he saw Régine every night and, notwithstanding, wrote her passionate letters every morning. Those letters, graphic in their detail, made clear to any reader the physical basis of their relationship – and one person who read them was Régine's father, a prosperous interior designer. Somehow M. Renchon got possession of the letters, devoured them at a sitting and brusquely summoned Simenon, now all of eighteen years of age, to the house.

The upshot was that, in the spring of 1921, Simenon and Régine became engaged. The young man introduced her to his parents. Désiré embraced her – "He was a man of many qualities, very civil, very cheerful," Régine now remembers. Henriette said: "My God, she's ugly!"

Régine wanted to go and live in Paris. She had already visited the French capital several times with her father on some of his business trips and felt, as many a young artist has done over the years, that only there could her talents really flourish and find fulfilment. The idea also appealed to Simenon. He felt that his development as a writer had gone as far as it could in Liège. Where better than Paris to learn his craft, to gain new experience and to try and establish himself? He did not want to be a writer restricted to his region, even though he would always say proudly: "I am a man of the North." "I cannot even say who first wanted to go," says Régine now. "Looking back, it seems as if it was always a mutual ambition."

Simenon, like all young Belgian men, would have to do a year's military service at the age of twenty, in two years' time. The young couple agreed that he should bring forward the period of his service and get it out of the way as quickly as he could. He would start it at the age of eighteen and a half in November 1921, and then go to Paris a year later, on his own, to set things up for their new life there as a married couple.

All was well planned, all seemed set. Then struck the tragedy that was inevitable and whose coming Simenon had done his best to try and forget. On the afternoon of November 28, 1921, the day before Simenon was due to go into the Army, Désiré dropped dead standing at his high accountant's desk in his office. At almost that very moment, Simenon was in bed with a girl in Antwerp, where his duties on the *Gazette de Liège* had taken him for the day.

On his return to Liège that evening, Régine and her father were waiting for him at the railway station. Simenon took one look at their faces and knew why they were there. He ran home. His mother was in tears. He went into his father's room, and there was Désiré laid out on his bed, fully clothed as if he were still at the office, a candle burning on either side of him. Simenon tiptoed forward alone. "It was the first time that I really saw anybody dead that close. I had just enough courage to kiss my father lightly on the forehead, and it was all cold. I looked at him for a few moments and then I left."

In recalling the moment sixty years later, Simenon acts out the words and purses his lips in imitation of that last salute. In the many hours of conversation with the writer of this book, it is one of only two occasions when he is in tears: the other is when he talks about the death of his daughter, Marie-Jo.

"I never want my sons to go through what I went through," he says. "I have written in my will that no one except Teresa will know the date of my death until after I have been cremated and my ashes have been scattered to join those of Marie-Jo in the little garden of my house. There will be no service, no journalists, no photographers, no speeches at the cremation. I do not want my sons to even know it is happening."

At the funeral of his father, Simenon shocks the onlookers by grabbing all the flowers and wreathes and throwing them onto the coffin before the earth covers it, instead of leaving them to be laid on top of the grave to bear witness to the wealth and generosity of their senders. Then he rushes out of the cemetery, runs home, throws himself on his bed – and cleaves his heart in two with sobbing.

Now there is nothing further to detain him in Liège. The thought of leaving his widowed mother does not – perhaps understandably – deter him for one second. He has to get through his year of military service as painlessly as he can, and then no longer will he live in this closeted provincial town. Over thirty years later, he tells his friend, Brendan Gill: "If I wrote so often of morbid people and things, it is to shake my fist in anger at the evils they have to suffer. I was born in the dark and the rain, and I got away. The crimes I write about – sometimes I think they are the crimes I would have committed if I had not got away. I am one of the lucky ones. What is there to say about the lucky ones except that they got away?"

CHAPTER 5

Paris in the Twenties

His year of military service was, at a physical level, no great hardship for Simenon. Because of his love of horses, he joined the Belgian cavalry and, after a month of initiation with the Army of Occupation which for a brief few years occupied the German Rhineland, he returned to Liège.

For the rest of his time in the Service, he was stationed in barracks in Outre-Meuse from which he could see his mother's house in the rue l'Enseignment and from which each day, in a somewhat unusual arrangement, he went to work, as usual, at the *Gazette de Liège*.

His nights of long, alcohol-flamed discussion with his fellow-members of *La Caque* were now over, but he still saw Régine most evenings. And still, after leaving her, he would – as before – often make his way into the mean, narrow streets bordering the moneyed, bourgeois area where she lived to find a prostitute, who would sell him her favours for a few francs. "I do not think that I am, or that I ever have been, someone that you could say was obsessed by sex," he claims in *Un homme comme un autre*. "Nor do I believe that I have had or have appetites in that direction that are more than normal."

But how many young men of twenty, or any age, having just made love to their fiancée, feel the compelling need to have sex again that same night – on the most animal basis with someone whom they have paid for the loan of their body – before finally reaching the haven of their own bed?

Simenon's year of enforced service in the Army was a wasted one, so far as the development of his talent was concerned. He merely marked time until he would be free to leave for Paris. Finally, in late November 1922, he walked out of the Outre-Meuse barracks, once again a civilian. On the evening of December 10, 1922, he boarded the night train for Paris.

Simenon has always been something of a chameleon, varying his colour to suit the setting in which he finds himself. When he reached London soon after the end of World War Two on his way to live in the

United States, as an established, successful author, Maurice Richardson, the English writer and critic, "got the impression that he was an actor playing the role that was expected of him. He wore a very smart brown suit, but with it a large weird floppy lilac bow-tie that suggested a teacher at a *lycée*. He was very amiable and polite and launched at once into a conventional old-fashioned spiel about how he adored your London with its fogs and how much he owed to 'your great Dickens'." When he was for five seemingly contented years in the nineteen-fifties living the life in Lakeville, Connecticut of a settled middle-aged man, happy in his farmhouse, surrounded by his wife and children, the American writer Brendan Gill found him completely at his ease, bedrock sure of his domesticity. So much so that he was saying he would find it impossible to leave – but within three years he had packed his bags and returned to Europe, leaving America for good.

In Switzerland in his late seventies, when he has adopted the role of Serene Elder Statesman, he is exactly that: kind, calm, courteous, absolutely innocent – serene.

So when, as a young man of twenty, he leaves his home town to go to Paris, "to mix the plaster" for his future career as a serious writer, as he later says to André Gide, he chooses to look the part. In his last few weeks in the army, he had let his hair grow long, in true "bohemian" style. He wore a large black-rimmed floppy hat. With his wide, loosely-tied necktie and cheaply-cut raincoat, he looked like something out of an imitation Toulouse-Lautrec poster.

Thirty-nine years later, receiving a reporter from the London *Observer* in his suite at the Savoy Hotel, where he had come in connection with the B.B.C.'s highly successful television screening of some of his *Maigret* stories, he says rather grandly: "I thought it was necessary to live in Paris. You have to make your first years of writing in Paris, to be a French writer."

The reality was something rather less prestigious . . .

The Paris of the twenties was indeed a forcing-ground for the talents of many and varied a young genius across the whole spectrum of the arts. It was also a marvellous place to live. People had fun there in the years before that word became debased into merely meaning a drink-oriented night out.

World War One had left the flower of French youth strewn across the muddy fields of Northern France. Three-quarters of the men who had gone to war were dead or wounded. Two and a half million of them were youngsters between the ages of eighteen and twenty-five. "Nothing else in the history of the Continent," has written Malcolm Cowley, "not even the Black Death, had produced such an extravagance of corpses." France, and above all Paris, wanted to forget the sadness and the anguish. These were *Les Années Folles*, the French counterpart of America's "Roaring Twenties". "When I look back over those ten years," Maurice Sachs was later to write, "it seems always to have been the Fourteenth of July. The tricolour was always flying."

Paris *après guerre* was a mecca, not only for the young Simenon and his fiancée, but for painters, sculptors, writers and musicians from all over the world. Emigré-Russians, Turks, Swedes, Italians, Spaniards, Britons, Americans – and Belgians – crowded the Left Bank and the upper reaches of Montmartre until the cafés sounded like the Tower of Babel with their mad confusion of tongues.

Yet none of this splendour was readily apparent to Georges Simenon, when on the cold and rainy morning of November 11, 1922, at first light, he walked out of the *Gare du Nord*, clutching in one hand a suitcase of synthetic material, wrapped around with cord because the lock was broken, and in the other a brown-paper parcel tied together with string. The streets were sad. The rain was persistent. People hurried by, their heads down, their hands stuck in their pockets. He had to find somewhere to stay; but, as he trudged through the wet, every hotel he tried was either *complet* or too expensive. Finally, at the Hôtel Berthe (which exists to this day, but now much improved) on the corner of the Boulevard des Batignolles and the rue Darcet, he found a small room on the top floor – with iron bedstead, washbasin, two chairs and no carpet – that he could just about afford: twenty-five francs a month, payable in advance.

In the years of his prime, there was always one thing – sex apart – in which Simenon could find solace, and that was food. He had a Belgian's trencherman appetite. And now, descending from his room, once again putting up the collar of his coat against the rain, he went in search of breakfast. In Liège, he was used to fried eggs, a large cup of coffee, slices of buttered bread and cheese; now for the first time he savoured the "marvellous taste" of croissants. He ate twelve in a sitting, and was conscious of everyone staring at him as he left the café.

That very morning, he was due to start work. For although this was to be his apprenticeship as a writer, he still had to earn his living, and he thought he had got things rather well planned. Through a friend of his father's, Simenon had been promised a job as secretary to Henri Binet-Valmer, now a totally forgotten French writer but in those days very well known and with a considerable reputation also as a right-wing political activist. Alas, when he arrived at Binet-Valmer's offices in the splendid building near the avenue Hoche where he also lived, Simenon found, to his dismay, that his real employment was not as secretary to an established writer but as a sort of glorified bellboy for the political league of which Binet-Valmer was president. Weak from lack of sleep and his long journey, the "secretary" spent his first working day helping to load lorries with Christmas presents for the children of French ex-servicemen, disabled in the war. A laudable occupation, no doubt, but not what he had come to Paris to do.

As he humped and loaded boxes, Simenon could not help smiling bitterly to himself at the thought of what his mother would have said, remembering her urgent command during his boyhood: "Never play with the children of workers!" In the six months that he worked for Binet-Valmer, his employer spoke to him no more than five or six times. The monocled frock-coated figure of the famous writer was far too aloof to make any serious contact with the newest member of his staff. "My job was to put stamps on envelopes, to go to the Post Office ten times a day and to take letters by hand to well-known, important politicians," says Simenon.

But at least he was earning money: 600 francs a month, of which he had promised to send 250 to his mother. It was not much for a healthy, lustful young man to live on. He used to eat a lot of camembert, because it was filling and cheap, and tripe, cooked *à la mode de Caen*, because the greasy sauce helped large quantities of bread to go down. "I don't want to talk about Christmas 1922," he says in *Un homme comme un autre*. "I know nothing more sinister than to be alone in Paris, with very little money in your pocket, on Christmas night, mingling in the street with people amusing themselves or looking at them through the windows of a restaurant. A long time afterwards the police told me that on Christmas night they always have most suicides. That does not surprise me."

New Year's Eve was equally grim. So was the morning of New Year's Day 1923. The streets of Paris were deserted, except for religious families on the way to church; most people stayed at home, nursing their hangovers. But around four o'clock in the afternoon came consolation – and in the form most acceptable for Simenon. He was standing, chilled and bored, his hands in the pockets of his raincoat, looking at the miniature models of steamships, advertising "holidays in the sun" in the window of a shipping company when he noticed, reflected in the glass, the face of a young, brown-skinned girl, with large sombre eyes, also gazing distractedly at this image of a happier world. She was a chambermaid at the Spanish embassy. They began talking. He invited her for a drink. Within an hour, they were in bed together in a hotel room.

It did not matter that the hotel was sordid, the room none too clean. Simenon already fancied himself as an accomplished lover, but this pert little Spaniard taught him delights he had not yet known. The two laughed in happiness at their sexual discovery of each other.

They arranged to meet again the following evening, at nine o'clock, on the corner of the avenue Hoche and the Faubourg St. Honoré. She did not turn up, and Simenon never saw her again. But she had welcomed him to Paris, and at last he began to feel more at ease.

The thought of being faithful to his fiancée never once seems to have entered his head. The need for sex was too compelling, too urgent a call to be denied. His earnings were so meagre he could afford only the cheapest, least attractive prostitutes on the less favoured streets; and even those not very often. Not often enough. In the novel, *Le Temps d'Anais* ("The Girl in His Past"), written in America in 1951, in strongly autobiographical terms, he describes how Bauche, like him a young man from out of town, first experiences the city: "Paris was dark, humid, with thousands of beings in a constant state of agitation for no reason, running after God knows what. The hotel he lived in . . . had a strong odour that suggested sordid things and was filled with equivocal voices.

"For months, his chief preoccupation was, not how to eat, but how to have the necessary number of francs in his pocket to buy himself one of the prostitutes who roamed the streets. The desire was so painful at times that he would weep."

With Simenon, early one morning, lying awake in his bed at the Hôtel Berthe, the need was so great that when he heard a chambermaid outside in the hallway cleaning the guests' shoes, he got up, opened his door, lifted up the girl's skirt and possessed her on the spot – while she was brushing away. She did not even stop what she was doing but merely said: "Oh, Monsieur!" Again, there are echoes in *Le Temps d'Anais*, when Simenon describes how the young Bauche had sex with Anais, a golden-skinned girl on the beach at Grau-du-Roi in the Lower Camargue where he lived: "It happened by chance. I really didn't know she was there on the deserted beach behind the stranded boat. The boats out on the water were too far away to see us. I went up to her and took her right away, without a word." Forty years later Simenon is to take Teresa, his second wife's personal maid, who is to become the last woman in his life, in exactly the same way: brusquely, from behind, without a word of endearment or preparation, when she is bending over to perform some household chore.

Paris, in those early months, was not all sexual yearning and occasional performance. Simenon truly fell in love with the city, with its streets, its houses, its people, its genuine gaiety at that time. An artist friend of his from Liège, a former fellow-member of *La Caque*, was already installed more or less successfully in a small *atelier* on the slopes of Montmartre. At first, Simenon visited him often and they used to spend evenings of discussion together, much as they had done earlier in their garret with the paraffin lamp near the St. Pholien church. But Simenon soon found that he preferred just to go and sit in a café and watch the world go by, or visit the Moulin Rouge and observe the endless pattern of movement and spectacle. Paris itself played a role as his tutor in his apprenticeship as a writer.

It was too early yet to attempt to earn his living at his trade, but every day he wrote one short story; for his own pleasure and without any intention of trying to sell them. He kept them all. They are now stored at the *Centre d'études Georges Simenon* at Liège University, and one day perhaps may be published.

Unhappy in his work with Binet-Valmer, needing to count every *sou* that he earned, living in a succession of cheap hotels or lodging rooms, he was glad nevertheless to be in Paris. There was no question in his mind of returning to live in Liège. But he had to go back for one brief visit: to get married.

The wedding was fixed for March 23, 1923, at the Ste.-Veronique church. Neither Simenon nor Régine wanted a church wedding; indeed, neither Régine nor any of her three brothers and sisters had been baptised. During Simenon's time in Paris, Régine had to be hurriedly baptised, make her first confession and, on the very morning of the wedding, receive her first communion. They both agreed to go through the ordeal of a church ceremony because of Simenon's widowed mother. For Henriette, nothing else would suffice and her son, for all the complex nature of their relationship, did not want to humiliate her in front of her family and neighbours.

As the day approached, Simenon found a lodging in Paris to which he could return with his wife; a room in a small apartment, belonging to an elderly homosexual who lived there with his young lover, who went around all day in women's clothes. They would have to go into the newly-married couple's room every morning, while they were still in bed, to use the sole washbasin in the apartment. It was hardly a propitious first home, but the young "bellboy" could afford no more.

Nor could he afford to purchase a new dinner suit, which his mother insisted he wear for the ceremony. He had to buy, on an instalment plan, a secondhand outfit from a Belgian journalist friend, working in Paris, that was at least one size too small for him.

Simenon would be the first to admit that he and Régine did not make too lovely a picture, as they led the wedding procession out of Ste.-Veronique on that overcast March day: the groom in his ill-fitting suit and the bride dressed in black (in respect for the dead Désiré), wearing a vast hat decorated with the feathers of birds-of-paradise. But why get married at all? Régine loved him sincerely, of that there is no doubt; but Simenon knew in advance that he could not be faithful to her, even as he took the oath of fidelity in church. The very evening before he left Paris to return for the wedding, he had taken part in a *carré à trois* with two Dutch women he had picked up in a *boîte*, where he had gone to celebrate a solitary "stag night".

Régine had insisted that they have no children, because she wanted to dedicate herself to her painting, and he had agreed – even though he has always maintained that, for him, having children of his own is one of the most fundamental needs of his nature.

So he knew that he was taking on a life companion who was denying him something essential to his being. He knew, by the evidence of his eyes, that she was far from physically atrractive. She had already told him that her idea of marriage was for her to have her own flat or studio and for him to have his, and that they should telephone when they wanted to see each other. Yet he still went through with the wedding.

Why? Simenon knew, deep down inside himself, that he was not really in love with Régine. "She was a good 'mate'," he says now. "Prepared to do anything. As a companion, she was alive, intelligent and thoughtful. One could not want for better." But her sexuality was low: from the start she made it clear to Simenon that their sexual couplings were not to be of outstanding importance in their life together. For reasons of her own, she simply was not all that interested.

Why choose a woman like that for one's life-long partner (and there can be little doubt that, as they stood there before the altar back in

March 1923, that is how Simenon regarded her)? In *Un homme comme un autre*, Simenon says that as early as the age of seventeen he was thinking of marriage as a protection against himself. "For me," he wrote, "the sole method of avoiding a catastrophe was to seek refuge in marriage." I think that is rhetoric. It reads well but means nothing. One has to try and search deeper for the significance of Simenon's union with Régine Renchon.

For the moment, as we see them clambering aboard the night train to Paris on the evening of their wedding (Simenon, on his own confession, somewhat drunk from the day's festivities), it seems bizarre for Georges, the arch-ram, the compulsive womaniser, to have taken as his bride a woman who, for all her great love for him, basically and in the quietest moments of the night preferred not to lie in his arms but to be alone with her own thoughts. The life of Simenon is more "black" than many of the stories he has unwrapped from his imagination.

Talking nearly sixty years later in Lausanne, with Teresa, whom he considers "the ideal love" of his life *but whom he will not marry*, sitting beside him, Simenon is bitter about marriage: "I am against marriage, completely against it. One of my son, Pierre's, friends is getting married next month and he has invited me to the wedding. I like him a lot and he often comes here to the house. But I have told him that I have only ever been to two weddings in my life – my own two. 'So please excuse me. I will send you a big bunch of flowers but I won't go to your wedding.'

"I consider marriage a swindle, a cheat. Take two beings who marry at twenty and twenty-three, like me and Tigy, for example – they are biologically two well-defined beings and they swear on the Bible, or on I don't know what, that they will stay together all their lives, for better or for worse. Well, that's a cheat because biologically those two people ten years later won't have the same cells in their bodies any more. They won't be the same people. And then at fifty, there is an even bigger change. They are not the same people at all.

"And yet you want to make them stay together all their lives! It's a cheat. I tell you!"

And with Régine there was another dimension to the unsatis-factoriness of marriage. "She was extremely jealous. It was a ferocious jealousy. And yet, because she didn't want to have children, she made me use a contraceptive for twenty years . . . with my own wife! It's not very nice. So, needless to tell you, I was unfaithful to her three times a day – but she didn't know. She announced to me: 'The day I find you have been unfaithful to me, I will commit suicide.' It was categorical. So what could I do? I had to lie."

It was a bizarre basis for marriage. Yet for many years, it worked – and worked well. Régine brought Simenon peace of mind. In a sense, she was the comforting mother that he never had. Her three and a half years' seniority may have helped; but, more importantly, the very absence of normal, full, sexual joy between them – "mechanical" is the word Simenon uses to describe their physical relationship – probably contributed to this calming and reassuring influence.

Most human beings, however free-rolling, need a home base: a centre for their existence, a gyroscope that always remains stable amid the ups and downs of life. This Simenon found at once in Régine. Even today something of this remains; she is "Mamiche" to his two sons by his second marriage, Pierre and John, and they visit her often in her home at La Rochelle. To her own son, Marc, she is a rock and a warm, loving grandmother to his children. In her eighties she is indomitable, as in her twenties she must have been both formidable and caring. She was no cook – they nearly always ate out – she was no *femme de ménage*. But somehow, almost from the moment she stepped off the night train from Liège with her new husband beside her, she gave him strength and an added sense of purpose.

Almost immediately upon his return from Liège, instead of just writing his daily short story for his own amusement and as a sort of academic exercise, Simenon went out and bought copies of all the weekly women's magazines that circulated in Paris, and beyond, at that time. They were *les revues galantes* – each with its own style of escapist "literature" for young French working girls and their mothers, in those days long before television and radio and the sophisticated mass-circulation national women's magazines of today, with their blend of stories about Hollywood and well-researched coverage of major world events.

Each *revue* had its own style. What was good for *Le Sourire* would not be appropriate for *Frou-Frou* or for *Rire*, or *Paris-Flirt* or *Mon Flirt*. They were trash, if you like, but good professional trash. Simenon set out to ape their professionalism. He wrote short stories in the individual styles of the different magazines, and sent them off. Within a short while, he was successful. He sold his first short story to *l'Humour* for a fee of a hundred francs – "which to me was marvellous!"

Within a couple of months, he was writing two or three short stories every evening in their little room and was contributing to a good half-dozen of the *revues galantes*. Régine, for all her dedication to her painting, was clearly not going to be able to help with their finances for a very long time (in fact, she only succeeded in selling one canvas in her entire time in Paris.). Even so, Simenon was beginning to think of throwing in his unpalatable job with Binet–Valmer and trying to exist solely by his writing.

Then, out of the blue, Binet–Valmer called him into his office. Simenon hardly expected the great man, resplendent in monocle and the inevitable frock coat, even to remember that he worked for him. Binet–Valmer looked the young man up and down rather disdainfully and told him that one of the aristocratic backers of his right-wing political league was looking for a secretary, and that he had mentioned Simenon to him. Next morning, at eleven o'clock, Simenon presented himself in the *salon* of the Marquis de Tracy, and was taken on at once. His duties were to commence at 9 a.m. the next day.

Simenon was bowled over with delight. Tracy was famous, one of the richest men in France, the owner of five or six châteaux as well as large properties in Italy and Tunisia. He even had his own newspaper, *Le Courier du Centre*, published in Nevers. He was the best kind of dilettante, using his vast inherited wealth not to live in luxurious idleness but to be truly a man of affairs. He was active in all sectors of French life. The key to a whole new world was being given to the young apprentice-writer, and almost by chance. What fresh experiences to savour, what new insights into people to be acquired!

It was in a self-confessed state of joyous exaltation that Simenon took Régine to dine that night in an expensive restaurant. It was perhaps also to be expected that later, on some pretext, he would leave their lodging "and offer myself to a jolly little girl on the Place de la Madeleine, which until then I had not dared to afford."

Simenon was with the Marquis de Tracy for a little less than a year. In a sense, it was something of a deviation from his set course as a writer, but in other ways it was an extremely valuable period in his development. He kept up writing his daily short stories, on top of his formal work as a secretary, and succeeded in selling more and more of them.

Tracy had a sympathetic personality. "It was very interesting to be with him and I was truly his secretary," says Simenon. The two men, though always employer and employee, became almost friends.

Simenon still wore his hair long, hanging over the back of his collar in a style that he thought appropriate for a young writer. Tracy said nothing until one day when they were alone, he stroked the hair at the back of Simenon's neck and said gently, "Mon petit Sim." That was all he needed to say! Simenon had his hair cut short and never again let it grow to "artistic" length.

Tracy moved around a lot from one château to another. His main home was a magnificent twin-towered mansion at Paray-le-Fresil in the Loire. Simenon spent a great deal of time with him there, having assured Tracy, who was something of a misogynist, that he had left his wife behind in Paris. In fact, he had taken a room for Régine and himself in a hotel in a small town some eighteen kilometres away, and every morning and evening he cycled there and back. He thought that Tracy knew nothing about it, until one day the Marquis asked him: "Do you like your bed?" Simenon blushed, and at once understood that his worldly employer knew everything. "You know there is a small house to let in the village. It has only two rooms," said Tracy. "But don't you think you and your wife would be more comfortable there?"

Indeed, Simenon and Régine were very happy at Paray-le-Fresil. It was summer. Simenon adored the countryside. He struck up a warm friendship with Tracy's bailiff, a burly, no-nonsense countryman who lived on the estate. Later he used him as the model for Maigret's father, with Maigret himself born on an estate based on the one at Paray-le-Fresil.

But as Tracy proved ever more reluctant to return to Paris, Simenon began to chafe at his enforced absence from the capital. As he has explained: "I began to feel I knew enough about this kind of life with the Marquis, this life of the artistocracy. And he was not enough in Paris for my taste. When I started, he said he would spend most of the year in Paris and just two or three months at the châteaux, but it was the other way round."

Simenon tendered his resignation and, in the spring of 1924, returned to Paris with Régine. There was no animosity with Tracy. In later years, they frequently used to see each other as friends – something that never occurred with Simenon's only other French employer, the pompous, bourgeois Binet-Valmer.

It was marvellous to be back in Paris. They found a small flat for themselves at 21, Place des Vosges, near the heart of the city. The work was really building up. Everything was good, everything was exciting. "I loved Paris madly," Simenon says. "But it was the victorious Paris, Paris after the First World War when the French considered themselves heroes, when they felt they had really won the war." He was to feel differently about the Paris he returned to after World War Two.

It was the period of Montparnasse at its best. It was the period in which the Americans discovered Paris and Paris discovered the Americans. It was the era of jazz, and the Simenons and their friends used to listen to all the latest records – and, with difficulty, to the radio direct from the United States itself. The music of New Orleans was all the rage. It was great to be young and alive, and beginning to succeed, in Paris at that time.

He now made the jump from short stories to full novels. To be sure, he was still serving his "apprenticeship". These were not novels in the *Acadamie Française* meaning of the term. They were *romans populaires*, potboilers that were full-length versions of the romantic, escapist material he had put into his short stories for *Frou Frou*, *Paris-Flirt* and the rest. The first one of this new style, *Le Roman d'une dactylo* ("The Story of a Secretary"), he threw off in typical express-train fashion in one morning, seated on the terrace of a café in the Place Constantin-Pecqueur, while his wife exhibited unsuccessfully at the nearby Foire aux Croutes. The novels instantly found a market. Simenon was not only learning his trade, but beginning to earn a good living for himself as well.

Then, on New Year's Day 1925, came the call to visit Tallandier, one of the leading publishers of this genre, for whom Simenon had already written several *romans*. He said to Simenon: "Listen, my young Sim. From now on I am going to order your *romans* ten at a time, and you can start at once by letting me have ten new ones for a special collection." It was something that Simenon, not yet twenty-two years of age, would never have dared to hope for: ten novels in one go!

For the first time in his life, he took a taxi back home to Régine, and he has never travelled in a bus or underground train since. It had taken him just over two years from his bedraggled arrival, in the rain, at the *Gare du Nord*, clutching his broken suitcase and brown-paper parcel, to reach the first rung of solid financial success. "From then on we had a very comfortable life," recalls Régine.

CHAPTER 6

Early Success

Success not only arrived very fast, so did its trappings. Gone were the days when at times Simenon and Régine would only eat when they had collected ten or so empty wine and mineral-water bottles and taken them back to the *épicerie*, the *consigne* of twenty *centimes* on each bottle providing them with a couple of francs to spend on food.

Now, although they remained for the next two years in the same small ground-floor apartment on the Place des Vosges, they ate sumptuously and went out every night to a restaurant or a *boîte*, or both. "The *Moulin Rouge* was our headquarters in the evening," recalls Régine, "and at that time we went a lot to *La Coupole* on the Boulevard Montparnasse, not in the main restaurant, but in the little bar on the left. All our friends were there. We danced the Charleston at *Le Jockey* club."

She has a vivid memory-picture of her husband at that time: "He was very busy, dynamic, full of life. Very attractive and always on the go. It was like a whirlwind. We never stayed at home one single night before the war – except when we had friends visiting us. We never had an evening together at home alone, just the two of us."

It was not her doing. "Georges liked to go out. He was attracted by everything that was outside the house. He needed to go out, to feel the people around him – the bustle of life." She claims that she always went with him: "He wouldn't have gone on his own." Was all this frenetic activity to his taste or to hers? "You know, we lived an intimate life together. We were very close. What he liked, I liked, and vice versa – except to stay home!"

And when they did stay home and friends visited them, it was often party time. They ranked among their friends in these middle years of the twenties some of the leading young actors, painters, writers and designers in Paris: Picasso, Jean Gabin, Marcel Pagnol, Marcel Achard, Vlaminck, Foujita, Paul Colin, Pascin and Kisling. The parties would

51

sometimes go on all night but every morning, party or no party, Simenon would start work. He would pick his way through the slumbering bodies and start tapping at the typewriter. Sometimes his guests sprawled on the floor would groan and moan for pity with every *click* of the typewriter's keys, but the automaton, seated at his desk, would hammer on.

For Simenon was really enjoying these hard-working years of his apprenticeship. His output was too much for a single publisher to handle, and soon he had six. He wrote eighty pages a day, every day. "That means eighty pages of typing a day, at ninety-two words a minute," he says. "You don't count in words in France or in Belgium, you count in lines. And they were novels of 10,000 lines each and I wrote them in three days! In French there are roughly seven words to a line, in English there are more because the words are shorter and in German there are less because the words are longer, but if you multiply by seven that means every novel was 70,000 words. In one month I once wrote five such novels. And when you remember that I was paid 1,500 francs for each one, you'll see that I considered myself rich."

At one time, he was juggling with seventeen pseudonyms, all registered with the *Société des Gens de Lettre*, since he could not positively flood the market with books by "Georges Sim". Some of the names are amusing: *Gom Gut* (a sort of yellow paint), *Plick et Plock*, *Poum et Zette*; others hearken back to Liège: *Jean du Perry* (named after the rue du Perry) or *Christian Brulls* (a throwback to his mother's maiden name, Brull); others just look suitably impressive: *Georges d'Isly, Maurice Pertuis, Germain d'Antibes*.

Some of the novels were Westerns, for which the French have always had a considerable appetite. They bore such titles as *La Panthère Borgne* ("The Dark Panther") and *L'Oeil de l'Utah* ("The Eye of Utah"). Others were adventure stories set in faraway places – *Le Roi du Pacifique* ("The King of the Pacific"), *Le Chinois de San-Francisco* ("The San Francisco Chinaman"), *Le Monstre Blanc de la Terre de Feu* ("The White Monster of Tierra del Fuego"). The rest were pure *roman galants* – what Simenon has called "juicy stories". The titles tell their own tale: *Orgies bourgeoises, Une petite très sensuelle, Fièvre, Nuit de Paris*. "It was the hot twenties and I made those novels as hot as I could," Simenon told Brendan Gill. "Some of them were illustrated, and oh, what a waste of the artist's time!"

But his output was not only novels. Sketches, short stories and novellas poured from him in their hundreds, all appearing under his various pseudonyms. He could have six stories in a single issue of a magazine, each story signed with a different name. Nor was he in the least disturbed that nearly all of this work was trash. He was learning his trade and being paid handsomely in the process. He also enjoyed what he was doing. "I liked writing those stories very much," he says blandly. "I would sit in front of the window in the flat in the Place des Vosges, then suddenly I would get up, go to the typewriter and write a story. Then I'd sit down by the window again. That happened up to eight times a day because I often wrote eight stories in a day."

It would be wrong to dismiss these years as mere commercialisation and the vulgarities of an *arriviste*. Doubtless there was an element of this; at one stage, for a publicity stunt, Simenon even offered to write a short story suspended in an iron cage on the terrace of the *Moulin Rouge*. But all the time he was applying himself with rare dedication and professionalism to his development as a writer.

As he said to his interviewer from the *Observer* in 1962: "I am not ashamed of what I wrote during those years. It was a way of earning my money and of getting to know how you make a book, how you sustain that interest of the reader, how you put a dialogue between two pieces of description . . . it is a lot of study."

Already, the very intensity of the creative process would cause his stomach muscles to knit together like steel, and he would be forced to break off from writing and run to the washbasin to vomit. Even in his later, assured years of success, this distressing symptom would constantly recur.

It was in 1925, in the first flush of exuberance at his new-found material wealth, that Simenon evolved two of the most important characteristics of his style. One is his use of a sort of flashback and flashforward technique in his writing: the way in which past, present and future tenses jostle each other, almost in the same sentence, and certainly in the same paragraph or page. "It comes from a very simple idea," he explains. "To my thinking, in my philosophy, past, present and future do not exist . . . It's as though everything happens at the same time. Because everything that we experience depends on what we have experienced before and prepares us for what we are going to experience." It is a technique that is nowadays quite often employed by those writing for the cinema but Simenon remains almost alone as someone who has consistently used it in popular novels.

As he wrote in a letter to André Gide in January 1939, the first time he attempted such a "flashback" and "flashforward" approach was in *M. Gustave*, a short story written in 1925. "You will see," he tells that great purist of the French language, "that I was already then haunted by a problem that has pursued me ever since: the three dimensions – the past, the present and the future – tying themselves together into a single action with a density of atmosphere and of complete verisimilitude that I had not achieved then and still have not today."

The second characteristic of the Simenon style that began to emerge at this time is the absence from his writing of anything resembling literature with a capital "L". He had been trying to get his short stories accepted by the newspaper *Le Matin* but, for once, he kept drawing a blank. Colette, the most famous French woman writer of her time, was then the paper's literary editor and it was she who kept rejecting his manuscripts. Finally, she said: "Look, it is too literary, always too literary." So Simenon followed her advice and wrote a story that was not "too literary" – and Colette accepted it at once.

He has been following that same advice ever since. He says that it is the only piece of general advice from a writer that has been of any use to him. He followed it when he was writing, and it was the main criterion when he was revising. He defines "too literary" as "every sentence which is there just for the sentence." All adjectives, adverbs and any other word which was there just to make an effect, he cut. "You know, you have a beautiful sentence – cut it. Every time I find such a thing in one of my novels, it is to be cut."

But having said what is to be cut, what is it important to retain? That which gives "a third dimension" to the writing. Simenon once explained to an American interviewer his theory in terms of painting. "A commercial painter paints flat; you can put your finger through. But an artist – for example, an apple by Cézanne has weight. And it has juice, everything, with just three strokes. I tried to give to my words just the weight that a stroke of Cézanne's gave to an apple. That is why most of the time I use concrete words. I try to avoid abstract words, or poetical words, you know, like 'crepuscule', for example. It is very nice, but it gives nothing. Do you understand? To avoid every stroke which does not give something to this third dimension."

On the surface, all was going superbly well for the successful young writer, with his artistic wife and circle of enterprising and stimulating friends. What else, apart from the children forbidden him by Régine, could he possibly want?

The answer, of course, was anything and everything; a corner of his soul was never still. The rue de Lappe and other streets around the Bastille, far from the comfort of his home on the Place des Vosges, were not tourist attractions then in the way that they are today. In the dance halls of the *quartier* they would pull a knife for "Yes" or "No", and Simenon once saw a woman's throat cut beside him in one of the bars.

Yet this was where he chose to go late at night, night after night (after having taken Régine home and under the pretext of looking for models for her), to seek out prostitutes, with whom he would then go off to a *hôtel de passe* – sometimes with men following at a distance, threatening him in the street. "It was a curious world," he has said. "One found girls there who had arrived in Paris from Brittany or Normandy only two months ago and were already on the streets."

He used to spend nights wandering, unarmed, on the old defence works that still existed near La Villette, on the rue de Flandre. He claims proudly that the infamous neighbourhood of the Canal St. Martin held no secrets for him, nor did the alleys of Montmartre or the narrow byways of the 12th Arrondissement. He made love in the streets and in the passageways, "where the unexpected arrival of a policeman could have changed my future."

In *Les Trois crimes de mes amis* ("The Three Crimes of my Friends"), written in January 1937 but never translated into English, he asks: "What gave us that taste for fallen women, the most disgusting love affairs . . . that unhealthy exultation between two glasses of wine?" He suggests that it may have been the fault of the First World War "that we lived through as children without understanding it and that marked us without realising it." The explanation rings hollow, as does his claim in an article entitled "The Novelist", written in 1946, that during those years in Paris he "realised that only what one has lived oneself can be transmitted to others through literature. I had to know the world from every angle, horizontally and vertically . . . know it in all its dimensions, come into contact with countries and races, climates and customs, but also to penetrate it vertically . . . have access to different social strata, to be as much at ease in a tiny fisherman's bistro as at an agricultural fair or in a banker's living room." This sounds very much like special pleading to mask the thrill of sexual adventure, tinged with danger, to be found in up-skirting a whore in a shop doorway.

In *Quand j'étais vieux*, he recounts that he penetrated a married woman in her own house, with her unsuspecting husband, busy in an adjoining room, talking to them through a half-open door. You do not take that sort of risk merely to gather source material for what eventually may go into a book.

Similarly, later, in Cairo, he wanders alone at night (with a revolver in his pocket, this time) in the red-light district. And it was the same "at Aswan, in Panama, in Guayaquil and almost all over the world." Simenon claims that at the time he never had the sense of running risks; that only retrospectively, looking back decades later, did he feel fear. One wonders if this was really so. One would have thought that the sensation of fear, if anything, was there at the time and heightened the sexual passion. And, if not, how much greater must the sexual compulsion have been to drive all thoughts of danger from his mind?

There was one woman in the mid-twenties with whom – as ever, unbeknown to Régine – Simenon had something close to a real affair. She was Josephine Baker, the St. Louis-born American negress singer and showwoman who *par excellence* represented *Les Années Folles* at their peak.

Leaving America for Paris at the age of nineteen as a member of a black dancing troupe, she had greeted the Old World with all the enthusiasm of the New. "When the Statue of Liberty disappeared over the horizon, I knew I was free," she said in later years. She certainly behaved freely enough, moving in with her first Parisian lover on the day of her arrival.

Within a year, she was the highest paid entertainer in Europe. She was the very embodiment of style, fashion and glamour, and retained her fantastic popularity for fifty years. Her funeral at the Madeleine in 1975 was a national event, complete with Mozart's Requiem and a 21-gun salute. "*Elle est morte, elle est immortelle*", came a voice from the crowd.

In those mad years of the twenties, Josephine was a "natural" for Simenon. Their animal attraction for each other must have been instant. "She was a beast for sex," her biographer Lynn Haney quotes a composer who knew her well as saying. "She was looking for the perfect penis, and she looked hard," recalls another old friend. "Sex was like champagne to her," says a third ex-admirer. "She didn't need conversation. It would last twenty minutes, perhaps one hour, but it was body to body the whole time. She was a free spirit 'way back'."

"Of course, Simenon was Josephine's lover!" says Régine. "I have learnt it since but I was ignorant at the time. We both knew her well. We went to her nightclub nearly every night." Lynn Haney claims, in her otherwise enjoyable and well-researched book, that Simenon was for a while, in his early days in Paris, employed as her secretary; but Régine says that is not so. "For a few weeks he helped her, when she was between managers, to set her papers and accounts into some kind of order. But that was all. He merely helped her as a friend. Josephine Baker, you know, was not exactly a business woman."

Their dalliance lasted for quite some time. The two were explosive together. Lynn Haney says that Josephine was quite possibly the most uninhibited woman that Simenon had ever met. Whether that is so or not, they certainly had similar tastes. She, too, loved love-making on the spur of the moment – standing up, alfresco, under water, "*n'importe comment*." They remained friends for the rest of Josephine's life and when, nearly thirty years later, at Lakeville, Connecticut, Simenon's second wife, Denise, by mistake goes into the guest bedroom without knocking, when Josephine is visiting their house, she finds the ageing singer's naked body, standing there just having come out of the shower, as taut and firm as in the days when she had *le tout Paris* at her feet.

There *was* another woman in Simenon's life at that time and, in a sense, there always has been ever since, throughout both his marriages and even now during his last tranquil union with Teresa. Her name is Henriette Liberge. She is from the Normandy coast of France. Her father was a cod-fisherman at Etretat near the small Channel resort of Benouville. In the summer of 1925, Simenon and Régine were holidaymaking at Benouville, high up on the cliffs facing England across the water. Every day they went down to Etretat to swim, and then had lunch with a friend from Paris, who was a restorer of paintings, and his wife who had rented a holiday-home for the summer in the picturesque little fishing village. The local girl they got in to help around the house was the pert, bright-eyed, seventeen-year-old Henriette.

"She was very nice, very much the country girl, she could hardly read or write at that time, but she was very straight . . . delightful!" recalls Simenon. "So I said to my friends, 'Do you mind if I take her back to Paris with us for a year? I want a maid to look after us back there.'"

So Henriette went to Paris with Simenon and Régine – but not just for a year. She has lived with the Simenon family ever since. At the moment, alert, forceful, still extremely attractive in her late seventies, she lives outside Paris with Marc, Simenon's eldest son. She cooks, helps care for his two teenage children, is, in a way, still a *domestique*, sleeping in her own quarters behind the kitchen. But they are very comfortable quarters, and when the family sits down for Sunday lunch, it is Mlle. Liberge, not Mme. Simenon (Marc's vivacious second wife, the actress Mylene Demengeot), who takes her place at the end of the table facing the head of the household. In a very real sense, she is the matriarch of the Simenon family; with Régine, as "Mamiche", on the sidelines at her home in La Rochelle.

According to Denise, Simenon has slept with all his maids who have let him; and that is probably true. Mlle. Liberge is no exception. Simenon is predictably frank about it. "I didn't want to touch her for three years. I waited for three years before we had a real intimacy, and then it was total – without Tigy knowing, obviously." He did with Mlle. Liberge as he has done with all the women who have been close to him: he remodelled her to his own liking. He did not approve of the name "Henriette" – perhaps it held too many memories of his mother – so he renamed her "Boule", and that is what the family call her to this day. She has never married. Says Simenon, "She has lived with one lover all her life . . . and that's me!"

It is significant that, although it took Simenon just over two weeks to establish intimate sexual relations with his first wife, Régine, and he had sex with his second wife, Denise, on the evening of the day that they met, it was three long years before he finally succeeded with Boule. "*Elle est vraiment formidable, Boule!*" says John Simenon, in a mixture of pride and affection. And he is right.

Life in Paris went on in the same whirl of activity as before. In the Spring of 1926 Régine sold the only painting for which she actually found a buyer. The price was considerable: 800 francs. "That's it!" said Simenon. "We're going to blow the money!"

And the three of them – Régine, Simenon and Boule – went off down to Porquerolles, a magnificently wild island off the Mediterranean coast near Toulon, then completely unspoiled, where Simenon rented a small villa facing the sea. They spent an idyllic summer there with Simenon, in shorts, typing his stories and potboilers in the early sunlight, then spending the rest of the day swimming or out in a small boat. There were parties, friends visiting, a whole new world of local fishermen to get to know, nude bathing; it was *Les Années Folles* in the blazing sun and balmy evenings of the Midi.

Simenon became so enchanted with the island that he kept on the villa indefinitely. Often in the years up to the Second World War he would suddenly, on impulse, flee Paris, or wherever else in France he might be, taking Régine and Boule with him, and seek the refuge of the small island in the sun.

Especially in the thirties, when he was in the early bloom of his truly creative years, the hurried departure for the south normally meant that he felt a novel was on the way and he required a change of atmosphere. Throughout his working life, Simenon needed challenge and a change of scene. He likes to think of himself as a chameleon, taking his colouring from his setting, able to fit in anywhere, whether with princes or paupers. But, in nature, the chameleon lives in only one habitat; he has to blend in with one set of surroundings. Simenon was a chameleon forever changing the backgrounds with which he sought to merge.

In the spring of 1928, the chameleon changed its colour again. Gone were the elephant-leg pants in a fetching shade of *bois de rose*, in which he used to dance the Charleston with Régine at *Le Jockey* club or watch Josephine Baker perform. Now he donned the faded blue denims of a boatman. For – with Régine, Boule and a massive Great Dane called Olaf – he set off on a five-months' tour of the rivers and canals of France. "I wanted to go right round France by water," he explains. "Now you can hire boats to do that, but then nobody did it." It took them the whole summer and well into the autumn, and they went through no less than 982 locks.

Why the desire to see France by water? Because ever since his childhood visits to his Aunt Marie's crowded bar-grocery store on the Coronmeuse quai at Liège, with its "invigorating odour of tar and resin", and the atmospheric grip that the River Meuse had upon his youngest memories, Simenon has been obsessed by boats, the water, canals and rivers. He has the theory that you can best see into the life of a country from the banks of its rivers: that is the back view which more accurately reflects reality; the front, which is the façade adopted to the world, looks out blankly on the road.

He bought a five-metres mahogany craft called *Ginette* that had once served as a yacht's lifeboat, and had it specially converted for the voyage. Riggings were fitted, along with sails and a small engine, and an auxiliary outboard motor (then just coming on to the market) at the back. An awning was installed that could be closed at night to make a cabin, where he and Régine would sleep. They towed a canoe containing mattresses, blankets, clothes, a little battery-oven, and a tent that could be set up on land at night for Boule and the dog. They must have been quite a sight, chugging dreamily along the calm river-waters of France.

Every evening, they would stop wherever the fancy took them. Boule, who was, and still is, a magnificent cook, served them a delicious dinner. Then they would bed down for the night. At about five o'clock in the morning Boule would wake Simenon with a large cup of hot, steaming coffee and take his place on the comfortable mattress beneath the awning, while he set himself up on the foredeck or on land with his typewriter and its large wooden box, which he used as a seat. Then he would work happily at some chapters of a book or a short story for the next two or three hours.

Very early one morning, when they were moored by the side of the Canal du Midi, he used the ground-floor window of a quayside house as a mirror so that he could shave himself. It was so dark inside the house that the plain glass adequately reflected his image. Then, after a while, it seemed to him that his face was changing in the reflection, that totally different features were meeting his eyes. Suddenly, the window was flung open and an astonished boatman's wife, in curlers and nightdress, cried angrily: "And what do you think you're doing?" He answered quite naturally: "I am shaving."

Another time, at Grau-du-Roi in the Lower Camargue (where, it will be remembered, in the novel Le Temps d'Anais, the young Bauche took the voluptuous Anais on the beach without a word), the Ginette rode on its mooring during the night and the unfortunate Boule had to bring Simenon his early-morning coffee from her tent pitched on the beach, wading out "with the water up to her breasts". One warm summer's night while they were there, Régine and Simenon changed into formal clothes in Boule's tent, and went off in solemn, bourgeois splendour to the local Casino. But they did not maintain their dignity for long. On the way back, they stripped off on the beach, "and it was in a state of candid nudity that we regained the shelter of the Ginette."

It was so hot in the Lower Camargue, and the mosquitoes were biting so viciously, that Simenon conceived the idea of covering himself with some bunting while he sat typing in the morning, pipe, as ever, stuck firmly in his mouth. All went well, and he remained unmolested, until some ash from his pipe set fire to the bunting and he was nearly severely burned.

It was not always sunshine and pleasing encounters. At one time, near Epernay, they struck a patch of persistent rain that endured for eight days. They had to huddle together, soaking wet, having only cold *charcuterie* for their meals, until a waterside housewife took pity on them and invited them in for a warming *pot-au-feu*. Even so, by the time they returned to Paris, Simenon had made his decision: the first stage of his life in the city, with all its bustle and gaity, was over. He felt that his apprenticeship was drawing to an end. At the age of twenty-five, he was quite literally ready to move on.

They had by now taken a larger, more luxurious apartment on the first floor of the same building at 21, Place des Vosges; but it was going to have to stand empty for a while. For the next year or more, Simenon, the two members of his household and his dog, were going to live on the water. He vowed they would not spend a single night on land in all that time.

In the winter of 1928–9, Simenon had a much bigger craft, a cutter called *Ostrogoth*, custom-built for him at the shipyards of Fécamp in Normandy. She was capable of going to sea, was ten metres long by five metres broad, and was constructed on the style of the French fishing boats used in the English Channel. She was powered by heavy cashew-coloured sails specially designed so that one man could hoist them, together with a large thirty horsepower auxiliary engine, and boasted a solid hull of thick oak.

Brought up the Seine to Paris in the spring of 1929, the *Ostrogoth* looked an impressive sight at its mooring off the *pointe du Vert Galant* on the tip of the *Ile de la Cité* within two hundred metres of Notre-Dame. No less a personage than the *Curé* of the cathedral was happy to perform the baptismal ceremony, with the fine-looking craft decked out in bunting – although its owner was not noted for his church-going.

A few days later, the boat slipped its mooring and, with Simenon's assured hand at the controls, began gently to make its way upstream. It was a voyage into the future – a future that was uncertain. Simenon and his companions knew only that they were heading north, towards Simenon's native land and beyond that towards Holland and the chill waters of the Baltic.

No one in the party – Simenon any more than the two women – knew how long they were going to be away from Paris. He had brought with him enough work to keep going indefinitely and, if he ran out, he knew that wherever they landed up he could easily get some more commissions simply by making a few phone calls to publishers.

No one knew then, or even suspected, that in a few months' time Simenon would sit down in front of his typewriter, set up by the water's edge in a small Dutch seaport, and, without realising that he was creating a character that would live in the annals of detective fiction, write his first Maigret novel.

CHAPTER 7

The Birth of Maigret

The voyage of the *Ostrogoth* was luxury in comparison with the previous year's experience on the *Ginette*. Simenon no longer needed to use the windows of irate waterside ladies' houses to shave; he had a comfortable warm cabin in which he could perform his daily toilet before starting work at the never-varied hour of 6.30 in the morning. He did his stint of typing to the accompaniment of appetising aromas from the galley, where Boule would be happily preparing late-breakfast. Even Olaf, the dog, was relaxed, laid out on the deck in the long afternoons, taking the sun.

"It was marvellous on board the *Ostrogoth*," recalls Régine. "It was to both our tastes, Simenon's and mine. In no way could you say I was an unwilling passenger on that boat."

In the evenings, replete from Boule's ravishing dinners, Simenon would, according to his self-declared need to "be as much at ease in a tiny fishermen's bistro as at an agricultural fair or in a banker's living room", take himself off to a waterside café, where he would chat with the fishermen over a drink and seek to enter into their lives. Often he would challenge one of the stalwarts to a wrist-wrestling match, hands clenched with elbows firmly placed on table, and generally he won. A strong, virile young man, still only twenty-six years of age at the time, he was, remembers Boule, "like a mountain!" Although there is no evidence to support this, it is more than likely that, at a certain moment in the evening, he would slink off to a local *maison aux filles* recommended by his new-found friends.

Life for Simenon, and for his companions, was idyllic in that long ago summer of 1929, when the decade of *Les Années Folles* and the "Roaring Twenties" was ending for many people on both sides of the Atlantic in financial disaster and total ruin. All that seemed very far away from the *Ostrogoth* and its contented crew. The peculiarly self-sealed existence of those who live by, and on, the water Simenon was later to recreate – especially in the nineteen-thirties – with his normal stylistic realism in such novels as *La Maison du Canal* and *Le Charretier de la Providence* ("Maigret Meets a Milord"), where the Parisian detective sits in a local café soaking up the atmosphere and inhaling "a distinctive odour, the nature of which was enough to mark the difference between this and a country café. It smelled of stables, harnesses, tar and groceries, oil and gas."

Even as late as 1962, when writing in Noland in Switzerland after nearly forty years spent elsewhere around the world, Simenon puts into the mind of René Maugras, the bedridden principal character of *Les Anneaux de Bicêtre*, ("The Patient"), a childhood memory of the quay Berigny at Fécamp, the northern French seaport where the *Ostrogoth* was constructed. Few experiences with Simenon, whether agreeable or otherwise, were wasted from the point of view of his work. Most found an outlet eventually in a character, a setting, or sometimes an entire novel.

Finally, as the burning sun of August 1929 paled into the more gentle warmth of September, the *Ostrogoth* sailed into the small northern Dutch seaport of Delfzijl. Completely unknown to Simenon, a new and vitally important stage of his life was about to begin.

The backcloth to the scene was picture-postcard in its beauty: a village of pink houses with roads paved with pink-coloured stones and an atmosphere of calm, all contained within giant walls that looked as if they were the remains of fortifications from long ago but were, in fact, massive protection against the invading waters of the North Sea. "Here, we'll spend some time!" announced Simenon. The setting was so attractive.

In the event, they stayed longer than he intended. For, despite what people say about the quality of workmanship today, when so many things mechanical or man-made seem to go wrong, the much-vaunted workmen of the twenties were also capable of a botched job. The *Ostrogoth*, for all the care and money spent on her construction, sprang a leak while riding at anchor in Delfzijl harbour. She was letting in too much water and could go no further. She would have to be put into dry dock and totally re-caulked. Simenon was told the job would take a month.

True to his oath before he left Paris that he would not spend a night on land until the completion of their voyage, Simenon and his companions continued to sleep in the boat marooned high above the water. But it was impossible for him to go on working there in the daytime. The hefty Dutch caulkers banging away at the hull made the cabin reverberate like the inside of a bell. So he found an abandoned old barge, half submerged in a nearby canal, and installed himself in it. He dragged into position a large packing case as a table for his typewriter, another for his backside and two smaller ones for his feet – and there, with the water lapping away at the base of his "furniture", he continued to bang out his *romans populaires* and magazine pieces every morning.

But after a few days time began to hang heavily on him. In the boat, on water, there was always something to do, as well as the stimulus of new scenes and varied stopping-places; but here there was little in the way of distraction. For some while now he had had the feeling that it was time his literary career changed gear, that he should start on the next stage of his development as a writer. The enforced, unaccustomed idleness of those balmy late-summer days, virtually shipwrecked on the flat Dutch seashore, added to the feeling that now might be the moment to experiment, to try something new; to move on.

But to where? To do what? Of late, he had written several short detective stories among his *romans populaires* and general potboilers. Indeed he was working right then on three separate thirteen-part series of short thrillers for Joseph Kessel's *Detective* magazine. A year or so earlier, he had written a long short story called *Train de Nuit*, in which a man was murdered on the night train from Paris to Marseilles with the crime solved by a policeman called "Commissaire Maigret". He was just a name, no more, and was not even given a physical description. The story was eventually to appear in September 1930, some six months before the first of the full-length Maigret novels, as yet another *roman populaire* under the pseudonym "Christian Brulls". There was no great contribution to literature in any of this; but it shows how Simenon was moving gradually towards a new dimension as a writer.

In later life, he has tended to foreshorten this development as being more or less a telescoped happening; a deliberate decision to plunge into writing full-length detective novels. But this is an oversimplification, viewed with hindsight. For instance, in the *Observer* interview in 1962, he rather airily told the reporter: "At the age of twenty-six . . . I have a feeling I was able to write better novels. But not enough to write a true novel, a plain novel, and that is why I start with Maigret, because a detective story is much easier, for many reasons.

"If one chapter is bad, people will go through the book anyway because they like to know the end. And equally you have a rope – the detective is a kind of rope, so you follow him. And because he is a detective he has the right to ask questions of people. He has the right to enter their houses.

"So I decided to write a Maigret series, one a month."

The reference to the detective as a kind of rope is a sound one; but for the rest this is not an accurate account of how Maigret was born. There was no blinding light on the road to Damascus or on the sand dunes surrounding Delfzijl. As so often with Simenon, the truth has to be extracted from a maze of sometimes contradictory pronouncements made by the man himself and from the independent documentary evidence. What actually happened is far more confused, and far more fascinating.

One day after Simenon had been some time at Delfzijl, instead of sitting down at his typewriter for his usual morning's stint, he took himself off to a waterside café of which he had become rather fond. He sat outside in the warm September sun, smoking his pipe and watching the world go by. He drank not one, not two but three glasses of neat, clear Dutch gin. Then – as he was always later to do when a story began to form inside him – he went for a long contemplative walk through the surrounding countryside; pipe clenched between his teeth, hands stuck firmly in his pockets.

As Simenon walked, a picture of his principal character came to him: a big man, powerful, a massive presence rather than an individual. He smoked his pipe, wore a bowler hat and a thick winter coat with a velvet collar (both later abandoned as fashions in police clothing changed). But he did not see the face. *Simenon has never seen the face of Jules Maigret*. "I still do not know what his face looks like," he says. "I only see the man and the presence." In none of the eighty-four novels and eighteen short stories in which Maigret appears is there any description of his face. When in 1956, twenty-five years after the first Maigret novel was published, the world's only statue of him was unveiled at Delfzijl in the presence of Simenon and five of the actors who had played the part in film or television adaptations, the coverings fell away to reveal a massive man of bronze wearing a bowler hat and a thick winter coat – but with a face that bore no recognizable features. This facelessness of Maigret is something to which we shall have to return when attempting to assess his true relationship with his creator. It is undoubtedly of profound importance.

His walk completed, Simenon returned to the *Ostrogoth* and spent the rest of the day enrapt in "a new atmosphere that invaded me, in a new setting that took place all around me."

The next morning, at 6.30, he sat down in his waterlogged barge and began to type the first chapter of a novel called, in French, *Pietr-le-Letton*, after the name of its principal villain, and in English, when it was eventually translated in 1963, "Maigret and the Enigmatic Lett". By eleven o'clock, the chapter was finished. Simenon had no plan, no notes, no plot worked out in advance. All he had by way of preparation was the names of the principal characters and of some important streets, written in haste on the back of an old manila envelope that he had found in the cabin of the *Ostrogoth*. Later this was to become an obsession with him. Before starting a novel, he would always have to jot down on a manila envelope the names of his characters, some essential facts about them, some vital addresses, and perhaps a plan or two of some of the main roads. Nothing more. In *Quand j'étais vieux*, he says: "I follow this whole routine because I believe it is necessary if I'm to set off the mechanism, so much so that it has become a superstition."

In all the books that he has written since *Pietr-le-Letton*, Simenon has never known the plot in advance. He has never known where the story will go from one chapter to the next; each chapter takes a day and each chapter he starts like the reader, not knowing what is to follow. If it is a murder story, he does not solve the mystery and discover the identity of the murderer one second before Maigret does: the two investigate the crime together, as it unfolds before them both. It is a unique partnership in the annals of detective fiction.

Already, in that first book, Maigret springs full-grown, like Minerva from Juno's womb, from the imagination of his creator. On the very first page we are told how he rises "ponderously" to his feet and lights a pipe. On page two, we learn that he is "a tall, burly figure, hands in pockets and pipe clenched between his teeth," with thick, dark brown hair with a few threads of grey at the temples. And chapter two opens with this splendidly vivid description:

> He had neither moustache nor heavy boots. His suit was of quite good material and cut: he shaved every morning and had well-kept hands.
>
> But his frame was plebeian – huge and bony. Strong muscles swelled beneath his jacket and soon took the crease out of even a new pair of trousers.
>
> He had a characteristic stance too, which even many of his own colleagues found annoying.
>
> It expressed something more than self-confidence, and yet it was not

conceit. He would arrive, massively, on the scene, and from that moment it seemed that everything must shatter against his rock-like form, no matter whether he was moving or standing still with feet planted slightly apart. His pipe was clamped between his teeth. He was not going to remove it just because he was in the Majestic (a supremely luxurious hotel in the centre of Paris).

It is not just a detective that is being created here, a mere device for the better unfolding of a yarn that will hold the reader's attention. It is a father-figure, a rock against which the turbulent waters of the world will lash, but which will remain firm and durable. The massive silhouette of Maigret may remind one of Simenon's great grandfather, the old blind miner Guillaume Moers – "Vieux Papa", sitting "monstrous in size and with hands like a gorilla" in a corner of his granddaughter's kitchen in Liège, his huge shoulders wrapped in a bear's skin. But the personal qualities of Maigret, his humanity, the idealised happiness of his marriage to Louise (she too is introduced in the first novel, complete with her "own plum brandy prepared every year in her native village in Alsace, where she always returned for the summer holidays") recall inexorably someone even closer to Simenon: his own father. In a radio interview in 1955, he frankly concedes as much: "When I wanted to create a sympathetic person who understood everything, that is to say Maigret, I gave him without realising it certain of my father's characteristics."

Maigret, like Désiré Simenon, loves his fellow men, understands and pities them. He believes they have killed or committed crimes because they are weak or unhappy, because they feel threatened, because they are frightened. The closer he gets to his prey, the greater his sympathy because he feels he understands him better. It is, to a lawyer's cynical mind, a completely sentimental, if not mawkish, view of the realities of criminal responsibility; but it is undeniably at the very forefront of the philosophy of Simenon *père et fils* – and of Maigret. In this very first Maigret novel, a somewhat contrived plot of look-alike twins and international crime, laced with fraud and murder, which has its denouement (and this will come as no surprise) in Fécamp, birthplace of the *Ostrogoth*, the detective does not end by arresting his man and charging him with murder – of his own brother, incidentally – but stands aside and allows him to shoot himself with Maigret's own gun.

He lets the man pass judgment on himself rather than allow society to do so. Not for nothing is the motto which forms part of the design of Simenon's personal bookplate, *Comprendre et ne pas juger*

("Understand and do not judge"). The basic theory of life to which Maigret (and Simenon) works is already full-minted, cogently stated in this first novel written in a half-submerged barge with packing cases as study furniture.

> The situation was ridiculous. The Superintendent knew there was not one chance in ten that his vigil would lead to any result.
>
> But he stuck to it, because of a vague impression; he could not even have called it a presentiment. It was more like a private theory, which he had never worked out but which stuck nebulously at the back of his mind; he called it the theory of the chink.
>
> Every criminal, every gangster, is a human being. But he is first and foremost a gambler, an adversary; that is how the police are inclined to regard him, and as such they usually try to tackle him.
>
> When a crime or felony is committed, it is dealt with on the strength of various more or less impersonal data. It is a problem with one – or more – unknown factors, to be solved, if possible, in the light of reason. Maigret used the same procedure as everyone else. And like everyone else he employed the wonderful techniques devised by Bertillon, Reiss, Locard and others, which have turned police work into a science.
>
> But above all he sought for, waited for and pounced on, *the chink*. In other words, the moment when the human being showed through the gambler.

It is part of the established Simenon legend that none of his novels – apart from the lengthy semi-autobiographical work *Pedigree*, which is in a class of its own – has taken him more than eleven days to write, with another three or four days for revision a week or so later. This first one was no exception, although there is a typically self-induced confusion by Simenon as to exactly how long it did take to write. In a short account of "The Birth of Maigret", written in September 1966, he says he completed the work "in three or four days"; when dictating *Un homme comme un autre* seven years later, he claims it took eight days; to the writer of this book he has said that it took four days. Either way it was a *tour de force* for a first full-length novel, with eighteen chapters, that introduced to the world a major figure in modern crime literature.

There is a far more intriguing riddle as to what precisely Simenon did with the manuscript, once he had written it. As so often, there are two different accounts, each supplied by the author himself; and it seems almost certain that neither of them is right. In fact, the truth is stranger than the fiction that Simenon has created around the event.

In *Un homme comme un autre*, he tells how after completing *Pietr-le-Letton* he went on to write three more novels with Maigret as the principal character, after which "I took the train to Paris. I handed over the four novels to *père* Fayard, who had the reputation of possessing infallible judgment." A few days later, Fayard called him to his office and an amusing scene took place, in which the publisher said that they were not real detective stories. They posed no almost mathematical problem that the public had to solve. There were no, in the modern vernacular, good guys or bad guys. There was no love interest. Nor was there a happy ending. "Very well then," said Simenon. "Give me back my manuscripts."

"Oh no!" said Fayard. "We're going to lose a lot of money but I want to risk it. Send me six more novels, and when we've got enough in stock to back it up we'll start to publish them at the rate of one a month."

Simenon returned to Delfzijl "with relief. I felt very good within myself. I set to to write the new series of Maigret books day after day."

In an interview (to two writers on Belgian television) given seven years after dictating *Un homme comme un autre*, Simenon repeats this charming story in a somewhat different form. In this second version, he says that he sent *Pietr-le-Letton* on its own to Fayard, but the publisher replied asking for "two or three more" novels before he could decide. Simenon then wrote those two or three more and sent them off to Paris. It was only then that Fayard called him to his office and they had their discussion about the books.

Both versions paint a cosy, Frank Capra-type story of "gifted-young-author-makes-good"; but it simply did not happen. At least, not like that. There was certainly some such conversation with Arthème Fayard as Simenon has described; that is not imagination. But there was no writing of Maigret books "day after day" in the autumn of 1929. And there was no (as per the second version) "two or three more" Maigret novels written on the trot after *Pietr-le-Letton* was completed.

The truth is much more fascinating and shows that Simenon, when he created Maigret, had no idea that he could serve as the central figure of further books. He was a one-off, the principal character of an experimental novel written by a young writer, still feeling his way in his profession and with time on his hands. Indeed Simenon, despite his public utterances to the contrary, has admitted as much in conversation: "When I wrote *Pietr-le-Letton* I did not think of doing a series. I had used the name of a policeman called 'Maigret' in *Train de Nuit* and I picked up the name again just because it crossed my mind. I did not think at the time of doing any other books at all on the same lines. That idea came from Fayard. It was he who thought of doing a series of books based on the same character."

This view of events is confirmed by Régine, who also says how Simenon came to light on the name of "Maigret", a not too common name in France. "There was a 'M. Maigret' who was a mild little man, who lived with his family in the same apartment building on the Place des Vosges as we did. I think he was some kind of civil servant. When the Maigret novels first appeared, he wrote to Simenon in some heat complaining that he had given his name to 'an ordinary policeman'!"

Simenon never talked to Régine about his new character Maigret. He gave her the chapters of *Pietr-le-Letton* to read as he wrote them – as he had always done with his *romans populaires* and was to continue to do with his novels thereafter – and they discussed the new material; but she "never gave him any directive." When she read the first chapter of the book, "clearly I thought it was something different and that he was finding himself – he was entering a new stage – but we only knew that he had something else to say by the time the first two Maigret books were launched so successfully on to the market. But that was eighteen months later. By then Simenon had already written five Maigrets in preparation for the launching, and we knew that he had definitely got out of his *roman populaire* genre; but it is difficult to say exactly when that was realised. Certainly not with that first Maigret. He didn't burst out and say, 'Now I have created this character Maigret and I can write a lot of novels with him because I know I have created something extraordinary.' There was nothing like that."

Régine's words reflect the reality of what actually happened at Delfzijl. Far from posting the manuscript of *Pietr-le-Letton* in haste to Arthème Fayard or hurrying himself to Paris, Simenon simply put the manuscript away and turned to completing his commissioned assignment of short thrillers for *Detective* magazine. Soon the *Ostrogoth* was completely re-caulked, the boat was put back in the water and they proceeded onwards to Wilhelmshaven, an important naval as well as civil seaport in northern Germany. It was here that Simenon's professional contact with a magazine bearing the suspicious name "Detective" led him and his party being expelled from Germany as possible French police spies.

German U-boats from World War One were quietly rusting in Wilhelmshaven harbour, forbidden by the terms of the post-war settlement from being put to any military or naval use. German susceptibilities were very much on edge because of this slur on the national honour, this reminder of their second-class status. Then, suddenly, this boat flying the French flag enters the port with its strange crew of one man, two women and a massive Great Dane. What is going on? The Germans can almost be forgiven for thinking that something was not quite right.

That evening some young German students saw Boule on deck. She was a stunningly attractive girl. In Simenon's rather charmingly old-fashioned expression, "they started to court her" and asked if they could come aboard. He agreed and they brought with them their gramophone and everyone started dancing and having a good time, including Simenon in his jaunty naval cap. Then the students' teacher arrived, followed by the police, and the young men were ordered off the boat. A somewhat chastened ship's crew settled down for the night.

Next morning, a German police inspector came on board and asked Simenon what he was doing. Apparently this was the first private French boat that had come into any German port since the end of the war. Simenon replied amiably that he was on his way to Hamburg as part of a pleasure cruise. "That is curious," said the German and then he spotted Simenon's typewriter. "What are you typing?" he asked. "Novels," said Simenon. "That also is curious," said the German, even more on his guard. "Yesterday you received a telegram signed 'Detective'. Are you typing official reports on our naval installations for the French police?"

"Really the whole thing was stupid," says Simenon now. "How could they seriously think I was a French spy?" But at the time it did not seem so funny. The inspector dismissed Simenon's reply that *Detective* magazine was nothing to do with the police and that they had merely telegraphed him a money order as payment for the stories he had sent them. "So they send you money, these detectives!" he snorted. "In that case, this afternoon at four o'clock precisely you will be kind enough to present yourself at the Police Headquarters in Wilhelmshaven!"

And so it was that a senior police official, erect in black uniform with monocle camped in his eye, ordered Simenon to put to sea within twenty-four hours and not to return to German territorial waters.

Simenon was no fool. He obeyed the command and went back to Holland, this time passing through Delfzijl and travelling across northern Holland through the canals to the small port of Stavoren on the Zuyder Zee, at that time still a wide expanse of water open to the

North Sea. There they dropped anchor for the winter. It was one of the coldest winters on record in that part of Western Europe, and every morning Simenon had to break the ice around the boat's mooring. But for years afterwards he would remember how marvellous it was to be in the warmth of the cabin and to smell the fried potatoes or the rabbit stew in white wine that Boule was contentedly preparing in the galley.

It was from Stavoren, two or three months after *Pietr-le-Letton* was completed, that Simenon sent the manuscript to Arthème Fayard in Paris. Why Fayard? Because the *romans populaires* with a thriller flavour that he had written before – including *Train de Nuit* – had been for that publishing house, so he thought they would be the people most likely to be interested in this new venture into the genre. It was as simple and straightforward as that.

In the event, Arthème Fayard not only gave Simenon a contract for the first batch of Maigret novels, he was also responsible for their appearing under the writer's own name. Simenon himself still did not consider that he was ready to have books with his name on the title page. In later years, he always referred to the Maigret books of the early nineteen-thirties as "semi-literary" novels. "That really amused the critics," he says. " 'What's a "semi-literary" book?' they asked. 'Listen,' I explained. 'A novel normally doesn't have to have limits, in other words it doesn't have to have rules. The writer can write just as he likes. Whereas in a detective novel you have to have a death, you have to have an investigator, you have to have suspects and someone who is guilty. So you cannot do exactly as you like. That is not what I call pure literature. Pure literature is when there aren't any rules.' "

So the young author, despite his delight at the publisher's confidence in his new creation and the splendid contract that he was being offered, sat in Fayard's office trying to think of a fresh pseudonym for this new series of books. They had bandied around some dozen names without success when Fayard, who, like practically everyone else in the Parisian literary world, called Simenon "Sim", said to him: "What's your real name?" "Georges Simenon," said Simenon. "Fine!" said Fayard. "What's wrong with that? That's the name we'll use." Simenon could hardly tell his publisher that he did not think his newly-commissioned books would be worthy of it.

CHAPTER 8

Maigret and the Art of Simenon

That winter, from the point of view of his literary work, was a barren one for Simenon. Iced up as if in an igloo in the warm cocoon of the *Ostrogoth*, he took time out from normal existence. He kept up to date with his three series for *Detective* magazine and his other commissioned obligations, but for the most part the typewriter remained covered and life was calm and restful. The *Ostrogoth* and its crew became so much a part of the accepted local scene that trawlermen returning to the tiny port at Stavoren, their boats laden with the latest catch, would throw live herrings to the tail-wagging Olaf, waiting patiently on the quayside. He devoured them in one gulp.

But with the spring, this period of relaxation had to end. The assault on Maigret had to begin. Simenon brought the *Ostrogoth* down to an anchorage at Morsang, on the River Orge near Corbeil, just south of Paris. And there in the summer of 1930, he wrote, on the trot, three full-length novels: *M. Gallet décédé* ("Maigret Stonewalled"), *Le Pendu de Saint-Pholien* ("Maigret and the Hundred Gibbets") and *Le Charretier de la Providence* ("Maigret Meets a Milord"). This was followed up in September by *Le Tête d'un homme* ("The Man in the Eiffel Tower"). "At that time I worked morning and afternoon, a chapter in each," Simenon recalls. "I said to myself: 'When it comes quicker, I won't be able to work any longer except in the morning,' and the time came when I could only work in the morning."

By working double-shift, as it were, he produced five Maigret novels before even one had been released to the public. Yet Arthème Fayard still delayed the initial launch, clinging to his original idea of having at least ten books in hand so that he could hit the public hard with a new title every month. He pressed Simenon for the delivery of more pre-publication novels; but it was simply not possible. Simenon was determined to wipe his work slate clean before devoting himself entirely to this new venture, and so the whole of the autumn of 1930 was taken up with completing his backlog of *romans populaires* and magazine pieces.

An interesting insight into Simenon's cavalier treatment of his new-minted hero, even at this late stage, is shown by the fact that among the *romans populaires* that he churned out that autumn were three more in which, as in *Train de Nuit*, an emasculated cardboard police figure called "Commissaire Maigret" appeared. It really was the most offhand way to treat the future Great Detective.

Finally, Fayard decided that he could wait no longer. The "real" Maigret would be unveiled to the public, even though he had only half the desired number of back-up books in hand. Simenon would simply have to work extra hard after publication day to keep up the sausage machine-like production rate of a new book a month. The strain on Simenon was made even greater by Fayard's decision to launch *two* Maigret books simultaneously for maximum impact.

Pietr-le-Letton, the first "Maigret" written, was not one of the two selected for the joint launch; it was the fifth novel to appear, in May 1931. The two chosen for the February launching were *M. Gallet décédé* and *Le Pendu de Saint-Pholien*. There was no particular reason for this, it just happened that way. But what it demonstrates, and what is really quite remarkable, is that the first five Maigret novels formed such a homogeneous unit, with the principal character – and his wife and junior police colleagues at the Quai des Orfevres (the headquarters of the Paris C.I.D.) – so firmly drawn that, for the purposes of launching the new series, as experienced a publisher as Fayard could consider them interchangeable.

At this stage, for all Simenon's subsequent somewhat lofty attitude to money (although a millionaire several times over, he guards all personal details of his wealth from public gaze and disdains to let his fortune bring in further substantial unearned income from investment because of his view that that would be "capitalism"), he was as concerned as Fayard to make the launch a triumphant commercial success. So he persuaded the publisher not to spend a *sou* on advertising, but instead allow Simenon to use all the money set aside for that purpose on organising an outrageous ball to launch the books. He called it a *Bal Anthropométrique*, naming it after that division of the Paris police that concerned itself with questions of identity and identification. The invitations were in the form of a police summons, all guests were fingerprinted when they arrived on facsimiles of police fingerprint forms (one famous music-hall actress declined and left the red lipstick imprint of her mouth instead), and the decorations had a law and order theme with handcuffs, police belts, batons and the rest hanging from the walls. Even the salad shakers were specially designed – by Paul Colin, a leading stage designer and close friend of Simenon's – in the form of miniature Black Marias (French slang for a police van is *panier à salade*).

To cap it all, the Ball was to take place, not in some prestigious, respectable *salle* on the Right Bank but in the Boule Blanche, a night-club in Montparnasse, where, as the newspaper *Le Figaro* somewhat sneeringly commented, "three hundred Martiniquans normally dance the *béguine*." Simenon invited four hundred well-known actors, writers, artists and other celebrities, including high officials of the police themselves. Their numbers were swelled by seven hundred gatecrashers who gamely fought their way in and didn't object to being appallingly overcrowded in the small *boîte*. *Le Figaro* reported: "A certain 'Tout Paris' was there, in evening dress, dinner jacket, apache cap and red scarf. Some women had tied a piece of velvet round their neck and their bolder male companions had reddened their cheeks with crayon."

It was the only publicity stunt that Simenon has ever organised, but it was a fantastic success. There were large quantities of caviar, whisky and champagne. At one in the morning, he made them open La Coupole, a big fashionable restaurant nearby, in order to get a few more cases of whisky and champagne, because the vast supplies that he had laid in had all disappeared down the throats of his guests. Seven hours later, as a faint drizzle descended upon Paris, the still-remaining revellers were served a magnificent champagne breakfast. Even the normally stoical Régine remembers the Ball with animation: "Oh, that was a truly formidable occasion!" she says.

It was also wildly expensive. Simenon had to dip into his own royalties as well as emptying Fayard's advertising budget to defray the total cost; but it was worth every franc. The Ball was the talk of France and Commissaire Maigret was famous before anyone had read a single novel in which he appeared. Within a matter of months, the novels had been translated into eight languages and Maigret's name was a by-word in Europe.

Shortly after the Ball, Simenon gave up the apartment in the Place des Vosges, which had remained unoccupied for the past two years, and together with Régine, Boule and Olaf went to live full time on the

Ostrogoth. During the next eight months, until October 1931, snug in his cabin, he almost kept to his impossible timetable and produced seven more Maigret novels, one of them, *La Danseuse du Gai-Moulin* ("At the 'Gai-Moulin' "), written in an incredible twenty-five hours.

In early August, he took the helm of the *Ostrogoth* and guided her up the rivers to Deauville on the Channel coast, then *the* chic summer resort for the wealthy French. Like all his earlier voyages on the Fécamp–built cutter, there was no other male crew to help him. But this time a uniformed chauffeur drove his chocolate-coloured Chrysler Imperial alongside on land.

For, on August 15, 1931, at the peak of the season, when *le Tout-Paris* had moved up north to become *le Tout-Deauville*, Simenon sat outside the Bar du Soleil on the seafront and, resplendent in specially-designed canary yellow shirt with wide blue stripes and *pyjamas de plage* trousers, signed copies of his books for two hours. This book-signing ritual was the high point of Arthème Fayard's publishing year, reserved for his best-selling writer of the moment. And it had never been so successful, with the elegant, the wealthy and the would-be fashionable queuing up in the sunshine to receive a smile (despite an agonising hangover) and a finely penned signature from the "Author of the Year". If Maigret was born in Delfzijl, his christening was at the *Bal Anthropométrique*, and his first communion was at Deauville.

Even better was to come. Driven away after a few days from Deauville by the persistent noise of late-night jazz and the daytime jinks of French "Bright Young Things", Simenon, still under the constraint of his gruelling production schedule, took the *Ostrogoth* down coast to the tranquil little port of Ouistreham. And there one morning, after he had finished his usual daily stint on a new chapter, a Bugatti roadster drew up on the quayside and out stepped Jean Renoir, son of the great Impressionist painter and himself well on the way to becoming one of the most talented directors in the history of the French cinema. He had come to buy the film rights of *La Nuit du Carrefour* ("Maigret at the Crossroads"). It had appeared only two months earlier, in June, but Renoir was beside himself with enthusiasm.

A deal was made. Simenon, who, apart from one brief occasion in the United States, has never used an agent, sold the film rights for 50,000 francs. Just over a year later the first of fourteen Maigret films appeared, with Jean Renoir's brother Pierre the first actor to play the part.

In those early heady months, it was success all the way. Janet Flanner, an expatriate American writer from Indianapolis who contributed a fortnightly "Letter from Paris" to *The New Yorker*, gushed to her readers about this "handsome" new writer who "always travels (always on his boat, and always on canals), hates heat and wants to go to Tahiti, and spends half a million francs of his royalties a year doing what his characters do: hiring a liveried chauffeur because his villain does; losing two hundred thousand francs at Monte Carlo because his hero must. For he says, 'I have no imagination; I take everything from life' (and from the exploits of certain of his acquaintances, who apparently include some of the liveliest crooks in France). 'I get up at half-past five; go on deck; start typing at six, with either a bottle of brandy or white wine at my side; and write a chapter an hour until noon, when I go on land and lie down in the grass, exhausted. My ambition is to arrive little by little in the class of a Jack London, or – who knows? – even of a Conrad?' " One does not know who is responsible for the hyperbole in this piece – the amazingly successful new novelist, biting joyously on the grapes of delight and consciously hyping his own success story, or the garrulous American journalist – but her verdict on the new literary phenomenon is un-challengeable: "Monsieur Simenon is mistaken; he is already in a class by himself."

The amazing thing about the first dozen Maigret novels written up to December 1931 (when Simenon at last sold the *Ostrogoth* and went to live in a rented villa in that Mecca of all successful people at the time, the French Riviera) is that already there is the assured stamp of an accomplished master on almost all of them. "Of course," writes literary critic Maurice Richardson, "he can't be expected always to keep up the same high level. Yet it is extraordinary how seldom he lets you down." Simenon was only to write seven more "Maigrets" in the nineteen-thirties, but Richardson's considered view (and that, inci-dentally, of Régine Simenon as well) is "that the pre-war Maigret books are the best."

At times, they are slipshod. Simenon kills off Torrence, Maigret's assistant, in the very first novel *Pietr-le-Letton*, only to bring him back to life subsequently, as he has admitted, because he had forgotten that he was dead! From the very early days he had good contacts with the C.I.D. at the Quai des Orfevres and got many of the ideas for his stories from police officers, but that does not prevent on occasions an almost reckless disregard for the realities of forensic science.

For instance, in *La Nuit du Carrefour* a vital question in the plot is exactly where the murder of a wealthy diamond merchant from Antwerp took place. His body, "a shot fired point-blank into his chest", is found slumped over the steering-wheel of a car parked in the garage of one of a small cluster of houses at the isolated Three Widows' Crossroads, fifty kilometres outside Paris. The car does not belong to the owner of that particular garage but to another local resident – in whose garage stands the car that *should* have been in the garage where the murdered man's body has been discovered. Why the switch around? – and in which garage (or where else) has the diamond merchant been shot? The whole novel unfolds without one word being written about the evidence of bloodstains, fingerprints or gunshot marks that might definitively have established whether the man was shot in one of the garages and, if so, which one.

When this is pointed out to Simenon (who, to be fair, does make token reference to forensic science material in his post-war "Maigrets"), he shrugs his shoulders and says: "That could be. But I was far more interested, and always have been, in the human beings involved and in their interaction with each other."

The pre-war novels are remarkable for their sureness of touch and mastery of Maigret's personality and temperament at so early a stage of Simenon's career. In *M. Gallet décédé*, the first book published, we already have Maigret saying the characteristic line: "I will know the murderer when I know the victim well." His role from the very start, unlike that of his greatest English rival, Sherlock Holmes, is not to reason, but to understand intuitively the mainsprings of human activity so that he arrives at a complete comprehension of how, and why, the victim and the murderer have behaved as they have done. "I never draw conclusions," he says in *Un crime en Hollande*, written in 1931. "I never think," he says in *La Pipe de Maigret*, written in 1945.

The characteristic Simenon style – concentrated, powerful, in some inexplicable way strangely *frightening* – is there at the outset. "No one noticed what was going on. No one suspected that a drama was being played out in the waiting room of the small railway station where only six depressed-looking passengers were waiting, amid the smell of coffee, beer and lemonade. . . ." begins *Le Pendu de Saint Pholien*. Immediately the reader is led into the action. "When, with a sigh of relief, Maigret pushed his chair back from the desk at which he had been sitting, the interrogation of Carl Andersen had lasted exactly seventeen hours . . ." starkly opens *La Nuit du Carrefour*. "It was on 27 June 1930 that Chief Inspector Maigret had his first encounter with the dead man, who was destined to be a most intimate and disturbing feature of his life for weeks on end. There were several aspects of this encounter, some commonplace, some harrowing, some unforgettable . . ." is the first trenchant paragraph of *M. Gallet décédé*.

The taut, atmospheric description of places is also there, as shown by this passage from *Pietr-le-Letton* telling us of Maigret's arrival at Fécamp in search of the "international swindler" and suspected murderer:

> La Bréauté station, where Superintendent Maigret left the main-line train from Paris to Le Havre at half-past seven in the morning, gave him a foretaste of Fécamp.
>
> An ill-lit refreshment room with grimy walls, and a buffet on which a few biscuits were mouldering and three bananas and five oranges were doing their best to form a pyramid. The storm felt more violent here. The rain was coming down in buckets. To get from one platform to another meant wading up to one's knees in mud.
>
> A repulsive little train, assembled from obsolete rolling-stock. Farms visible in faint outline in the pale daybreak, almost concealed by the streams of falling rain.
>
> Fécamp! A dense reek of salt cod and herring. Stacks of barrels. Masts beyond the railway engines. A foghorn moaning somewhere.
>
> "The Quai des Belges?"
>
> Straight ahead. He had to go on walking through the slimy puddles where fish scales glittered and fish offal lay rotting.

You are there! Trudging through the rain with Maigret on this damp, grim morning in northern France. "The settings never fail", says crime writer and critic Julian Symons,* "giving always an impression of personal involvement with Paris or Antibes, a shop by the Belgian frontier or a *guinguette* by the Seine. The weather is described with such vigour and pleasure that it is, again, as though the writer were actually soaking up the rain or sun that he is writing about. Simenon's susceptibility to physical experience of this kind is greater than that of any other contemporary novelist. And the characters grow in this thick soil of sensuous experience, they fit perfectly into sleazy or criminal city life, a small town's close provincialism or the uneasy potential violence of a port. They take colour and conviction from their surroundings, and there seems absolutely no limit to the kinds of people Simenon knows, and into whose personalities he can enter."

It is this quality of Simenon's, of being able to enter into the

Bloody Murder from the Detective Story to the Crime Novel: A History (Faber & Faber, 1972).

personality of other people, that he himself attributes (and rightly so) to Maigret. In *La Première enquête de Maigret*, written in October 1948 and supposed to be describing the future commissaire's first case as a young detective, back in 1913, after his father's untimely death has cut short his early career as a medical student, he speaks of Maigret already having acquired the ability "to live the lives of every sort of man, to put himself inside everybody's mind." As American Professor Lucille Frackman Becker of Drew University says in her study of Simenon, written in 1979★: "This ability remains constant throughout the Maigret cycle, as do Maigret's methods. While the technique remains essentially the same, there is a change in emphasis from the early novels, where Maigret is solely a sympathetic witness, to the later works in which he occupies the entire novel and his reactions, rather than the case at hand, hold the reader's attention."

For all the virtues of the post-war Maigrets, *that* is what Régine means when she says that she prefers the earlier novels: "In those first Maigrets it is not Maigret himself who is important. It is his memories, his experiences, what he has seen, understood, lived through, etc. The action unfolds through his eyes and one reads only of what he knows, and knows well. Afterwards, the later Maigrets take on a more philosophical tone. They are different from the first ones and, for me, less satisfying." Julian Symons is more blunt: the later Maigret novels, he says, are "sometimes ramblingly philosophical." "Rambling" is a somewhat pejorative epithet to use of a writer with a style as economical and concentrated as Simenon's; nevertheless it is accurate.

Why is there this difference in "feel" – in texture as well as in content – between the early and the later Maigrets? It is not merely a question of greater maturity on Simenon's part or even perhaps a more expansive attitude to life itself. It goes deeper, much deeper, into the truly bizarre relationship that developed between the writer and the creature of his imagination.

Many people have said, and written, that Maigret is Simenon and Simenon is Maigret, that they are one and the same person; that all that Simenon had to do to create the character was to put himself down on paper. That is moonshine. Simenon himself has always rejected the idea, and he is thoroughly in accord with the facts to do so. Indeed, as we have seen, the almost cavalier way in which the character was

★*Georges Simenon*, Twayne Publishers (G. K. Hall & Co.) Boston.

created; the way in which the manuscript of *Pietr-le-Letton* was set aside for several weeks, if not months, before being submitted to the publisher; the way in which Simenon cynically went on to use the name "Commissaire Maigret" for a character in three more *roman populaires* after the "real" Maigret books had been commissioned: all this shows that, at least to begin with, Maigret was just a device – a "rope", to use Simenon's word, to hold together the narrative flow of a detective story.

In fact, in June 1933, after completing his eighteenth Maigret novel, Simenon stopped writing "Maigrets" altogether. He felt ready to move on to what he called a *roman dur*, a "hard" or "plain" novel, psychological thrillers still dealing with the darker side of human nature but without a detective as a central, linking character. "You are mad!" said Fayard. "Look, you are like Conan Doyle. He always wanted to write a 'plain' novel. But you'll always regret it. It has never happened that a detective novelist can be successful in another field. Certainly you will come back crying."

After that, although there were many "plain" novels, there was a gap of thirteen years before Simenon produced another full-length Maigret. That was in March 1946, when, living briefly in Canada, he wrote *Maigret à New York*. Yet for most of that time, including the war years, he continued to write Maigret stories, either in novella or short-story form, for his own amusement – and because of what seems to have been a deep personal *need* to do so – even though they did not appear, at his publisher's insistence, in book form until several years later. Once Simenon returned to the full-length genre, he carried on with it until he finished writing novels altogether in 1972. It is not without significance that the last novel he ever wrote, his farewell to creative writing, was a Maigret story: *Maigret et M. Charles*, where the detective is himself tired, thinking almost longingly of his own retirement.

Yet Simenon has, in his public utterances, always chosen to underestimate the role that Maigret has played in the working out of his literary genius. He has consistently denied its importance. The *Observer* interview is typical and can serve as a standard text:

"Around 1939 I got so many letters from people who asked for more Maigret. They said: 'Look. It isn't nice of you to let this poor chap disappear. Please give us one in a while.' So I said: 'Why not?' My serious novels tire me very much. So I decide, about once a year I will write a Maigret – for fun. I do it after the holidays, Christmas, New Year's, when I do nothing but play with the children. So to start again,

I start with Maigret. It makes my fingers familiar with the typewriter again to start with something light, to start in a more optimistic way.

"Now I write four or five books a year – four plain and one Maigret."

That is total rubbish. It is hard to know whom Simenon was fooling more, the interviewer or himself. The "Maigrets" after *Maigret à New York* were not written at the rate of one a year, "after the holidays", just to get his fingers nimble again. Before he covered his typewriter for good in 1972, he wrote fifty-three more Maigret novels over a period of twenty-six years as against sixty "plain" novels. In other words, nearly half his total output were "Maigrets".

One can understand that there could well have been a financial reason for this. Claude Nielsen, Simenon's present publisher, says that with the possible exception of those non-Maigret novels which have been made into successful films (of which there are several), the Maigret books sell better than the others, for all Simenon's Conan Doyle-like desire to be known as something more than the creator of a great detective. One has only to wander into a paperback stall at a railway station or airport, almost anywhere in the world, to see that this is so. There is far more likely to be a Maigret novel on display than a non-Maigret. That is a fact of life.

But the reason why Simenon returned throughout the rest of his working life to Maigret goes deeper than purely monetary considerations. After all, the man could have afforded to stop writing decades ago.

Simenon could not leave Maigret alone because he could not leave a part of himself alone. Maigret is not Simenon in any simple, straightforward way, but I believe that over more than four decades of close identification with the same character, with whom he had considerable similarities anyway (the intuitive way of working, the basic humanist philosophy, the pipe-smoking, the childless marriage – Simenon did not become a father until ten years after *Pietr-le-Letton* was written – the early flirtation with medicine as a possible career, etc), Simenon found that Maigret became, in psychological terms, his *alter-ego*; an essential part of his life and of his personality. Simenon himself, at any conscious level, would most certainly deny this; but that does not prevent its being a viable hypothesis.

For his part, Simenon derides the significance of Maigret. "I consider the Maigret books as semi-potboilers," he says in *Quand j'étais vieux*. Just occasionally, he will turn about and put Maigret on a pedestal, describe him as "a mender of destinies" and make the point (which is a valid one) that in his Maigret novels he often takes up subjects that are more serious than those dealt with in his other books. But for most of the time he treats him with a casualness bordering on contempt.

He either genuinely cannot appreciate Maigret's true significance for himself or, more likely perhaps, realises it full well but does not want to accept it, like the alcoholic who never admits to drinking or the anorexic who never acknowledges that he has not eaten.

It is perhaps not too strong a claim to make that at times Simenon is in torment when seeking to delineate the interrelation between himself and Maigret. It does not seem in any way strange that after forty years of entering "into the skin" of Maigret, the fictitious character of the detective should become a real being within his creator's own skull, to some extent actually taking him over. An actor, during a "long run" in the theatre, may feel himself becoming something of the person whom he is portraying: he thinks like him, talks like him. Why should this not be equally so with an author during a "long run" that lasts for decades and in which, unlike the actor, he does not merely speak lines written by someone else but forges both the lines and the character itself from within his own imagination?

Such a phenomenon can occur, and it would seem to have done so with Simenon. That is why, although the later Maigret novels contain many typically Simenonien delights of style and acute observations of human character, they *are* often discursive and rambling. Both Simenon and Maigret are getting older and the battle for supremacy between them inside Simenon's psyche is becoming all the more tiring for the writer and undermining his talent. In a rare moment of personal insight in *Un homme comme un autre*, dictated in 1973 after he has ceased to write his novels, Simenon describes a curious dream that he has had. "More exactly, it was not entirely a dream," he says. "I was still in a voluptuous state of half-sleep and I saw with curiosity a man of whom I could only see the back. He was taller, with broader shoulders, fatter than I. Although there was only this back view, I could feel emanating from him a calmness that I envied.

"He was dressed in linen blue trousers with a gardener's apron and wore a battered old straw hat. He was in a garden, and along a low wall that separated this garden from the adjoining one there had been planted a whole lot of aromatic herbs, which he was busily engaged in hoeing.

"It took me quite some time, in my half-sleep to realise that this was not a real person but someone from my imagination. It was Maigret, in his garden at Meung-sur-Loire, a Maigret in retirement – like myself."

Simenon has even written an entire novel *as Maigret*. In *Les Mémoires de Maigret* ("Maigret's Memoirs"), written at Lakeville in September 1960, the ostensible author is Jules Maigret, who declares himself at the beginning of the book as "welcoming the occasion at last to explain my dealings with one Simenon by name." In what Julian Symons has called "this very witty book", he writes not only of his childhood, courtship and early career in the Paris police, but also of his slight resentment at some of the minor liberties that Simenon has taken with him. He claims that he very rarely wore a bowler hat and does not remember "the famous overcoat with the velvet collar" of the early stories, although he admits that he may at one time have possessed it.

The scene, in which is described the first meeting between the two men, reminds one of those old-time Hollywood movies in which the same actor played two parts, usually twins, and the split-screen technique had to be employed when one character encountered the other. Xavier Guichard, his chief, has called Maigret to his office:

> "Come in, Maigret."
> The daylight was so dull that morning that the lamp in its green shade was alight on his desk. Close by, in an armchair, I saw a young man who rose to offer me his hand when we were introduced to one another.
> "Chief Inspector Maigret, Monsieur Georges Sim, who's a journalist . . ."
> "Not a journalist, a novelist," the young man protested smilingly.
> Xavier Guichard smiled too. And he had a whole range of smiles which could express all the varied shades of what he was thinking. He also had at his disposal a sort of irony, perceptible only to those who knew him well and which, to others, sometimes made him appear a simpleton.
> He spoke to me with the utmost seriousness, as if we were concerned with an important affair, a prominent personality.
> "For his novel-writing, Monsieur Sim needs to know how Head-quarters functions. As he has just explained to me, a good many dramatic stories wind up in this house. He has also made it clear that it's not so much the workings of the police machine that he wants to study in detail, for he has been able to get information about these elsewhere, but rather the atmosphere in which these operations take place."
> I merely glanced at the young man, who must have been about twenty-four and who was thin, with hair almost as long as the Chief's, and of whom the least I can say is that he seemed to have no lack of confidence about anything, least of all about himself.

With all respect to Julian Symons, the reaction of many people is likely to be one of uneasiness rather than amusement at the somewhat pedestrian wit. The entire novel has an eerie quality – like this passage, describing another encounter some years later:

> Simenon is now just about the age I was when we met for the first time. In those days he tended to think of me as a middle-aged man and even, in his heart of hearts, as an elderly one.
> I did not ask him what he thought about that today, but I couldn't help remarking:
> "Do you know that with the course of time you've begun to walk and smoke your pipe and even to speak like *your* Maigret?"
> Which is quite true and which, you'll agree, provided me with a rather piquant revenge. It was rather as if, after all these years, he had begun to take *himself* for *me*!

The nearest that Simenon has gone to acknowledging anything like what I believe to be the true relationship between himself and Maigret in the long discussions that I have had with him is to call the detective "mon brave Maigret" and to say that, with the passage of years, he no longer knew who was Maigret and who was himself: one had merged so much into the other.

There was also this significant passage in our dialogue, when we were discussing Maigret in relation to some of the other great detectives of fiction, Sherlock Holmes and Hercule Poirot among them:

> *Simenon:* Sherlock Holmes I've read. I read him a lot when I was young. I haven't tried since. The others I haven't read. I didn't want to be influenced.
> *Bresler:* You never read about the other Belgian, Hercule Poirot?
> *Simenon:* No.
> *Bresler:* That's interesting. But Sherlock Holmes, whom you did read, was a detective with a completely different style . . .
> *Simenon:* The opposite.
> *Bresler:* And also with his Dr. Watson. Your Maigret doesn't have a Dr. Watson.
> *Simenon:* No. It isn't necessary. *It's me who serves as Dr. Watson.* [F.B. italics]

Dr. Pierre Rentchnick, the Swiss psychiatrist who with four colleagues spent a whole day questioning him for the analytical study, *Simenon sur le gril*, is convinced that he has a double personality. "We all thought that he was schizoid," he says, "but we did not want to write that. During the midday meal, for instance, Simenon said something – and it doesn't matter now what it was – and one of my colleagues said, 'But in such-and-such a novel Maigret does it,' and Simenon replied, 'Yes, Maigret can do it, but not me!' " That statement

e Brull

Désiré Simenon

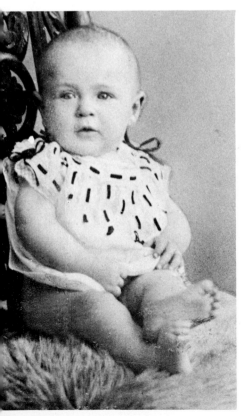

rtrait of G.S.

G.S. (*right*) with younger brother Christian

of 1910. (G.S. second from right, front row.)

918, aged 15

Newspaper reporter Simenon with
Russian students and anarchists, 1918

Henriette and Désiré Simenon

G.S. with Josephine Baker, Paris 1926

Launching of the *Ostrogoth*, Paris 1929

The *Ostrogoth* on the River Orge near Corbeil,
where G.S. wrote *M. Gallet Décédé* in 1930

ng fishermen repair their nets at Ouistreham,
ady, 1931

; friends with the pygmies, Belgian Congo 1932

Au Grand 13 by Gom Gut, one of Simenon's more c
pseudonyms

M. Gallet Décédé: one of two novels published
simultaneously in February 1931 to
launch the character of Maigret

is for Dr. Rentchnick the key to the relationship between Simenon and this creation of his own imagination.

"On the psychiatric level," says Dr. Rentchnick, "Simenon is an obsessional compulsive. The way in which he prepared and wrote his novels clearly shows you that. Only an obsessional man could tell you about all the stereotyped minutiae of his working pattern: the manila envelopes, the four dozen sharpened pencils on his desk, the 'Do Not Disturb' sign on his study door, and all the rest. He showed us his vast collection of clothes stacked neatly in his wardrobe: a manic depressive could never have arranged everything like that. It can only be the obsessional compulsive: rigidity with order, then the strain gets too much – and there is a sexual outburst, as always happened with Simenon after he completed a novel.

"An obsessional compulsive is introverted. He keeps diaries and so on, as Simenon did in his notebooks for *Quand j'étais vieux* and, in a sense, his dictated memoirs. Such a person needs to invent an extrovert character, if he is a writer, or to have a brilliant adviser, if he is a politician. You have Nixon-Kissinger, Hitler-Goering. They are compensatory needs, and so Simenon invents Maigret who can do things that he cannot do. Above all, he can experience a great love – a long, lasting love – with the same woman, Mme. Maigret, that he, Simenon, in his life, never experienced."

In case all this seems too fanciful, too far gone along the path of psychiatric jargon and high-flown theory, just pause and consider what Simenon's own son John has to say on the subject. "Of course, there is an awful lot of my father in Maigret. He disclaims it entirely, but that's not true. It's probably also a projection of some of the things he would like to be himself. He's made Maigret a very calm person, for instance; *he* is anything but that! I think Maigret is a lot of what he is himself and of what he would like to be – and what his father was."

Back in the summer of 1931, no one could have foreseen such a development with the creator partly being taken over by the creature of his imagination. The seeds were there but the burgeoning of the buds was well into the future. Even so, what already existed was enough to ensure this new series of detective stories an instant success. The Art of Simenon almost at once achieved public recognition.

Unlike in the English language, where there was a long tradition of detective fiction running back by way of Conan Doyle and Wilkie

Collins to Edgar Allan Poe, in French this was a neglected genre and what little coterie of writers there had been at the beginning of the twentieth century had dwindled since the war. By the early thirties, Edgar Wallace and Agatha Christie had made their mark in England but there was no such contemporary rival in Europe for Georges Simenon.

Yet by July 1932, an enthusiastic reviewer was able to state in the *Nouvelle Revue des Jeunes*: "Let us pay homage to M. Simenon who, with spirit, has introduced truly French characters into a genre where, since the war, the Anglo-Saxons have known the greatest success." The years of triumph were at hand – and Simenon was still under thirty years of age.

CHAPTER 9

The Early Years of Triumph

Success went to Simenon's head, there are no two ways about it. The young author was the toast of Paris, if not the whole of France, and the bubbles in the champagne made him dizzy. He was intoxicated with his own triumph, and he continued in that heady state for most of the decade.

His success was just too dazzling, and for a while it had a bad effect on his personality. In later life he was the first to admit as much. "There is a period in my life," he says in *Un homme comme un autre*, "the years of the thirties, of which I keep a bad memory and even an aftertaste in the mouth." The man who thereafter was to claim that his search through life was to find "the naked man", covered his own naked body in the finest silks and styles, had his suits cut in London, wore a pearl tie-pin and had the conceit to send press copies of the first two Maigret books to the greatest writers and critics in France with the presumptuous greeting "Cordially" inscribed to them, as if (he later admits) overnight he had become their equal.

He had a custom-built Chrysler Imperial limousine shipped over from the United States, hired a chauffeur and, with the arrogance of new-found wealth, dressed him in a sailor's uniform so that, as he drove around Paris on his master's errands, he was accorded all manner of vehicular liberties by the police on the assumption that he was driving for a high official of the Ministry of Marine.

The basic philosophy of the new-look Simenon was trenchantly pronounced when, on a brief visit home to Liège, he declared to his mother as they walked arm-in-arm down a street in Outre-Meuse, "You see, Mother, there are two kinds of people in this world: the shitters and the shat upon. I prefer to be on the side of the shitters." Forty years later, when dictating *Un homme comme un autre*, he was to say: "Those words today still fill me with bitterness and continue to humiliate me." But at the time they accurately summed up his philosophy. Just as with his boundless nervous energy he lusted after women to the full, so it was with the equally physical delights of success. Simenon did nothing by halves.

In December 1931, within ten months of the launching of the first two Maigret books, Simenon sold the *Ostrogoth* – as an elderly widow's caprice for her would-be *macho* young gigolo – and rented a sumptuous villa called "Roches Grises" at Cap d'Antibes. There were not more than about a dozen villas built there at the time, and in winter the place was almost deserted. The only other inhabitant was the old Aga Khan who would wave at the soon-to-be-millionaire author as the two of them took their regular morning walks alone beneath the pine trees.

In the three months that Simenon was at "Roches Grises", he wrote three Maigret novels and worked on the scenario of two Maigret films: *La Nuit du Carrefour* with Jean Renoir and *Le Chien Jaune* ("The Yellow Dog") with Jean Tarride.

Despite the different setting, Simenon had lost none of his Liège and Paris acquired skills in engineering furtive sex. He had engaged a local female secretary to help him with the film work and, as he recalls with obvious relish in *Point-Virgule* ("Semi-colon"), his fourteenth volume of memoirs dictated some forty-five years later: "There was time, between completing my Maigret chapter for the day and the arrival of Jean Renoir, to make love."

The fate of the two films proved somewhat amusing. *La Chien Jaune* was a considerable commercial success but an artistic disaster, with the director's father, Abel Tarride, a veteran of the stage, completely miscast as Maigret and giving a far too over-ripe performance as the essentially humanistic and unflurried detective. In contrast, *La Nuit du Carrefour* sank without trace at the box-office but has now become a cult Jean Renoir film and is shown to admiring audiences in intellectually smart cinema clubs throughout the world. As brilliant a director as Jean-Luc Godard has called it "the only great French detective film ever made."

In his autobiography, *My Life and My Films*★, Jean Renoir describes how his "aim was to convey by imagery the mystery of the starkly mysterious tale, and to subordinate the plot to the atmosphere. Simenon's book wonderfully evoked the dreariness of that crossroads situated fifty kilometres from Paris. I do not believe there can be a more depressing place anywhere on earth. The small cluster of houses, lost in a sea of mist, rain and mud, are magnificently described in the novel. They might have been painted by Vlaminck.

"My enthusiasm for the atmosphere Simenon had evoked caused

★ Collins, 1974.

me to discard my own views in the matter of basing a film on a work of literature. We rented one of the houses at the crossroads, which happened to be empty, and there set up our quarters. A good many of the team slept on the floor in the living-room. We had our meals there. When the darkness was as mysterious as we wished we aroused the sleepers and went to work. Within fifty kilometres of Paris we led the life of explorers of a lost land. In the matter of mystery the result exceeded our expectations, particularly since, two reels having been lost, the story was pretty well incomprehensible, even to its author."

The fiction of the two lost reels has entered into the folklore of the French cinema. One critic has even claimed that their absence has enhanced the film: "To the dramatic disjunction corresponds an aesthetic discontinuity." This is, of course, pretentious rubbish and profoundly amuses Simenon, who has always had, with very few exceptions, a feeling very close to contempt for most French critics ("I rarely have the impression that the critic has understood my work," he writes in *Quand j'étais vieux*. "They interpret everything in their own way. And when they talk to me about my novels . . . I no longer recognise them.")

What actually happened to that first Maigret film was really rather sad – especially, as in Simenon's view, Pierre Renoir's performance was one of the finest in the part – but, out of respect for Jean Renoir, who became a close friend, Simenon never revealed the truth during his lifetime. "Even now I don't want to speak ill of him and his death upset me greatly," Simenon says, "but when they were making the film, Jean was in the middle of separating from his first wife, Catherine Hesling, the actress. He was very depressed and in the morning he started to drink and drink and drink, and he was nearly drunk most of the day. He directed the scenes that he shot very well but he forgot some, and when they saw the whole thing it was too late because they were already engaged in another film somewhere else." There were no "lost" reels, they were simply never shot.

So the producer summoned Simenon to a meeting and offered him 50,000 francs – as much as they had paid for the film rights in the first place – to come before the cameras and, at strategic moments in the story, explain what was happening and thus fill in the gaps in the plot. Simenon may have been an *arriviste* but he did not have the standards of one: "50,000 francs was a lot of money in those days," he says, "but I refused. I had no desire to ridicule myself even for 50,000 francs."

Surprisingly, Simenon's early flirtation with the French film industry, unlike his later substantial success in the forties and beyond, was something of a disaster. It is ironic because the earlier Maigrets read almost like film scripts. They contain much more dialogue than the later novels and the action moves from scene to scene with almost cinematic swiftness. Yet, apart from *Le Nuit du Carrefour* and *Le Chien Jaune*, Simenon was involved in only one more filmed adaptation of his work throughout the whole of the thirties – and that also was a minor catastrophe.

In April 1932, it was announced in *Vu*, a leading French cinema magazine, that "M. Georges Simenon, the well-known author of numerous detective stories, will himself direct *La Tête d'un homme*, one of his latest novels, of which the principal role will be taken by the great artiste, M. Inkinijoff." In the end, *La Tête d'un homme* did appear on French screens, being premiered in Paris the following February, but it was a totally different film from that undertaken by Simenon. Funds ran out before they even started shooting and the project was taken over by another producer with Julian Duvivier, an experienced director, replacing Simenon behind the cameras and the great Jewish actor, Harry Baur, coming in for Valery Inkinijoff as the third film Maigret.

Simenon lost all interest. Duvivier insisted on re-writing the script, creating characters who were not in the original book and expunging some who were. And the producer insisted on a famous *chanteuse* of the time, named Damia, appearing on the screen, completely out of context and having nothing whatsoever to do with the story, to sing a song so that the production company could issue a record of it and cash in on the film's publicity. That was a common, somewhat dishonest tactic of the French cinema industry in those early cowboy years, and Simenon had had enough of it. In *Point-Virgule* he recalls his bitterness: "I made a decision, to which I remained faithful for more than five years, of not selling the film rights in any of my works to anyone, whatever the increasingly large amounts I was offered." It was the only blemish on the gloss of his amazing success.

Simenon's new-found wealth allowed him to choose where he wanted to live, without restriction of area or limitation of price. The man, who for millions of people around the world has created an unforgettable picture of Paris, chose to reside three hundred miles away in the southwest of France, at a little hamlet close to the Atlantic Ocean called Marsilly. It is near La Rochelle, the thirteenth-century walled seaport that stands amid flat, sparsely cultivated sand dunes like those of Simenon's native Low Countries. Surveying the scene today, one can understand why this "man of the North" found so strong a *rapport* with this terrain of the South; the landscape for miles around is almost identical.

It was, indeed, the landscape that attracted Simenon. Like many a person born and reared in the town, he yearned to live away from its noise and pace. After three months in the splendour of their rented villa on Cap d'Antibes, he and Régine climbed into their luxurious Chrysler Imperial and drove back to Paris; but by a long, meandering route looking for somewhere to live.

That is how they came by way of La Rochelle. Simenon was fascinated by the city with its ancient wall, its two watchtowers guarding the harbour and its narrow stone-laid streets. But it was the countryside around that he adored. "We're going to find a house here," he said to Régine, "but in the country."

And so they found this delightful manor house called "La Richardière", standing in its own grounds, with small farm, lake and woods, by the sea at Marsilly. It had a single tower pointing to the sky with an internal spiral staircase in white stone. Above the room that was to be Régine's study was a stone-walled dovecote in which birds, of all kinds and from all countries, came for temporary lodging. It was a dream house, and they both fell in love with it.

The Simenons wanted to buy it but Régine recalls that the owner said he was only prepared to give them a three years' lease – at the end of which time, he promised, he would sell it to them. The house was semi-derelict, so they put in electricity (Simenon himself installing the generator) and spent a small fortune on turning the place into a true home. In the visitors' book of the Café de la Paix in nearby La Rochelle, Simenon on a later visit to the town wrote: "*Au souvenir du temps le plus heureux de ma vie.*"

In *Quand j'étais vieux*, Simenon characteristically clouds the reality by saying of their departure from Marsilly: "I cut the cord. The umbilical cord." He implies that by his deliberate act the family moved on. Régine remembers it differently: "Sadly, at the end of the three years' lease, the owner refused to sell it to us. His promise was, after all, only verbal. We had to go – but we both adored that house and, if we had been able to buy it, who knows how our life might have been different?"

In addition to the normal country household of several cats and dogs, Simenon bought five horses and spent much of the day riding, "because I did my military service in the cavalry. So the horses were marvellous for me." His favourite was a pure-blooded white and grey Arab steed, bought from a circus, that would let no one else ride him. Simenon used neither spurs nor riding whip; he would talk to him, his legs holding firm to his flanks, and the animal would show he understood by moving his ears. When they returned to the house, Simenon would unsaddle the horse before entering the courtyard and the animal would trot off to his quarters, knocking at the kitchen window with his snout on the way so that Boule could hand him his regular pieces of bread or, on occasions, small cakes.

Simenon bought a small trotting-cart and liked to go into La Rochelle with it to do his shopping. He became such a familiar figure in the town that the mayor had a ring fitted on the pavement for him to tie his horse. It was there until the late nineteen-seventies, but then disappeared when the pavements were renewed.

In the lake at the back of the house that received, at high tide, its ration of water direct from the sea, five hundred ducks happily lived out their lives. Behind the vegetable garden, white rabbits were reared. Fifty or so large white turkeys, the biggest and most authoritative of which they called "Maigret", circulated peacefully in the ground, amid the geese and chickens. In the woods, they raised pheasants that Simenon never allowed to be shot and which became so tame they would eat from their owners' hands. He planted trees, including walnut trees which would take twenty years to produce their first crop, so certain was he that this agreeable setting would be his home for a long time to come.

It was an idyllic existence for Simenon and for every member of his household, human as well as animal. He and Régine had decided that they would, in those early hectic years of the thirties, travel a great deal and see the world together; but La Richardière always remained their base, with Boule staying in charge to keep it going and ready for their return. Coming back from a visit to Turkey in June 1933, as part of a tour of the Black Sea area (during which, among other things, he interviewed Trotsky, living under strict guard on a beautiful island in the Sea of Marmara near Istanbul, for the newspaper *Paris-Soir*), Simenon brought with him, to swell the ranks of his animal friends, three wolf cubs. He had bought them on impulse when "a sort of tramp" had stuck his head over the garden wall of the French Embassy at Ankara, while the Simenons were there, informing the Ambassador that he had just captured them.

They transported the three little beasts in a sack in the sleeping-car of their train and, as they grew, had cages built for them in the grounds at La Richardière. The female had to be put to sleep when she contracted a skin ailment that turned her vicious. One of the males was hurt and also had to be killed. But the last of them lived for several years and used to follow Simenon on a leash on his long country walks, and in the evenings played in his study.

At La Richardière, Simenon positively flowered, both in mind and in body. He played golf, canoed, had a punchbag installed so that he could keep himself in training for boxing. He was no effete young novelist. Everything was so right for him there that, in the eleven months between May 1932 and April 1933, he wrote no less than ten novels – during which time he was out of the country for more than two months, touring in Africa with Régine on an assignment for the magazine *Voilà*. Of the ten novels only two were Maigrets written as part of his contract with Arthème Fayard for eighteen novels featuring the detective. They were the last two due under the contract. The crunch had now come for Simenon in his progress towards his next stage as a writer, no longer writing "semi-literary" novels but psychological novels – the real thing, to his mind.

Few, if any, writers on Simenon have stressed the importance of the fact that, as early as July 1931, while still living on the *Ostrogoth*, he wrote his first "hard" novel, *Le Relais d'Alsace* ("The Man from Everywhere"). This shows that as early as five months after the Maigret series had been launched on the public, he was already at work preparing himself for the next step of his career. But it was at La Richardière, in the comfort and contentment of the marvellous new home that he thought would be his for ever, that he really found himself inspired to write his new style of novel, without the central prop of the Maigret character.

It was in the late spring of 1933, after he had finished *L'Ecluse No. 1* ("The Lock at Charenton"), the last of his eighteen contractual Maigrets, that Simenon travelled to Paris to tell Fayard that he did not want to write any more of them. One can well sympathise with the publisher's feelings of anger and frustration. One can understand why he lashed out verbally at this "difficult" author, who felt that he had come to a crucial crossroads in his professional life and no longer wanted to supply the goose that was laying them both such large golden eggs. Simenon was able to mollify him somewhat by producing the manuscripts of the new non-Maigret novels that he had already written. It was not as if he was naively wanting to put all else behind him and see if he could take on something new. He could prove that he already *had*.

Reluctantly, Fayard agreed to publish *Le Passager du Polarlys* ("Danger at Sea"), the first of the non-Maigrets to have been written at La Richardière: and, for his part, Simenon agreed to supply one more Maigret to round off the series, with the detective, by now retired, called back to solve one last case. Written at Porquerolles, in their rented summer home, in June 1933, the novel, called simply *Maigret*, was published by Fayard in March of the following year.

But by then Simenon had another publisher.

Before coming to the story of how, and why, Simenon changed pilot so soon after setting up river in pursuit of his "literary period", one has to pause and look at the phenomenal amount of travelling that he undertook in the early and mid-thirties. For someone who in later life was to become almost an agoraphobic, frightened of crowds, reluctant to travel more than a few kilometres from his Swiss home and content to see the world only as projected on to the backcloth of his memory, his wanderlust and genuine sense of adventure in those pre-World War Two days seem even more extraordinary.

For a start, he was very lucky – or simply very astute – so far as the cost of it all was concerned. He travelled at his own expense, but before every trip he arranged with the editor of a well-known newspaper or magazine that they would take so many articles from him, which would cover his costs. Nowadays, successful journalists are negotiating such deals all the time but in those days Simenon, as ever, was well ahead of his contemporaries. He did the same thing in the summer of 1934 when he hired his third boat, a 100-foot schooner called the *Araldo*, with a crew of seven, and cruised in the Mediterranean for a couple of months (he actually chartered the boat for a whole year but his crowded schedule only allowed him to use it for that comparatively brief time).

Few novelists have written more, earned more, spent more and travelled more than he contrived to do in such a short time – or attempted to assimilate and respond to so many and such varied cultures.

In the summer of 1932, he and Régine spent several months (though he cannot resist exaggerating it in *Point-Virgule* to "over a year") touring in Egypt and down through and across Central and West Africa. It was a voyage worthy of an explorer. Régine insisted on their going to see the Pyramids, but that was their only concession to anything like a tourist trip. Otherwise it was hard – if not dangerous – going all the way. They flew down from Cairo to the edge of the Belgian Congo in an early British monoplane of Imperial Airways only 2,000 metres above the land from which, if they crashed, there was slight hope of being rescued.

The plane had the sort of windows that you could open yourself, as in a train or a bus; but if you did, a wadge of torrid air hit you like a damp sledgehammer. Each one of the thirty passengers was supplied with a small waterproofed box that they were told to keep ever-ready on their knees, and by the time they finally touched down at the Belgian Congo frontier town of Ouadi-Halfa, after several stops on route, each one of them had used it for the purpose for which it was clearly intended. In that climate, air pockets were inevitable and everyone was sick.

At Ouadi-Halfa, they transferred to a battered old Fiat car that Simenon bought on the spot and later sold at a profit at Stanleyville, the next stopping-place on their journey. They travelled across untamed country in a terrifying drive over dust-covered roads, with a young black African who had only been driving for a month at the wheel. At Stanleyville, they boarded a steamship that looked as if it had come straight off the Mississippi River and steamed down the Congo as far as Matadi, the principal port of the Belgian Congo – where Simenon's brother, Christian, was waiting for them on the quayside. For he too had long since left Liège and had what Régine calls "quite a good position" with a Belgian company at Matadi; he was to spend over twenty years there.

"I never noticed any sort of jealousy between the two brothers," she recalls. "They didn't have the same character. Christian was very easy going and pleasant, cheerful. He came to visit us in Paris quite often and he was always very good and jolly."

Simenon speaks of him in *Point-Virgule* in somewhat muted terms. He describes a club in Matadi, reserved for the "more or less important" local Belgian administrators, to which Christian for some reason chose not to take him, but where the habit was to drink only whisky or champagne, as their sole distraction, which gave the officials a bad reputation when they returned home on leave to Belgium, often to quite modest family circumstances. When asked in some discreet suburban household in Liège or Ghent what they would like to drink, they would grandly reply: "Champagne." "My brother Christian was no exception to that rule," comments Simenon, "and his wife spent her whole days lying on a hammock, calling for one of the boys to

97

bring her something of so little importance as a glass of water or just to light her cigarette." She did not even have to look after their only child, a boy: he could not take the tropical climate and had been shipped off back to Liège for Simenon's mother to bring up.

The humanitarian in Simenon reacted strongly against the way in which the Whites lived and ruled in Africa; and not only the Belgian colonial administrators but the French and the British as well. In his report on his journey that appeared in *Voilà* on his return, under the prophetic title "The Hour of the Negro", he wrote:

> Living in Africa, the white men sweat, complain, succumb to apathy and end up hating the world and themselves. Once able to go back to France, they swear never to return to Africa again. But they do return, and not because they can't obtain employment elsewhere. They return for a multitude of reasons, chiefly an ambience they no longer can do without.
>
> But the time of colonial Africa is running out. We are living in the transition period between adolescence and maturity. Tomorrow the black who has today bought a fuschia-coloured suit at a French department-store will be dressed in impeccable black and take his seat at international meetings, dignified and unbending. The native lieutenant of today, proud of his stripes and the prizes won on the range, may become a general. Not in a foreign army – in his own.
>
> What kind of recollection will the African have of us white colonists? Will he remember gratefully the railroads paid for with the life of one labourer for each tie beam? The banks that gave him paper money, knowing full well that paper wouldn't last in the humidity of the huts and that the blacks would have to exchange it for coins at a rate of five francs for three? Will we be remembered as benefactors because we introduced the Africans to spirits much higher in alcoholic content and much more expensive than their native palm wine? Or for having sown the country-side with small beings of mixed colour?

So much for the public man on the African journey: defiant, tolerant and admirably liberal in his sentiments. There was also, of course, the private man, "the naked man" – and, even though accompanied by an unsuspecting Régine, he was able to slink off into the dark places of the cities that they visited and find the enjoyment that "was more necessary to me than I might have wished for my own peace of mind." In Cairo, he wandered alone in the red-light district at night, armed with a gun (which he knew well how to use), following women down furtive alleyways to houses that he would never be able to find by day, and it would be the same more or less wherever they went in the world during those years of frenetic travel. (Paradoxically, his most exciting coloured woman was "an admirable Negress" that he encountered in a *maison aux filles* on the rue St. Sulpice in the heart of Paris shortly after his return from Africa. As he says, he "ought to have been blasé" by then with attractive coloured girls, but this Paris-based whore he ranks number two in his sexual souvenirs. He has always had the habit of referring to women with whom he has had sex rather in the terms of a big-game hunter or collector of tourist curiosities.)

The African voyage was followed, in the spring of 1933, by a "panoramic tour" of the major countries of Europe that was also written up in the magazine *Voilà*. It's title: "Europe '33". As chance had it, Simenon stayed in the same hotel in Berlin, the Albion, where Hitler was living in the weeks prior to his assumption of power as German Chancellor. It was the best hotel in the capital and, on two occasions, Simenon observed Hitler in the tearoom in earnest conversation with a "very distinguished and beautiful woman with silver-white hair and a fine face." They talked for a long time in whispers and seemed well content with each other's company. It was the *Kaiserine*, the wife of ex-Kaiser Wilhelm II. He was forbidden to re-enter Germany from his exile in Holland, but she was allowed to travel freely between their home in the small Dutch town of Doorn and her husband's former empire. The fact that she was sitting there quite happily with the uniformed Nazi leader showed, as Simenon himself says, that Hitler was not always at variance with the Kaiser; an interesting footnote to history, one might think.

"There was nothing extraordinary about Hitler," Simenon recalls. "He was always in that brown uniform of his and with that slightly ridiculous little moustache. He took the lift with everybody else but he would never look at the other people. He would always stand there, waiting for his floor, looking straight ahead. He was a lot less impressive, I thought, than the Germans, the officers I had known during the first World War, when Belgium was occupied and they strutted around the streets in their helmets with the tall points, their grey capes, a monocle in their eye and a duelling scar on their cheek."

In the hothouse atmosphere of those Isherwood-days in Berlin before Hitler's advent to power, he found himself unexpectedly, and somewhat bewilderingly, involved in a real-life "cloak and dagger" situation, like something out of a spy novel of later years. The story has never been told before. What happened was that, prior to his visit, he had obtained a letter of introduction to the secretary of the local Communist Party in Berlin because he wanted to inform himself as deeply as he could of what was actually going on in the German capital at that time. He was told that it would be dangerous for him to come to

99

Party Headquarters. An assignation was made for a "tiny bookshop that was all dirty in an obscure back street." He went up to the first floor and there were three men waiting for him. Their leader said to him: "You can do us a great service." "What service?" asked Simenon. "You can save at least fifty thousand human lives," was the somewhat flamboyant reply. "Me?" said Simenon. "How?"

They explained that they had managed surreptitiously to install a hidden listening device in the room where Hitler regularly met with his leading henchmen. Eight days earlier, they had overheard a conversation in which it had been decided that the time had come to make a strike for power and that the best way to do it would be to engineer a situation, on some pretext or other, that would provide an opportunity to exterminate the upper echelons of the German Communist Party. Once that militant opposition was removed, the rest would be easy.

But how to do it? The first suggestion had been to fake an assassination attempt. Hitler had proposed himself as the would-be victim but Goebbels had argued against that on the basis that it might give others the idea to try the real thing. So Goebbels had suggested, and the others had agreed, that instead of a phoney assassination attempt upon an individual, there should be a real attack upon a public monument or institution that was dear to all Berliners and, indeed, to the German people as a whole. It was due to take place in two days' time.

In the murky atmosphere of that first-floor room over the seedy bookshop, the leader of the three Communist workers told Simenon: "We don't know what form that attack is going to take, but if it happens we are finished – and so is Germany. The Nazis will set it up in such a way that we are blamed. We shall all be killed, and the door will be open for Hitler. We know you write articles for *Paris-Soir* [then the newspaper with the largest circulation in France]. You must get through to the editor and tell him to publish this story. Then the whole world will know about it in advance and they'll have to call off their plans. You *must* help!"

Simenon hurried round to the French Embassy, demanded to see the Ambassador and told him to warn the French Government and to send a coded telegram to the editor of *Paris-Soir*, asking him to splash the story front page across all editions next morning.

But nothing appeared in *Paris-Soir*. Two days later, the Reichstag, the German Parliament building in the heart of Berlin, was burned down by the Nazis. The Communists were blamed. Hitler came to power and, as Simenon had been warned, thousands of Communist Party members were slaughtered. Why did *Paris-Soir* do nothing?

100

The editor, a good friend of Simenon's, wrote to him later with the explanation that if they had published the story nothing would have happened (which was the point of the whole operation anyway!) and that they would then have been accused of irresponsibly passing on to the French public false information. So they had thought it better to print nothing. Thus, can weak men always find reasons for their inaction.

The following spring, after his interview with Trotsky on his heavily guarded island home near Istanbul, Simenon was off again; this time on a visit to the countries of Eastern Europe for a series of articles for the magazine *Le Jour*. The title, chosen by himself, was "Hungry People" – in those days almost a taboo subject for a prosperous French bourgeois publication.

Simenon travelled through Poland, Czechoslovakia, Hungary and Rumania. In Warsaw, he took the opportunity to search out Niota, one of his mother's student lodgers from the old days in Liège. Now she was married and lived more or less contentedly with her husband and baby son. Simenon could not help smiling to himself when she told him the child's name: Christian. For he remembered that when, as a teenager, Niota had lived with them, his brother had fallen madly in love with her but had received no more than superficial favours, as was entirely appropriate for a respectable young Jewish girl keeping herself intact for her future husband. But here she was, nearly twenty years on, married comparatively late in life to a man with thick black hair and giving birth to a baby boy whose mass of blond hair was just like Christian's – and whom she called by the same name. Simenon wondered if perhaps she had persuaded herself that the child might in some way be the son of Christian Simenon, born later as if by a miracle.

But he did not spend much time in such novelist-like musings; soon afterwards, he was being taken by Niota's brother on a characteristically vigorous visit to the best whorehouse in Warsaw. Nor was that his sole dalliance while in the Polish capital. In *Un homme comme un autre* he relates how, while walking one afternoon down a busy street, he saw the figure of a blonde young woman, with dimples, standing behind the gateway to a house. She seemed to him "appetising", so he entered the courtyard and followed her upstairs: to her room on the second floor where their sexual enjoyment was so great that, even though it endured for less than an hour, he claims nearly half a century later he can remember every tingling minute of it.

Finally, in early 1935, came the ultimate in his wanderings: a tour of the world accompanied by Régine that took him, by way of the United States, to Panama, Colombia, the Equator, the Galapagos Islands in the Southern Pacific, Tahiti (where he spent two months), New Zealand, Australia, the East Indies, India, the Red Sea and back through the Mediterranean. "Even if I were physically able to," he now says, "I would not want to make such a journey again. I don't want to see the whole world again turned into concrete. When I did it, there weren't planes to go from one place to another. One went by boat, sometimes by cargo boat. I saw a completely different world. And when I watch, in the news on television, the African towns, for example, or the South American, it is no longer what I saw."

In Panama occured an incident that sounds like a scene from one of his novels, although it is not referred to in any of his published writings. At that time, he was being plagued by pirate editions of his work that appeared in the Spanish language across all of Central and South America and even as far east as the Philippines. He was being defrauded of very substantial sums indeed, and he did not like it.

He discovered that the source of it all was a somewhat seedy office in Panama City. So, having previously armed himself with a revolver, Simenon walked in, drew his gun and told the startled man sitting behind a desk who he was and that he had made an exact calculation of how much was owed to him for the thousands of his books that had, without permission or payment, been translated and distributed. "I'll give you an hour to get the money and hand it over to me," he said. "But that's impossible!" spluttered the man. "I'm poor, I haven't got so much money. Besides, I can't possibly get it in that time. Can't you come back in a week?"

"No," said Simenon. "I propose waiting here with you for exactly one hour. You can make whatever telephone calls you like to get the money but you are not to leave this room. And if at the end of the hour I do not have my money, I will shoot you with this gun!"

The man made six or seven telephone calls. Within half an hour, another man walked in with a bag containing the money. It was handed over to Simenon, and he left. *End of story.*

It is difficult not to agree with Boule when she says, of the young Simenon, that he was "a mountain of a man".

CHAPTER 10

Prelude to Happiness

It is difficult to assess the importance, so far as his work is concerned, of Simenon's almost frenzied outburst of foreign travel in the thirties. In all, at least nine "exotic novels", as the critics have called them, and several novellas and magazine articles have been directly based on the experience of those years.

Simenon himself says, in *Un homme comme un autre*, that he took his typewriter with him everywhere and that in Tahiti and in Panama he sat down and wrote a full-length novel. "I discovered countries that were entirely new to me," he says. "I tried ferociously to enter into the reality of wherever I was. But I wrote not a word of my almost daily discoveries. No. Seated before my machine, I wrote of the rue Lepic in Paris, of Bourges and of La Rochelle."

As so often with Simenon, this is almost totally untrue. He wrote no novel whatsoever in Panama and, as for Tahiti, the one that he wrote there was not set in some town or city back home in France, but in the torrid, scathingly humid Galapagos Islands, from which he had just arrived. That novel, *Ceux de la Soif* ("The Thirsty Ones", but untranslated), was the only one actually written while he was away.

In fact, if the "exotic novels" have any validity at all as an entity, it is that their setting, their colour, their local atmosphere is, of course, exotic and tropical and totally out of the ordinary. But the stories that they tell are typically Simenon, as are the people that they describe – characters who are troubled, disturbed and anguished, and whom we are used to meeting in the rooms and cafés of the back streets of Paris or small French provincial towns. As the Belgian critic, Michel Lemoine, has said: "There is hardly a character in all the Simenon canon who does not ask, 'Who am I? What have I done with my life?'" That is absolutely true of the "exotic novels". Simenon claims that while he was on the other side of the world he wrote about Frenchmen living out their lives in France. The truth is that after he

103

had himself returned home, and "recollecting past events in tranquility", as William Wordsworth said of his poetry, he wrote about those same Frenchmen *transported to exotic places*.

Albeit with their problems and anxieties accentuated by the local setting, the characters are living through exactly the same trauma from which they would be suffering if they had never left home. It is as if they spend their lives in a vacuum-wrapped, pre-sealed Simenonien atmosphere of despair that they take with them wherever they go.

In a series of articles, *Les Vaincus de l'aventure* ("Adventure's Failures") published in *Paris-Soir* in 1935 and later in book form under the title *La Mauvaise étoile* ("The Evil Star"), Simenon describes these "banana tourists", as the locals call them, who go to the tropics because:

> One fine day when they are disgusted with their mediocrity, or frightened by impending destitution, someone tells them: "In the islands, you can still live as if it were heaven on earth, without money, without clothes, without worrying about tomorrow . . ." They sell everything to pay their passage. When they disembark, the prudent authorities, who have often been burned before, require them to deposit enough money for their return fare.
>
> The next day, every good banana tourist has already bought a sarong and a straw hat. Half-naked, disdainful of the town and of the "colonials" who wear white suits and detachable collars, he takes himself off excitedly to the endless beaches.
>
> He is evidently then a bit astonished to see that the natives are also wearing detachable collars and are riding bicycles, and he is indignant when buses full of Kanaka Indians pass him on the road.

The message is: *Plus ça change, plus ça reste la même chose*. One cannot run away from oneself. The internal torments remain the same as in the West, just as the externals, apart from the exotic colourings of the vegetation or the pile-driving heat, also do not change, with their detachable collars, bicycles and buses.

As sound a judge as Maurice Richardson rates one of the "exotic novels" – specifically called *Touristes de bananes* ("Banana Tourist") – as among Simenon's twenty best books. Set in Tahiti, although written in Simenon's rented summer home at Porquerolles on the Mediterranean in June 1937, two years after his return, it is an admirable example of this genre.

The "banana tourist" of the title is a disillusioned wealthy young man called Oscar Donadieu who first appears in a novel called *Le Testament Donadieu* ("The Shadow Falls"), written at Porquerolles a year earlier. Fleeing the family scandal and business intrigue in his native La Rochelle with which the earlier novel ended, he is bound for Tahiti on a vessel belonging to his family's shipping line. He is seeking a different lifestyle from that which he has known. "All his life, ever since he was quite small, he had been trying to discover a way of life that was beautiful, pure, serene. Searching for something, or was it rather escaping from something? Perhaps both at once." He knows of the expression "banana tourist" — but he rejects it as applying in anyway to himself.

The sombre mood of the novel is set in the very early stages when a few days off Papeete, Tahiti's capital, his ship heaves to and a new passenger comes aboard. He is Ferdinand Lagre, captain of a sister vessel of the same line, who, on a homeward journey to La Rochelle, has killed one of his ship's officers and is now being taken back, as a prisoner, to stand trial for murder. The reason for the killing: jealousy over a sultry Tahitian prostitute named Tamatéa. Donadieu knows Lagre as one of his late father's most trusted employees, and is saddened by what has happened.

Nor does he find Papeete the sun-drenched paradise for which he had hoped. He is greeted by a torrential downpour that lasts for three days. The little waterfront hotel where he stays, kept by a hardened French provincial woman, is frequented by prostitutes (Tamatéa among them), whose friendly casualness only serves to accentuate his melancholy. Soon he realises that the sordidness and corruption that he discovers all around him are merely a replica of what he has fled from in La Rochelle.

Captain Lagre's trial opens, and Donadieu cannot resist attending the proceedings. He is sickened by what he sees and hears, for it soon becomes obvious to him that the outcome is a foregone conclusion. The governor, the judge and the lawyers on both sides have conspired to make an example of the white man who has dared to break the rules of colonial life by killing another white man for love of a coloured woman. Although in France the perpetrator of such a *crime passionel* would walk free from court or receive only a nominal sentence, Donadieu is told (while the trial is still going on) that Lagre will be gaoled for ten years. (There are few, if any, sympathetically drawn court scenes in Simenon's work. Like Maigret, he views with suspicion all the formal trappings of conventional justice.)

This particular trial is even more hypocritical than most depicted by Simenon: the judge himself, for all his courtroom dignity, is a former client of Tamatéa's! Donadieu feels disgusted with himself for not jumping to his feet to protest at the heavy-handed farce being played out before him, and "pale with indignation fling his challenge at these callous brutes."

Instead, he does nothing. The people around him believe that he has become one of them, a "banana tourist" who has finally learned how to play the local sordid game. In reality, he has decided just the opposite: that life has no longer any meaning for him. "Suppose he took to drink, living like the others, it would not help. One day, sooner or later, he would feel disgusted with everything, as now, and with himself as well – which would be still worse. Wasn't it better to get things over before he reached that stage?

". . . It was intolerable that he should have struggled as he had struggled, only to come to this. Even if it went against the grain; even if there would be a sickening, agonizing moment to endure."

He takes Tamatéa to bed. They have sex and then, while she lies in a half-drunken sleep beside him, he kills himself with a razor. When she wakes, she runs screaming from the blood-spattered room – but the "banana tourists" barely shrug their shoulders.

The British writer who comes immediately to mind when considering the "exotic novels" is Somerset Maugham; but Simenon says that, although they became firm friends when both were living in the South of France in later life,★ he never read him and was certainly not influenced by him. Although Maugham's doomed tea-planters and passionate women expatriates have a surface similarity to the characters of Simenon, there is a fundamental difference between the two. With Maugham, one gets the feeling that the tragic and on occasions ironic encounters in his stories only happen to the people concerned because they are living so far from home in the totally alien environment of the Far East. Such things would never have happened to them in Cheltenham or Surbiton. Their experiences come in upon them from outside. With Simenon, however, it is the other way round: Oscar Donadieu would surely have killed himself eventually, even if he had never left La Rochelle. The characters of the "exotic novels" carry their own private hells around with them. Their lives *would* have been the same in the French equivalent of Cheltenham or Surbiton.

★One evening at dinner in Simenon's home at Cannes in the mid-fifties, Maugham was telling him about a pathetic letter he had received from a blind girl who wanted to be a writer and needed the money to buy a Braile typewriter, when Simenon said, "Wait a minute!" got up, went to his files, came back and said, "Oh yes, I've got that one too!" [Source: *Somerset Maugham* by Ted Morgan (Cape)]

Indeed, Simenon maintains that he did not deliberately go in search of the picturesque in his travels. "I say that when one lives in a place, a tree is a tree, whether it's called a kapok tree, a flame tree or an oak." Even in old age, on his seventy-fifth birthday, he says to an interviewer, looking out at his beloved cedar tree in the garden of his home in Lausanne: "I speak of my tree, not my cedar." In *Quand j'étais vieux*, he attacks the critics for claiming to see too many convoluted motivations in his work: "I was travelling a great deal at that period. And quite simply I told about what I was seeing as, in the first Maigrets, written on a boat I talked about canals, about the North, about the ports, etc."

He was never a tourist, as such, going to see all the sights and landmarks. Régine says that she nearly had to drag him to visit the Pyramids, although he was impressed enough when he actually got there. He never carried a notebook or made notes, although (with one exception as we have seen) all the books based on his travels were written after his return and sometimes at a distance of several years. He was always content to carry his impressions in the computer of his brain – and sometimes it played him tricks.

That is the explanation behind a famous lawsuit brought against him in May 1934, when a French woman hotel proprietor from Libreville in Gabon came especially to Paris to sue him for libel, over his all too candid portrayal of her in *Coup de Lune* ("Tropic Moon"). The novel, written in the spring of 1933 but based upon his visit to Africa a year earlier, had incensed the local French officials and settlers because of its etched-in-vitriol description of the arrogance and corruption of their lives. They subsidised the plaintiff's travel to Paris in their thirst for revenge.

The story was half-vicious, half-comic. The alleged libel was said to lie in the fact that Simenon recounted how Adele, the name that he gave to the voluptuous ex-Parisian prostitute who owned the hotel in Libreville, always wore a tight black cotton dress *beneath which one could see she was totally naked*. "How could M. Simenon possibly have known that unless he had seen me take my dress off and we had had sex together? I have never had sexual relations with this man. It would be a slur on my reputation to say I had done so" was the somewhat surprising import of her complaint before the Parisian court. In the event, Maître Garçon, Simenon's expensive and highly successful lawyer, was able to pour scorn on the discomforted woman's complaint. She did not challenge the rest of his thinly-veiled fictitious story: that she played fast and loose with men and cuckolded her complaisant husband with sordid ease; that finally she had killed a man and avoided being put on trial by sleeping with the local chief of police. Oh no, she denied none of that; but she still maintained she had been libelled by the innuendo that she had slept with one of her hotel guests: to wit, Georges Simenon! Garçon had the case literally laughed out of court, but nonetheless Simenon only had himself to blame for all the trouble he was caused.

Searching his memory for the name of her hotel – so that he could choose something else for the fictitious one in his book – Simenon could not remember what the establishment had been called. So he thought he would play safe. He knew that the hotel was right on the edge of Libreville, within a few hundred metres of where the virgin jungle started, so he called it "Hotel Central" – for nothing could be *less* central. But – just his luck – that *was* the name of her hotel!

(Incidentally, did he ever really sleep with "Adele"? In his published comments on the affair, he studiously avoids supplying the information. When asked the question direct, he replies: "No. It never happened. I would tell you, if it did.")

She must have been about the only available woman in all his travels with whom he did not have sex. Even in Tahiti, there was a real-life Tamatéa who had to jump naked out of the bedroom window of his beach-side bungalow when Régine was heard approaching from a party outside, come to see where her husband had disappeared to. As Brendan Gill has written in *The New Yorker*: "In the photograph albums that Simenon preserved from this period, neatly named and dated, are snapshots of pretty black girls in the Congo, pretty brown girls in Tahiti, pretty yellow girls in the Orient and pretty white girls in Cannes. As much as he contrived to change from one civilisation to the next, his eye never faltered."

It is not only for Simenon's "banana tourist" that one may say, *Plus ça change* . . .

Of Simenon's nine "exotic novels", only the first three were published by Arthème Fayard, the original publisher of Maigret and of the early non-Maigret stories. In October 1933, his commitment for the first eighteen Maigret novels completed and operating for the non-Maigret successors only on an *ad hoc* basis with no contract, Simenon was approached by the other outstanding publisher in France at that time, Gaston Gallimard: then fifty-four years of age, at the peak of his powers and already overtaking the ageing Fayard. Simenon was pleased to receive the call. He was still trying to get away from being identified exclusively with Maigret and being thought of only as a "popular" detective-story writer, which was Fayard's speciality.

He went to see Gallimard, but made it clear at once that he was prepared to talk business on his own terms. Not every writer is so fortunate, or so sure of exactly what he wants.

Gallimard greets him with the words: "My dear friend, please do sit down. We are going to talk about your contract. I really want you to join our house, to be among our authors. André Gide [then one of France's most prestigious authors] is one of our writers, you know, and he much appreciates you. He would very much like to meet you." "We'll see to that later," replies the wary Simenon. "Do you have a long contract with Fayard?" asks Gallimard. "No," says Simenon, "I don't have a contract. I give him what he wants, but I don't have a contract. I don't believe in signing lengthy contracts with a publisher."

"Good, good!" says Gallimard, obviously very satisfied. "Could you start as soon as you have finished your current project?" "Yes," says Simenon, "but it would depend on your terms."

"Oh, well," says Gallimard expansively. "We'll have lunch in a good restaurant some time next week to talk all about that!"

At once, Simenon lets him know exactly with whom he is dealing. "Monsieur Gallimard," he says. "Let me tell you something. Firstly, we will never have a meal together. I have a horror of those business lunches where you talk about everything except business and then you fix another business lunch. The contract I will discuss with you in your office, with a typist present, the door closed and the phones switched off – and in half an hour we will agree everything. On top of that, I will never call you 'Gaston', as everyone else around here seems to do, and I will never address you as 'my dear friend' because I hate all that kind of words.

"So when you want to have a meeting, tell me the time and day. I'll come to your office. We'll discuss everything. But after that *you'll* come to me! When you want to renew the contract, you'll come and see me."

As Simenon recalls, Gallimard was bewildered. No one, least of all an author, had talked to him like that before; but he still knew a mammoth money-earner when he saw one. The following week, when Simenon came to his office, he offered what Simenon himself calls "an amazing contract" for six books a year, which the writer knew he could accomplish in only a quarter of that time. He further-more agreed to Simenon's "very tough conditions" (his own des-cription) of a fifty-fifty sharing of the net profit. "I always impose very tough conditions," explains Simenon, "but I also know how much it costs to publish a book because I have studied how to put a book together, how much paper costs, how much printing costs, how much for transport, the percentage for the bookshop, etc., and I know how much is left for the publisher. And so I can claim to take half of it."

The contract was to run for one year, and thereafter it was renewed every twelve months – with Gallimard travelling across France to meet with Simenon wherever the writer happened to be, just as Simenon had laid down from the start.

The French critic Bernard de Fallois has said that Simenon's work is to be divided into three main phases, in keeping with his three main publishers: the Fayard period, the Gallimard period (which lasted until 1946) and the Neilson period that followed. De Fallois and others claim to see individual characteristics in the books of these periods that differentiate one publisher's influence from another. Gilbert Sigaux, the veteran critic, who knows Simenon well personally and perhaps understands him the best of all the academics that cluster around his name, disagrees. "There is no aesthetic difference between the novels of Simenon in any of his so-called 'three periods'," Sigaux said in public debate at the Simenon Exhibition in Paris in January 1982. "The difference in his relationship with his three publishers has been purely contractual."

Simenon himself has said much the same thing. He has always been cynical of those who read too much into his novels and of the different circumstances in which they were written. In a letter to Sigaux, written in September 1960 and later incorporated in *Quand j'étais vieux*, he castigates a writer who "speaks of my Balzac period, in some way allowing it to be understood that in *Le Testament Donadieu*, I was trying to imitate Balzac. Actually, I was talking only about what I was discovering by living at La Rochelle, and by being the friend of the big shipowners of that city. As to the length of that novel, [it is, in fact, by far his longest, apart from the autobiographical *Pedigree*] that was decided, not that I attach any importance to it, by the fact that it was an assignment from the magazine *Le Petit Parisien*, which requires very long novels.

"Also, all the novels of that period are characterised not by my desire to create 'suspense' but by the fact that they were all intended to be published as serials."

Simenon is a genius of formidable dimensions; but he is also one of the most practical, down-to-earth men ever to have earned a living by conjuring up creatures from his imagination. In no way is this better shown than in an incident that occurred after Arthème Fayard died.

Fayard had been succeeded by his nephew, a financial man whose father was the head of the Credit Lyonnais and whose instincts were not those with which Simenon felt a great deal of sympathy. To this very day, the House of Fayard and its subsidiaries still publish the first eighteen Maigrets and the early non-Maigret novels – *but only in French*. Some time after Arthème Fayard's death, Simenon bought back from his nephew all the publishing house's translation rights, which entitled them to fifty per cent of the profits. And the way in which he did it was quite dramatic.

The nephew lived in a superb mansion on the Avenue Foch, then called Avenue du Bois, leading down from the Etoile to the Bois de Boulogne. Unannounced and unexpected, Simenon went to see him on a Sunday morning carrying a large briefcase stuffed with bank notes – "because I knew my man, I knew how much of a miser he was."

He told him that he wanted to buy back Fayard's percentage of the translation rights: "It is such a bother for you to have to calculate the exact amount every time and to sort out the different returns from all the foreign publishers who have bought the books." The nephew was inclined to agree; but could it not wait until some time during the following week, when they could talk the matter over properly and perhaps more suitably in his office? "Oh, no," said Simenon, "let's sort it out here and now. I think your rights are worth a million francs!" And with that he opened his case and spread out in front of the man's amazed eyes one million francs in neatly tied bundles of hundred franc notes. "Here is the agreement that I want you to sign," he said, producing from his pocket a water-tight legal document that he had drafted himself, and proffering a pen.

The nephew signed, and took the money. "If I had written out a cheque, it wouldn't have had the same effect," recalls Simenon. "It was the sight of all that money in cash in front of him that he could not resist – but he must have lost at least ten million francs that day. Oh no, much more than that when I come to think of it. Not only are all the early Maigrets published in so many foreign countries, but there are all the television adaptations as well! There have been Maigret series in

111

Russia, one in France, one in Japan, there was one in England and one in Holland – and there have been two in Italy. Everyday I still earn money from the foreign rights in early Maigrets without giving a penny to the publisher. That was the best single day's business I have ever done in my life!"

Thinking in millions of francs came easily to Simenon at that time. By the mid-thirties he was enjoying a lifestyle appropriate to a man of extreme wealth.

Realising that the owner of the manor house at La Richardière, now that he had a marvellously refurbished and modernised building at his disposal, was not going to honour his verbal promise to sell them the property at the end of their lease, Simenon and Régine moved out – sadly – in the autumn of 1934 and ensconsed themselves with Boule, their horses and all their menagerie in another rented home. This time it was the Château de la Cour-Dieu, in the forest of Orleans, near Ingrannes, a splendid old building that was, in fact, an ancient Cistercian abbey with a ruined church standing in its grounds. It was intended to be only a temporary lodgement, as Simenon also bought a clearing, a few kilometres away, in the middle of the forest, with a delapidated farm in it, where he had the idea of building a new "house of his dreams" – a huge one-storey edifice with a large interior court, stables, kennels, etc. He even rented a nearby hunting preserve of some ten thousand kilometres so that, like a true country gentleman, he could enjoy the delights of the chase; although wounding a young deer at the first beat and being forced to finish it off, he at once conceived a revulsion for the pastime and never went shooting again.

Meanwhile, Boule was left in charge at the Château while he and Régine went off on their world tour. By the time they returned, the place had lost its enchantment for both of them. They decided to return to Paris. In *Un homme comme un autre*, Simenon says the decision was taken largely because Régine wanted it, complaining of life in the country. For her part, she maintains that it was her suggestion because she thought it was not a good thing that Simenon had no real home, and that he needed a headquarters: "Georges jumped at the idea and it was he who found this immense flat in the Boulevard Richard-Wallace."

Now intervened a bizarre three years in the life of Simenon. For this Man of the People, this seeker after "the little joys", selected as their home a most luxurious apartment in the most fashionable part of Paris, in the district of Neuilly, facing the Bois de Boulogne. Even today a Parisian taxi-driver will tell you that only the most wealthy and *le plus snob* will have their homes on the Boulevard Richard-Wallace, where the building that housed Simenon's apartment still stands in solid, moneyed splendour.

Simenon is the first to admit that he became a typical resident of that area, wearing only the most elegant clothes, visiting only the most fashionable restaurants and night clubs, doing only the "in"things. He drove a pale-green Delage convertible, wore a fitted long blue over-coat, sported a grey homburg and white gloves. He had his regular table at Maxim's and took cocktails every evening at five o'clock on the terrace of Fouquet's. He attended all the premières and, as he says himself, "did not miss any chance to dress in tails and high hat."

Why did he do it? In *Quand j'étais vieux*, written in the early nineteen-sixties, he said that he was flabbergasted "by that dispersion which left me nothing but confused memories . . . I don't recognise myself very well in this picture." In his *Mémoires intimes*, written twenty years later, he says that his apartment was "too sumptuous" and admits that at the time he liked what he was doing – even though "when I wanted to take my sacrosanct long walk, which furnished the idea still vague of a new novel forming within me, I had to cross the bridge at the end of the Boulevard and plunge into the populous streets of the Puteaux and Billancourt suburbs where I drank, in the bistros and with counters made of real zinc, with the workers of the Renault factory and others such, with whom I felt more at ease than with my friends."

He seemed to be able to lead two different lives at the same time; but not perhaps without an element of self-delusion. It is rather like a militant left-winger who feels that he somehow has to explain why he has acquired a liking for champagne or caviar: "We came alive at night and slept during the day," he says. "I wanted to study a certain sort of people, what was called *le Tout-Paris*. I was part of it at that time and every evening at Fouquet's I met people like Raimu, Pagnol, Arletty and all that group. I wanted to see them all close to.

"I knew all the Rothschilds, for instance. They came to my house at Porquerolles and one afternoon when one of them and his wife were having coffee in the garden after a lunch of *bouillabaisse* she said something to him, I don't know what, and he smacked her so violently across the face that she fell. There were rocks behind and I was terrified that she would fall on the rocks. As it was, she fell flat on the ground and could hardly pick herself up. You see how refined those people were . . . I much preferred the local fishermen, with whom I played boules, to the people of *le Tout-Paris*.

"But I did it to get to know about those people really well. I did not particularly enjoy myself."

Well, one wonders. Simenon has always had a knack of doing for his "art" what he wanted to do for his pleasure and enjoyment anyway. In *Quand j'étais vieux*, when writing about his theory "that men reveal more of themselves when they are having a good time than when they are at work", he was perhaps rather more honest: "In my bar on the Place des Vosges I forced cocktails on my guests in order to produce more quickly the release that would permit me to see them naked. But the evenings when I drank myself? Wasn't it just an alibi then? And if, during the small hours of the morning, I arranged it so that several women were naked, was that just to study the behaviour of the other males, or for my own satisfaction?" Posing the question is itself to give the answer; Simenon has always been an astute provider of alibis to cover his spirited search after his own fulfilment, whatever form that may take.

"During all that time, I never spent an evening at home," says Régine. "Our flat was very luxurious, very spacious and very comfortable but still for Georges it was a cage – a 'box', he used to call it. He needed to feel the bustle of the crowd around him, the atmosphere. He couldn't stand being shut in – while nowadays that's what he does all the time in his 'little pink house' in Lausanne. I can't understand him any more. He is no longer my Simenon."

She recalls how one evening she insisted that they were going to have a quiet supper together at home and afterwards she was going to read a book. "Oh, well, alright!" Simenon said – and then immediately remarked that such and such a film was being played at a local cinema that night. "Oh fine, we'll go and see it tomorrow," Régine said determinedly. He agreed. "But he kept on nagging throughout supper and afterwards about that film until finally I said, 'Alright. Let's go!' and we went, although really we could just as well have seen it the following night. There was absolutely no urgency."

He did very little actual writing in the apartment. Boule remembers how suddenly, sometimes in the middle of the night, and in winter not only in summer, he would announce: "Right, better get dressed. We are going down to Porquerolles!" He duly honoured his contract to Gaston Gallimard of six novels a year but only two of the eighteen books that he wrote in the three years they lived on Boulevard Richard-Wallace were written there. Most were written at Porquerolles, which he particularly loved at that time, where he used to spend the nights deep-sea fishing in a boat with a pointed bow which he had had built at Cagnes-sur-Mer, accompanied only by a local sailor named Tado; while the days he would spend typing away in his study, at times ending up naked and glistening with sweat in front of his machine.

His novels of that period are, in the view of many critics, not among the best. In a letter written to André Gide in January 1939, some months after leaving the Boulevard Richard-Wallace, he says to his illustrious colleague (to whom Gallimard had introduced him at a cocktail party in Paris some three years earlier) that he still felt, at the age of thirty-six, that he had yet not written his "first true novel". "I have suppressed my ringmaster, Maigret, but I remain still with a feeling of restriction of my powers. I work only two hours a day, as before. I still vomit as I did at the beginning. I still enter into the same 'state of grace' as I have always done: I *am* my main character. I live his life for those two hours. Then I feel myself emptied. I sleep. I eat. I await the moment to plunge again into the bath of creation.

"But I still arrive at only being able to support one character at a time. I still can only enter into the skin of one person in a novel. My aim is that one day I shall be able to do so for three or four of the principal characters, not just one."

(There is a large element of charm in his correspondence with Gide, which continued almost up to the older man's death in 1951. Simenon throughout began his letters "Mon cher Maître," and valued highly Gide's judgments upon his career and talent. In this same letter of 1939, he says how he felt himself inadequate when recently he had "enjoyed the pleasure of re-reading your works." In fact, as he admits in *Quand j'étais vieux*, when they first became friendly he had tried to read Gide, "I couldn't. I have never read him." Gide's highly stylised form of writing was not to his taste.)

Throughout these later years of the thirties, Simenon never lost his spasmodic urge to escape from the luxury of the Neuilly apartment that both enraptured and stifled him. It would be nothing for Simenon and Régine to drive out to Le Bourget airport in the late hours of the night and, without baggage, board the next aircraft scheduled to leave, whether its destination be Prague, Bucharest or Vienna. In *Un homme comme un autre*, he says that all his departures have been flights. But flights from what? Perhaps he gives the answer in that letter to Gide: "I must try and explain myself to you, which is far more difficult than to explain a character in a novel. Is it that the only forbidden territory of knowledge is oneself? That is often my thought and that is why often I cheat with myself. I pretend not to know the truth in order to avoid confronting reality." He was both running away from – and in search of – himself.

In the end, according to Simenon, the falseness of his life in Paris just became too much for him. In *Quand j'étais vieux*, he describes how "one day, disgusted, unable to work in Paris, I left in a car for the North of Holland to find a simple house somewhere along the seashore where I could live like a peasant. I used to say, I remember: the house one would have liked to be one's grandmother's." In *Mémoires intimes*, he gives much the same version: "One morning I said to Tigy [his name for Régine], 'I want to work somewhere else, in a little house, personal to me, far from towns and tourists, close to the sea . . .' " – and he tells how on impulse they departed, past the Hispano-Suizas, the Rolls-Royces and the Packards parked in the driveway of their smart apartment block to find a simple home for themselves.

It is a dramatic picture; but it may not be the true one, for Régine remembers it differently. The idea to leave was hers, not his – and it was not supposed to be for good, although that is how it turned out. "With all our to-ings and go-ings from the apartment, we were really only living in Paris in a sporadic way," she says. "So I suggested that we look for a place in the country where we could come to when he felt like writing; and when he had finished writing, we could go back to Paris. He agreed, and we began looking along the Atlantic coast, starting up at Delfzijl, where he wrote the first Maigret, until we arrived in the area of La Richardière near La Rochelle. There Simenon said, suddenly all very nostalgic: 'Ah, that's the countryside I like!' So we got in touch with a friend of ours, a doctor, and he said, 'Yes, there is something on the market now at Nieul,' which we knew to be only a few kilometres along the coast from La Richardière – and that's how we got the house in which I am living now!"

Régine's present home at Nieul really is "a grandmother's house". They both fell in love with it: solid, old, the stone-built remains of an ancient priory with niches for saints in what would be Simenon's study. Unlike their previous homes, they did not lease it but bought it outright. Although the apartment in Paris was kept up for a while, they were never to live there full-time again, and on Simenon's increasingly rare visits he would no longer dress "like an English gentleman." He even occasionally forgot his five o'clock appointment for cocktails at Fouquet's.

A great deal of work had to be done on the house at Nieul; walls had to be torn down, bricked-up windows opened. As in the old days of the *Ostrogoth*, the "family" of Simenon, Régine, Boule and the now ageing Olaf, set up home in a small villa on the outskirts of La Rochelle, from where every morning the two women set off for Nieul to supervise the jobs being carried out and do their share of the necessary labours, while Simenon stayed behind to put in his daily two-hours' stint at the typewriter before joining them. So great was his excitement at the new venture that he did not have the concentration to write full-length novels. Long short stories of fifty pages each, one per day, flowed from his machine – including his first Maigrets for six years, written partly because they were easier for him and partly because Gallimard had for a long time been urging him to return to his original money-spinner.

In the afternoons, Simenon himself worked on the house, almost re-building it with his bare hands. He completely re-laid the garden, aided by an attractive young secretary he had just taken on, the eighteen-year-old Annette de Bretagne: "With great laughing eyes and a gourmand mouth," he describes her in *Mémoires intimes*. "She was gourmand of everything, not only of what she ate but of the sun, of movement, of colours. I can see her now, one afternoon, bringing from the farm opposite wheelbarrow loads of hot manure that we spread on the flowerbeds." She too remembers those days. "There was happiness in the air," she says.

And there were two very good reasons for that. First, Simenon was at last making a real home for himself. Second, Régine had agreed, after fifteen years of marriage, to give him what he had always yearned for: a child. At the age of thirty-eight, in the summer of 1938, as war clouds gathered across the skies of Europe, she told him that she was pregnant.

The conception of the child that was to be Marc Simenon was a deliberate act. We have already seen that before their marriage Régine had made it a condition that they should not have children. Their mechanical (to use Simenon's word) sexual couplings had always been with Simenon wearing a contraceptive: "Not very agreeable," as he ruefully recalls.

Yet soon after they had moved into the old priory at Nieul, a house warm and serene enough "for children to visit their grandmother in", as Simenon put it, Régine turned to him and said: "Listen, do you really want a child?" "Yes," he replied without hesitation, although in truth he was rather frightened because of her age. "Well," she said, "I'm ready!" Simenon still remembers there were rays of sunshine coming through the window as she said those words. Gently, he led her into their bedroom and, as he says, "I made a child. I didn't make love but I made a child." For the first time he had sexual intercourse with his wife without using a contraceptive.

Why? What had made Régine change her mind on something so fundamental and on which her attitude had always been so rigid? Partly it was because she genuinely loved her husband and he seemed so happy in their new home that she wanted to give him the one thing, above all others, that she knew would complete that happiness. Partly it was because of the influence of the house itself; furnished afresh and newly laid out, with its vast stone fireplace and marvellous old rooms, it was, in essence, a family house, made for the laughter of children.

But there was also a stronger reason: "She did it to save the marriage," says Simenon bluntly. "For some time, she had felt that things had been strained between us."

That tension dated back three years – from the time that Simenon and his wife were returning from their world tour on a ship bound from Australia. The journey to Europe took forty-two days, and in that time Simenon fell hopelessly in love with a sixteen-year-old Australian girl. Her mother and father were also making the crossing, in a cabin next to hers, but that did not stop Simenon joining her night after night in his pyjamas. They did not make love. He was too conscious of the age gap and, besides, for once this was no casual sexual bout. He genuinely wanted to marry her. He conceived the idea of divorcing Régine as soon as they arrived back in France.

The girl did not speak a word of French. At that period, he had no command of English. However, with the aid of a pocket dictionary, he stammered out his devotion as they whispered their mutual affirmation of undying love to each other in the middle of the night. The spectacle of the earnest thirty-two-year-old married man, incongruously clad in his pyjamas and clutching his dictionary, and the eyes-aglow teenage girl, anxious lest their voices carry to her sleeping parents in the next cabin, has in it elements of both the romantic and the ridiculous.

Nor did Simenon take much pains to hide his feelings. One evening, on the forward deck, he had a fist fight with a young man who had asked the girl to dance. On another occasion, he almost jumped overboard because she had spurned him. In the end it was the child, rather than the older man, who had the sense to finish the relationship. She was in London, he was living in Paris, and she simply stopped answering his letters. The sweetly sad, unconsummated affair petered out — but Simenon knew from that moment on that one day or another, in one way or another, he would divorce Régine. Alone among all his dalliances, Régine knew of this girl and of his fevered, half-fanciful, half-real plans to marry her. For the first time, she too felt that their marriage was at risk.

But all such thoughts were put aside in the sheer joy that she gave Simenon with the news that she was pregnant with his child. Few would-be fathers were in as idyllic a state as he was; even his subconscious was infused with a warm glow of serenity and inner contemplation. It is surely not without significance that, in addition to some Maigret short stories, of four novels that he wrote during Régine's pregnancy, two (*Chez Krull* and *Le Bourgmestre de Furnes*) were set in his native Belgium while the others (*Les Inconnus dans la Maison* and *Malempin*) were the story of a father's love for his child.

Les Inconnus dans la maison ("Strangers in the House") deserves special mention. It is one of his few novels to have been made into two different film versions: one (with Raimu) in French and the other (with James Mason) some years later in English. In the new spirit of hope engendered by the impending birth of his child it is one of his more "upbeat" novels: the story of an *avocat*, Hector Loursat, who, after eighteen years of self-imposed drunken exile from his profession after his wife had abandoned him and their small child, returns to the courts to secure the triumphant acquittal of his daughter's lover, wrongly accused of murder.

"I have just finished reading your stupefying *Les Inconnus dans la maison*," Gide was later to write to him. "It is a long time since I have been so strongly impressed by a novel." Published in translation in the United States (but oddly not yet in Britain), the warmth of its portrayal of the father, saving in effect both himself and his daughter's lover at the same time, has a poignant, almost wish-fulfilment quality, that one does not often find in Simenon's work.

In the event, Marc was born — on April 19, 1939 — not in the old priory at Nieul but in Belgium; at a clinic in Uccles, a suburb of Brussels. But as Régine says, "it was nothing to do with our wanting

119

our son to be born in our native land. The story of Marc's birth is really a poem."

For what happened was that Simenon, anxious for the welfare of his wife, who was then in her thirty-ninth year, was not satisfied with any of the clinics in La Rochelle. A good friend of both of them, who visited Porquerolles every summer with his family, was a medical professor at a leading Strasbourg hospital. Simenon telephoned him for guidance and he told him to bring Régine to Strasbourg. So Simenon, Régine – and Boule – climbed into their enormous old Chrysler Imperial and they travelled right across France to that grim city of *choucroute* and *pâté de foie gras*, where the amiable Professor Pautrier had rented them a château for Régine to await her time.

But the château was twenty miles away from the city; Hitler had just invaded Czechoslovakia, the panic of impending war – allayed since the appeasement of Munich the previous autumn – was now again in the air, and Simenon grew worried for his wife's safety. He suggested to Pautrier that they should move to Strasbourg itself, lest there be unnecessary delays when Régine's time came. But the professor countered that with the recommendation that they should seek the refuge of Paris: Strasbourg and its environs were just too close to Hitler's Germany with the Nazi frontier guards only the other side of the River Rhine. "Everybody is leaving the area already," he said. "It's possible that, when your wife is going to give birth, all the hospitals will be evacuated and she will have nobody really to assist her. You had better leave now!"

So leave they did, but not for Paris. They drove in the other direction – towards Belgium, which was not only much nearer, but where, after all, they both had family that could help them. They travelled with a midwife in the car, ensconced beside Boule, so close to her expected time was the stoically calm Régine.

Within a short while of arriving at Brussels, where Régine's brother Yvan and his family lived and warmly greeted them, the child was born. "Are you happy, Georges?" were the first words that Régine said when Simenon, trembling with joy, tiptoed into her room like a youngster, full of reverence, entering a church. He played his car horn like a trumpet, as he sang all the way back to their rented apartment, where he threw open the door and cried out to Boule, who was pale with emotion: "He's born! I have a son!"

He had waited so long for this moment that it seemed to him almost sacrilege that others should touch the child. When his mother-in-law, the ageing Mme. Rechon, who was already a grandmother many times over and had brought up five children of her own, took her latest grandson in her arms, he could not stop himself exclaiming: "Be careful. You're holding the baby too tight!"

At last, it seemed that he really could be happy. He was genuinely fond of his wife. He had the son – and the home – of his dreams. He was approaching the plenitude of his powers as a writer, full of hope and confidence in his ability. Life was – almost – as he had ever wanted. If he did not have the moon, at least the stars were there shining in all their glory.

And then, sitting in a bistro in La Rochelle sipping a glass of white wine, with Annette de Bretagne beside him, on a routine visit to the town one warm Sunday morning in early September 1939, he heard the announcement on the radio that France, and her ally Great Britain, were at war with Nazi Germany.

CHAPTER 11

The Early Days of the War

In that little bistro in La Rochelle, the trembling hand of the young Annette, who knew nothing of war, sought Simenon's hand for reassurance. They sat for some while, then drove back to the house, where Simenon broke the news to Régine. They had both lived through the First World War, they both knew what this new conflict could mean. They looked at their five-month-old son, and they were afraid.

Yet, for all their apprehension and Simenon's dramatic gesture of opening several bottles of champagne "to give us the courage to look the future in the face", he was soon back at work as usual. Bent over his typewriter and immersed in the lives of his characters, he put the international situation out of his mind and, in his regulation ten days, wrote *Il pleut bergère* ("Black Rain"), a tale in which war and thoughts of mass destruction figure not at all.

In fact, the Second World War hardly enters the writings of Simenon. In only two novels, *Le Train* ("The Train") and *Le Clan des Ostendais* ("The Ostenders"), both written after the war, does he tell a story set against a background of wartime events. Even then, in the more successful of the two, *Le Train*, the German invasion of the Low Countries in May 1940 serves only as a catalyst provoking thirty-two-year-old Marcel Feron, a radio repairer and "petit bourgeois" in a small town in Northern France, to flee, almost with joy, his home, together with his baby daughter and wife Jeanne, pregnant with her second child. It is his "turning point", that familiar device in a Simenon novel, enabling him to make a break with his past life. On the crowded refugee train taking them south, he loses his wife and daughter and has a "time-out" brief affair with a young Jewish girl, who is making the same journey. After arriving at their destination he eventually succeeds in rejoining his family, his wife having by then safely been delivered of a son.

The Ferons return to their home in Northern France, where Marcel picks up the routine of his ordinary life. Several years later, towards the end of the war, he sees the young Jewess again in the street. She is now fleeing desperately from the Gestapo and asks him for help; but he refuses. "I understand, Marcel," she says. A month later, he reads a notice on the wall announcing that she has been shot. It leaves him neither sad nor happy, living out his life with his wife and his children in the same little house over the radio repair shop in the small northern town.

Le Train is a powerful story, later made into an impressive film with Romy Schneider, the Austrian actress, as the young Jewess; but it is as if Simenon can only feel or relate to *individual* tragedy, particular experience, not that of the crowd. Although he continued to live in France throughout the war, one would never know from reading the many novels and stories that he wrote at the time that Hitler existed or there was such a thing as the German occupation. There are no concentration camps, no aerial bombings, no fear of the knock on the door in the middle of the night.

In August 1940, soon after the fall of Paris, with hundreds of thousands of young Frenchmen languishing in prisoner-of-war camps, with the cities and countryside of Northern France devastated and the aged puppet Marshal Petain installed in fascist splendour at Vichy, Simenon wrote *La Vérité sur Bébé Donge* ("I take this Woman"), a novel that he himself, in *Mémoires intimes*, describes as "without war, without noise, almost without drama, full of sun and of harmonious gardens."

Denis Tillinac, a young French writer, has commented on what he calls "the a-historical quality" of Simenon, with major current events almost totally missing from his work and hardly touching the lives of his characters. In his critical study of Simenon*, he says: "His indifference to 'great events' is that of the man on the street. One can read all the hundreds of novels of Simenon without knowing that in 1917 the Russia of the Tsars became the USSR . . . One can read his novels without knowing who in 1939, declared war upon whom."

But it goes further than that. There is almost a perverse refusal by Simenon to accept the reality, in his writings, of the Second World War. In *Signé Picpus* ("To Any Lengths"), for instance, a Maigret novel written in the summer of 1941, after a year of German soldiers strutting in the streets of Paris and with all foreign tourists long since disappeared, he writes of "the roar of the traffic on the Ile de la Cité" and of the rue Auber "with cafés jostling on either hand and gay

Le Mystère Simenon ("The Simenon Mystery"), Calman-Levy, 1980.

crowds jostling each other on the pavements." As Maigret goes about his investigations, "charabancs packed with foreigners threaded their way through the streets of Paris, with a guide bawling through a megaphone pointing out the sights."

Was this deliberate escapism or a blockage in his own mind that prevented him from seeing things as they really were? If he chose to continue to write at all during the war and the grim years of the Occupation (and there is no evidence that he was compelled by financial necessity or by either the French or the German authorities to do so), one would have thought he might have written something nearer the truth and not painted this fairytale picture of a Paris and a France that had cruelly ceased to exist. Says Simenon: "I did not write very much during the war. There were not many books published. There was no paper." The facts belie this. David Pryce-Jones, in his *Paris in the Third Reich**, quotes Otto Abetz, Hitler's representative in Paris, as being "proud to record" that "in spite of shortages, French publishers received substantial allocations of paper; from 1941 to 1944 the average annual production of purely literary, artistic and scientific books was not inferior to what it had been in peacetime. In 1943, at the height of the war, French publishing led the world with 9,348 titles, ahead of America with 8,320 titles, Britain with 6,705 titles, and Switzerland with 3,325." Yet Simenon says there was no paper!

The Germans, throughout the years of the Occupation, established an official censor, Gerhard Heller, with headquarters on the Champs Elysées in Paris. But, as David Pryce-Jones says, "Heller made a practice of passing virtually everything." Although a decent enough man, it was not his liberalism that allowed him to do this but the supine weakness of the French publishing world as a whole, too hastily complying with what they thought might be his demands. As Heller himself says, in his book *Un Allemand à Paris†*, published in France in 1981: "The French applied between themselves a sort of auto-censorship." It is not generally known outside France even today that, within three months of the fall of Paris, the *Syndicat des éditeurs français*, the professional organisation of French publishers, signed an agreement with their Nazi masters by which they bound themselves not to publish books written by Jews and Freemasons (to which was later added Communists) and, in return, they would only have to submit to German censorship "books on which they had their doubts."

*Collins, 1981.
†("A German in Paris"), Seuil, 1981.

Notable among the publishers who was a party to this agreement was Gaston Gallimard.

It is not a pretty story. Journalist Sam White, a veteran observer of the French scene, says: "People overlook the fact that at one time during the Occupation Jean-Paul Sartre, the arch-radical, had two plays running at the same time in Paris – and one of them was at the Théâtre de la Cité, renamed from the Théâtre Sarah-Bernhardt because that great actress had been Jewish."

For most people in the world of arts and entertainment, life carried on as usual – or as close to it as they could make it – throughout the years of the Occupation. As Sartre himself later said, "The Occupation was intolerable but at the same time we adapted ourselves to it well enough." Writers and dramatists such as Sartre, Simone de Beavoir, Marcel Aymé, Jean Anouilh and Marcel Pagnol continued living, and working, in Paris. Sacha Guitry, then the best known actor–dramatist on the Parisian stage, appeared to like the company of Otto Abetz so much that he was a frequent visitor at his embassy in the rue de la Lille, with the triumphant German flag flying at the masthead. The choreographer Serge Lifar was honoured by a gala performance at the Paris Opera, at which he did not disdain the plaudits of uniformed high-ranking Nazi officers. Maurice Chevalier lived mostly outside Paris but came in for singing engagements, in particular on Radio-Paris, for which he was heavily paid (but for which he was to pay in public censure more heavily still after the war). Edith Piaf found it convenient to rent the entire top floor of a brothel for herself and in one night's stage performance earned up to twenty thousand francs, the equivalent of an office worker's annual salary. Neither she nor Chevalier flinched at visiting Germany and giving concerts to French prisoners-of-war, flanked by their steel-booted captors.

Alfred Cortot, the pianist, saw nothing wrong in giving recitals in Berlin and famous artistes such as Danielle Darrieux, Vivianne Romance and Albert Préjean (later three times to play Maigret on the cinema screen) accepted invitations to be fêted in the Nazi homeland.

The Comédie Française functioned throughout the war, with Marie Bell, Mary Marquet, Madeleine Renaud and Jean-Louis Barrault among its loyal troupe of performers. Le Tout-Paris did its best to act as if the hostilities were but a memory; the great restaurants such as Fouquet's, Lapérouse, the Marquise de Sévigné, the Tour d'Argent and Le Grand Véfour remained exactly what they had always been. Maxim's, although taken over by Horcher, a celebrated Berlin restauranteur, was outwardly the same as ever. Night after night, prominent or visiting Germans, Goering above all, and their French friends, were shown to their table with fawning courtesy by the old pre-war headwaiter. One evening, at a splendid dinner party in a private house where the Duc d'Harcourt and Coco Chanel, the couturier, were among the guests, Mlle. Chanel got into a long tirade against the Jews, from which "fortunately she was sidetracked," as one of her fellow guests noted in his diary, "when everyone agreed that Catherine d'Erlanger's emeralds are nothing but bits of green bottles." In the words of David Pryce-Jones, "(Jean) Cocteau and (Jean) Marais, in the apartment they shared in the Palais Royale, lived much as though the war was passing them by. 'How will I get my opium?' was Cocteau's first priority."

In the cinema, it was much the same message of "life as usual". Veteran actors such as Raimu, Pierre Fresnay and Jules Berry, and newcomers like Serge Reggiani, Gerard Phillipe and Daniel Gelin, pursued their careers. As one French historian of those wartime years comments, not without bitterness: "The Resistance found only a feeble echo in the world of the cinema."[*]

The feeling of shame among some Frenchmen is still etched deep today; forty years later the newspaper *Le Figaro* can still publish a review of a new book on the Occupation under the headline: "Le Temps de l'humiliation". But not everyone behaved in such a complaisant fashion. After the Fall of Paris, such gifted and distinguished people as René Clair, Louis Jouvet, Jean Gabin, André Maurois, Fernand Léger and the composer Darius Malhaud managed to get away to the United States. Vladimir Nabokov escaped to New York on the last liner out ahead of the incoming Germans. Jean Renoir, one of Simenon's closest friends, also contrived to make a hazardous departure. When asked if she and Simenon did not think of trying to leave, Régine responds with what seems like genuine surprise: "No," she says. "There was nothing to be done. We were being Occupied."

After the war, Simenon did not escape unpleasant accusations. In Maurice Richardson's telling phrase, "after the Liberation the Communist poet Aragon was darting his forked tongue all over Paris telling everyone that the model for Maigret was an arch-collaborator." You will find no mention of any of this in his writings, but Simenon has admitted: "I wasn't stopped from making my films in the war. They continued to make Maigrets. I asked myself why actors shouldn't

[*]Jean-Pierre Agéma: *De Munich à la Libération (1938–1944)*, Seuil, 1979.

be allowed to go on making their living because there was a war. So I let my films be made. But some people found it – how shall I say? – in bad taste."

In fact, some of his films were produced by the notorious Continental Film Company, set up by the Germans under the aegis of Dr. Goebbels, the Nazi Propaganda Minister, and affiliated to the Nazi-dominated U.F.A. in Berlin. *Les Inconnus dans la maison* was banned for a time after the Liberation because the screenplay by Henri-Georges Clouzot, with its strong undertones of anti-Semitism, was held to constitute "anti-French propaganda." The undertones are *not* present in the original text of Simenon's novel; but he had to approve the sale of the film rights. He is famous for not taking care with what happens to his stories once they are bought for screen adaptation; by then, he has genuinely lost interest in them. He does not usually bother to see the finished movie. "Take the money and run" would be a sordid but not entirely inaccurate way of putting it. Even so, in the context of the German Occupation and of what was happening in his adopted country, ought he not in those circumstances to have taken greater care?

When criticised by a journalist after the war for having ignored the events of those years, Simenon retorted: "I do follow closely current events – but they don't affect me. Out of curiosity, I will turn on the TV when I am too tired to read, and I will watch it vaguely. But I will be at pains afterwards to tell you what I have seen. Current events repeat themselves: the same winners, the same losers. I hope that one day the losers will be the winners – and I hope too that before that we do not have to go through a more reactionary period than the present one."

That seems an adroit side-step of a difficult question, but perhaps the truth is that Simenon genuinely suffers from a sort of "tunnel vision". He sees life only through blinkers. He searches after the truth – not least, about himself – but he is, in essence, interested in events and other people only insofar as they affect *him*. Simenon is the God of the Simenonien world; there is no room for any other.

His good friend Dr. Jean Martinon (whom, to be fair, Simenon has instructed to speak freely and withhold nothing which might be of interest to a biographer) tells how, when Simenon and his second wife Denise were living in Cannes in the mid-fifties, "Simenon had a way of behaving that made it difficult to separate the truth from the untruth. They were both a little bit hypocritical. They said, 'We are sacred monsters' and this formula allowed them all sorts of things." Simenon would no doubt protest at the allegation, but the evidence would indicate that this applies to his activities during the war years as well. Ordinary standards do not apply to him; at least, that is what he would like to believe.

Régine's verdict on her former husband during that difficult time is characteristically more generous: "Current events do not interest him from the literary point of view, since he concentrates his study on 'the naked man'. On a personal level, it's another matter; he suffered a lot during the war. He doesn't study man in the frame of political events. He studies man for his desires, his illusions, his sorrows, his joys. And whether there is a war on or not, doesn't reflect on what he writes."

So what did happen to Simenon during those appalling years of the Second World War? What is the truth about his experiences? With hand on heart, how would he answer the up-dated question: "What did you do in World War Two, Daddy?"

He would no doubt reply quite simply: "I lived." Like millions of other Belgians and Frenchmen, he was neither a hero nor a coward, neither a saint nor a toady. Unlike Serge Lifar he did not visit Germany three times in one year, with Hitler, Goering and Goebbels receiving him with admiration and flattery.* Indeed, he had refused to sell German rights in his books after his own publisher there had been forced to flee the country, and he stuck to this throughout the war despite many tempting offers.

There are, no doubt, quite a few men and women of his age still living in Europe today who can look back on the war years with greater cause for honour, but there are many more who can look back with far less pride on how they behaved when the time came for their mettle to be tested.

For a start, until the Germans invaded Belgium and the Netherlands on May 10, 1940, Simenon was, as a Belgian citizen, not really at war with anyone. But, as soon as the frontiers of his native country were breached, he rallied at once, if in somewhat melodramatic style, to its defence.

Within hours of the German invasion, the Belgian Government called up for the armed forces all male nationals under the age of fifty, with orders to proceed at once to their local barracks or areas of military command. Simenon was then thirty-seven; he had long since lost the uniform he had worn as a cavalry man during his stint of

* In 1947, Lifar was officially exonerated from a charge of collaboration.

National Service, but he had kept his old army cap with its coloured pompom. Wearing that cap, and dressed in riding breeches, boots and tweed jacket, he kissed Régine and the baby Marc goodbye and boarded the train at La Rochelle en route to Liège via Paris. But when he arrived at the Gare Montparnasse in the French capital, there was a large notice displayed: "All Belgians are requested not to continue their journey to Belgium but to go and make contact with the Belgian Embassy, rue de Surenne." Pushing his way through the crowds, he hailed a taxi, only to find the scene at the Embassy one of complete confusion.

He managed to get to the First Secretary, whom he knew quite well and who expressed surprise at seeing him there, dressed in such splendid operetta-style. "I'm going to rejoin my regiment like every-body else!" replied Simenon, although he had to admit that he had no idea where it was. "I haven't either." said the First Secretary. He explained that the position was absolutely chaotic, with the Army saying that all the men who reported for duty should be sent at once and the Government saying that it was impossible to get through because the roads were already cut. "Every half an hour there is a contradiction. I just don't know what the position is," said the First Secretary. "Listen, you must have some friends still left in Paris. Go and have lunch with them. Come back this afternoon at three o'clock, and by then I'll have a definite answer for you, whether you can carry on or not."

This was Simenon's last lunch before he knew not what. He was not going to waste it just on food. He hastened round to the wife of one of his wealthy aristocratic friends from La Rochelle, whom he knew to have a town apartment nearby, overlooking the Seine. She was alone; her cook prepared a delightful meal which they ate with great pleasure and then, sitting beside each other on the sofa, he said to her: "Listen, I have never touched you, as you know, but you have such very beautiful legs and you know that I am very fond of you. I want to stroke your legs now so that I can keep a beautiful memory of that, no matter what may happen." She smiled her acquiescence and very tenderly his hands stroked the silk of her stockings and fondled the flesh of her thighs before sliding out from under her skirt. Then they embraced and he departed.

Simenon tells the story of this encounter in *Mémoires intimes*, but what he does not say there is that the woman, although married, was, as he well knew, a lesbian. "That made no difference," he says now. "In my relationship with women, that is really all I have wanted.

Tenderness. In that instance, the tenderness of stroking those beautiful legs of someone I was truly fond.''

Back at the Belgian Embassy, the First Secretary told him there was to be no stirring departure to the field of battle. All the roads really were cut. Yet there was still a way in which he could help. The French Government had nominated the area of Southwest France in the region of La Rochelle as a reception centre for the hundreds of thousands of Belgian refugees that were fleeing from the German armies by train, by cart, and by every possible means of transportation. Did Simenon know the local Prefect? "He is one of my close friends. He was dining with us the day before yesterday," was the reply. Did he know the Military Governor? "He too is a good friend and we visit each other's homes." "Good!" said the First Secretary. "In that case, with the agreement of the French Government, I will nominate you High Commissioner for the Belgian refugees. You have *carte blanche*. You can sign whatever you like in the way of orders, you can requisition whatever Belgian-owned property you may consider necessary, you can bind the Belgian Government to pay the French for whatever goods or services you deem appropriate.''

Without spending a whole night away from home, Simenon was back in the house at Nieul by four o'clock the next morning. "I have a great deal of work to do," he told Régine.

For the next three months, Simenon was totally caught up in his involvement with the refugees. He enlisted the aid of the local Mayor and Prefect; he had pre-fabricated buildings erected in the forecourt of the railway station at La Rochelle to give temporary housing to the hordes that arrived by train. He slept on a bench on one of the station platforms because the trains were coming in at all hours of the night and he needed to know as early as possible how badly damaged they were. He would be told, for instance: "This next one is a bad one. It's been machine-gunned three times and there are a lot of wounded, and there is also a woman on board who's likely to give birth at any moment" – and he would then arrange the necessary hospitalization.

He requisitioned all the cars and lorries bringing in refugees, and used them to re-distribute fresh arrivals throughout the region. By the time that Marshal Petain's Government had signed an armistice with the Germans on June 22, 1940, and the Army of Occupation had begun to arrive in La Rochelle, Simenon had been responsible for the reception, temporary housing and medical treatment of no less than 55,000 homeless men, women and children. He had even managed to find some of the younger, able-bodied men well-paid employment in local factories. Then he was called to the office of the Prefect, introduced to a polite young *Oberleutnant*, who spoke excellent French, and told him that the Germans were going to repatriate the lot of them!

"Fine. I'll ask them if they want to go," said Simenon, and it turned out that they all did. "You know, the Belgians have a real attachment to their little houses," he explains. "They work all their lives to get one. Like my mother, who spent the entire war in her own little house in Liège, which she had worked so hard to obtain. They all wanted to go back to their own homes, however ravaged by the war they may have been."

It was Simenon who supervised the massive task of repatriation. He went with the *Oberleutnant* in a German army car to the military headquarters at Bordeaux, where he explained to the officer in command that in each train there would need to be at least two first-class coaches for women or old people who were sick and for babies – "the other coaches I wasn't worried about" – and that he personally would be responsible for using his requisitioning powers to ensure that each passenger would be given sufficient bread for a three-day journey and two kilos of butter, together with a sum of money. Simenon said that he would also organise, from among the refugees themselves, a doctor, a nurse and a Boy Scout for every train. The Germans agreed with this and asked him to draw up a detailed evacuation plan, which he did. "So they all left in a very good state," he recalls, "but it took a month and after that I was absolutely exhausted. I was dead tired."

The house at Nieul had lost its enchantment. La Rochelle, whose dry docks were admirably suited for the repair of German U-boats, had quickly become a prime target for RAF bombing sorties. Air raids were frequent and once, returning to the house, Simenon had to run through a stream of flaming petrol spilling across the road from a large storage tank hit by an Allied bomb. To add to his discomfiture, a German officer had been billeted in his study and was using it as a bedroom.

Régine and Simenon decided to leave their dream house. In August 1940, together with Marc and Boule, they moved to a little farm in the Forest of Vouvent in the nearby Vendée countryside, remote from Allied air raids and German soldiers. Here they stayed for two months, living in the farmhouse, while the wife of the farmer, who had been taken prisoner by the Germans at the Front, and her small son occupied one of the outbuildings. It was in the hayloft of this temporary rustic home that Simenon wrote the sunny and harmonious *La Vérité sur Bébé Donge*, in which there is not the slightest echo of wartime clamour.

It was also while staying on the farm that an incident occurred which was to blight the next four years of Simenon's existence; but for a reason that had nothing at all to do with the war. If anything, it only served to make him turn even more upon himself and block out the wider horrors from his mind. Cutting a large piece of wood to make a toy for Marc, it slipped from his hand and gave him a nasty blow on his chest. He felt some mild pain at the time but the following morning it was very much worse. Never having forgotten that his father had died of heart disease and obsessed with the morbid idea that he too would die at the same early age (forty-four), he decided that at all costs he must have his chest X-rayed.

With no petrol available for his car, he walked eleven miles to the nearest sizable town, Fontenay-le-Comte, where the telephone directory gave him the name and address of a radiologist. There he received perhaps the most famous wrong diagnosis given by a medical man in the history of literature, for the radiologist told him that his most secret fears were true: he *was* suffering, like his father, from serious heart disease. "You have a badly enlarged heart," he told him. "Provided you cut out all wine, tobacco, rich food, any form of physical exertion – and that includes making love – you may perhaps survive for as long as two years."

Crushed, Simenon staggered back to the farmhouse in the forest. When he broke the news to the two women who loved him, Régine quietly put her hand in his. Boule burst out: "*Mon petit monsieur joli,* I shall never leave you!" Simenon spent the greater part of the war under personal sentence of death. Even when the two years had passed, and he was still surviving, he put it down to his good fortune and not to any failure in the dread diagnosis.

Why did he so easily accept the assurance of his impending demise? He says in *Mémories intimes* that he subsequently consulted a general physician in practice in Fontenay, who merely telephoned the radiologist who confirmed his earlier reading of the X-rays. "You would do well to consult a heart specialist in Paris," the doctor told him. But Simenon counters in his memoirs: "It was easy for him to say that. But it was in the war. We were foreign nationals having in principle to sign the register every day at the local police commissariat. We did not have the right to leave the town."

Régine says differently: "He *could* have gone to Paris if he wanted to, though there were less trains. He would not even have needed a special permit to leave the town. That was only if you wanted to go to the coast, which was, of course, fortified."

As we shall see later, in February 1944, Simenon *did* travel to Paris – apparently without a permit – and got a second opinion from a leading Parisian cardiologist that exposed the radiologist's error and removed any possibility of an early death. So why not, even on Simenon's own version of events, at least try and get a travel permit from the authorities back in that summer of 1940? He does not even seem to have asked.

The truth is that Simenon, like many another, has always been a hypochondriac, congenitally prone to accept that some dire illness has befallen him. Even the faithful Boule has to admit: "Georges Simenon was always very much concerned about his health." He would probably even admit to that himself.

Although the story of the radiologist's mistaken diagnosis is well known to all those familiar with the tale of Simenon's life, what is not well known is that, almost from the start, Régine was trying to convince him that it simply was not true. But he would have none of it. "I thought it must be nonsense," she says. "So I went to see that radiologist myself as soon as I could and I asked him what on earth it was all about. He had put my husband into a terrible state. He said, 'Oh, there is nothing serious about it. It's not that alarming.' But he couldn't give me any explanation of why he had given Simenon such a wildly exaggerated diagnosis. It was cruel! Simenon truly was very alarmed, despite all that I did to try and persuade him to the contrary. I simply do not understand that doctor even now. Perhaps he was jealous, or a sadist. It was ridiculous to tell Simenon what he did."

Nevertheless, the damage was done. As millions died on the field of battle or their bodies were blown to smithereens by bombs falling from the skies, Simenon learned to live with his own private sadness – even if it was partly of his own making.

133

CHAPTER 12

The War Begins to Bite

In September 1940, Simenon and his family exchanged the simplicity of their small rented farmhouse for a luxurious apartment that occupied half an ancient château. It was at Fontenay itself and to this day the large, magnificent structure of the Château de Terre-Neuve, dating from the sixteenth century, dominates the small country town, looking down on it from a high ridge on the other side of a river banked with trees.

Nowadays tourists can pay seven francs to enter the building, which has opened its doors to charabancs to help pay off death duties or the cost of maintaining the fabric. But even a handwritten sign "Bar Crêperie" on the side of the building does not detract from the feeling that one is protected from the rigours of the world by this solid monument to wealth and local power. The turrets and noble stone statues of the façade overlook a terrain of trees, lawns and geraniums in their ancient pots. There is an atmosphere of tranquillity and security.

It is easy to believe that, living in a building and in grounds such as these, the war – at least, at first – did not touch Simenon and his family too closely. There were German soldiers in the area but camped some distance away. One saw very few in the town itself. The impact of the Occupation was muffled in this small community of only 5,000 inhabitants.

Simenon himself has said, in *Mémoires intimes*: "We lived for nearly two years a calm and sheltered life in that calm and sheltered corner of Southwest France, with its discreet charm." It is interesting to compare what he says of his contact with the local population with what *they* say. In his memoirs, he relates how he used to play bridge most afternoons with some cronies – a doctor, a lawyer and others of that kind – in the Café du Pont. (For once he remembers a name almost correctly. It was, in fact, the Café du Pont-Neuf, now pulled down.) He also frequented another café, more buoyant, more vulgar, where the customers would often break out into great gales of laughter and

134

where he would, "in a voice full of shame", summon up the courage to request a small glass of white wine "to defy my pedantic radiologist who lived in the 'best part of town', reserved for the *grande bourgeoisie*, and did not deign to show himself in either of these cafés."

But you do not enter into the life or heart of a town by merely frequenting its cafés. Says M. Jim Dindurand, the owner of Fontenay's leading bookshop: "I remember that Simenon would come to town in his car or on foot. He would stop at the newsagent, or at the café for a glass of wine, then go back home where he shut himself up again in his ivory tower." M. Pierre Chaigneau, one of his few remaining bridge companions, says: "Yes, that is true about the sessions of bridge in the Café du Pont-Neuf and we could go up to the Château as well to play. He was very familiar with everybody. Everybody knew him. He was no snob at all. Yet he was living somehow in isolation in respect to Fontenay, not mixing in the town's life."

In *Je me souviens*, the first book that Simenon was to write while living at the Château, he tells his infant son, Marc, never to forget their humble origins: "You live in a château, you have a park at your disposal . . . a distinguished governess follows your every step . . . I clutch hold of the fragile chain which links you to those from whom you are descended, the little world of little people who struggled in their turn – as tomorrow you will in yours – confusedly seeking a means of escape, a goal, a reason for existence, an explanation for good luck or misfortune, a hope for an improved condition and for serenity."

Yet, even in the middle of a war, the barrier of wealth and fame was too great for Simenon to surmount, however genuine may have been his efforts. The other townsfolk also lived comparatively well, having friends or relations who cultivated crops or reared livestock on the surrounding farms. All they had to do was pay a visit to the countryside and come back fully laden against the rigours of a notional rationing; but, as Simenon's ex-bridge crony says, "He did not need to go into the countryside. Having money, he could buy all the food he wanted."

When, in 1942, there was of all things a "world première" at "L'Eden", Fontenay's crowded little cinema, of *La Maison des Sept Jeunes Filles*★, a film based on Simenon's novel of the same name that had been published in the previous year, everyone turned out in their best clothes to do honour to the distinguished man of letters temporarily in their midst. Jean Tissier, one of the actors in the film, stayed with Simenon at the Château and it became an item of gossip in the town how at breakfast he was seen emptying the sugar bowls into his

★("The House of Seven Young Girls") though as yet not published in English.

135

pockets because the Simenon household had plenty and there was a shortage in Paris.

Simenon really thinks that he is "a man like any other", that he can make true contact with ordinary people and enter into their lives. Since the early years of his success that notion has, in reality, been a myth in which he somehow needs to believe. More than ten years later, when living on the other side of the world, in Lakeville, Connecticut, he wrote *Maigret a peur* ("Maigret Afraid"), a murder story set in a Fontenay that he describes as an unsympathetic, narrow-minded sort of place with, as the cover blurb says, "its undercurrents of personal, social and political animosities." Yet that has made no difference to the feeling of pride, tinged with awe, with which the local populace still view him. "No, they did not find it shocking when the book, and later the film based on the book, appeared," says M. Jim Dindurand. "Indeed, they rather enjoyed their notoriety. He even took my family name and gave it to some character in the novel who is not a very nice person, but I didn't mind."

To be a "man of the people" when you are a famous millionaire living in a château is to chase after a will-o'-the-wisp.

But it appears that Simenon did make close contact with at least one of the inhabitants of Fontenay. And, despite his radiologist's orders to refrain from physical exertion, there are no prizes for guessing what sort of contact it was. "Mme . . .," and M. Dindurand names a local widow only recently dead, "could have said so much about Simenon. She was a beautiful woman, especially in her prime, with lots of past successes." Local gossip has her firmly cast in the role of Simenon's mistress in the town. (One day she was talking to her bookkeeper in her shop when she saw Simenon come in and excused herself with the words: "Oh, give me a minute. Here comes my poet!")

At the première of Simenon's film, he arrived at the cinema with this well-known Fontenay tradeswoman on his arm. She was resplendent in local traditional costume: clogs, short skirt and a high headgear with white flaps. Régine was also there, and tongues clacked. As in many small provincial towns the locals were used to affairs, but they were usually of the "behind closed curtains" variety. This was flaunting the relationship in public, and in the presence of his wife (although Régine's normal dignity prevented anyone from knowing whether she was aware of what was apparently going on or not).

Even if Simenon had not been restricted by the radiologist's grim warning, Fontenay is not the sort of place in which a married man interested in other women would have had many opportunities for dalliance. An attractive widow would be just the sort of person who could provide loving friendship, the nearest to a relationship possible in the circumstances. There were certainly very few other options open to him. As it was, local scandal fed upon the fact that (as one old lady still living in the town remembers) Simenon used to walk around his apartment in the Château with practically nothing on in front of the maids – and some of them did not like it!

This then is the setting in which, on December 9, 1940, Simenon sat down in a little wooden hut in the grounds of the Château that he had rigged up for himself as a study, opened a large notebook and wrote (in French) on the first page:

PEDIGREE
OF
MARC SIMENON

WITH THE PORTRAIT OF HIS FATHER, HIS GRANDFATHERS AND GRANDMOTHERS, HIS UNCLES, HIS AUNTS AND HIS COUSINS

It begins "*Mon cher garçon*", and takes the form of a long letter to his infant son, Marc, in which he recounts the events of his own past life. It was never meant for publication. Written entirely in longhand, it was Simenon's attempt to explain himself to his son, still only twenty months old, whom he never thought he would live to see grow to manhood.

This is a literary device that Simenon was to use again, in a fictitious context, in *Le Fils* ("The Son") a novel written at Cannes in December 1956, in which, with poignant effect, another father, this time a man named Alain Lefrançois, writes a long confessional letter to his sixteen-year-old son, Jean-Paul, to explain to him, on the occasion of the funeral of the lad's grandfather, the truth about his family. "I am a Lefrançois," he writes in the early pages, "just as you are one, as my father was before me and his father before him. It makes me smile, without any melancholy, to imagine you at my age perhaps pre-occupying yourself in your turn with what your son thinks of you and of your grandfather."

137

Marc Simenon, who is now a film director in his forties, living in a rambling country house just outside Paris with his glamorous actress wife Mylene Demongeot, Boule and his two children by his first marriage, did not, in fact, read *Je me souviens* (as the letter-book to him was eventually called when Simenon was persuaded to publish it after the war in December 1945) until he was seventeen. "I started rather late reading my father's books," he says, "but it drove me to read other works of his. When he wrote it, he thought he was going to die and he was a man in torment. We are both very close to each other – he had waited a long time for me, after all! – but then he is very close to all his children.

"Did he succeed in explaining himself to me? Well, undoubtedly he tried in *Je me souviens* but I think he is still trying in all his books. You see, I think my father needs to communicate with people. He had a short, very warm contact with his own father but he did not really know him for long. He died when my father was eighteen – just at the age when he could have started getting to know him so much better and understand him. He may have tried to find, in his relations with his children, something he had known with his father. I think that's why, when he thought he was going to die, he started to write and try and explain himself to me so that I wouldn't find myself in the same position as he had been with my grandfather, when he died so young. And with his dictated memoirs it's the same. They are all more or less self-analysis. He didn't want them to be published at the beginning – just as with *Je me souviens* – but in the end he didn't refuse because deep in his heart he always wants some form of communication."

In a later preface to *Je me souviens* (not, incidentally, Simenon's own title), Simenon says that when he re-reads "the primitive text" he finds himself rather embarrassed. "It is not at all a literary work, but a sort of document. The style is rather a spoken style, that of a father talking to his son more than the written style of a novelist." Yet, although never translated into English, it is a strangely powerful work and when nearly thirty years later Simenon came to write his last published book, the massive *Mémoires intimes*, he chose to do so in the same documentary style – this time in the form of a letter to his only daughter, the twenty-five-year-old Marie-Jo, who had killed herself two years previously.

For all its merits, *Je me souviens* has been largely over-shadowed both in France and other countries by its sequel: a long, rambling novel called *Pedigree*, which was an enormous financial success. What happened was that Claude Gallimard, Gaston's son, visiting Simenon,

138

saw the manuscript of *Je me souviens* lying around and, with the author's permission, took a copy to show to André Gide, then living with his characteristic elegance on the Riviera. Gide had expressed an interest in what Simenon was currently working on, but when he read the stark narrative of the autobiographical text, he was horrified. He wrote an urgent note to Simenon counselling him in the strongest terms to stop what he was doing at once and start again on the same material – only this time as a novel, written in the third person and with ostensibly fictitious characters.

Simenon, although he may have found the "Master's" own literary works virtually unreadable, venerated his judgment and promptly did his bidding; the printed text of *Je me souviens* ends almost in mid-sentence. There was, however, another reason for such swift action. The larger-than-life characters of his early childhood in Liège haunted his imagination, blocking the full fruition of his talent. He had to exorcise them and leave space free in his sub-conscious. Freed from the restraints of an authentic biography, that is exactly what he could now do. As he later told André Parinaud in a series of radio interviews: "When I wrote *Pedigree*, I had a second reason for doing so . . . When it was finished, I said to myself: 'I've finally finished with all those people. Now that I have put them into a book in the flesh, they no longer encumber me and I am going to be able to write about new and different characters'."

The result of all this was a lengthy tome of some five hundred pages. Ironically, Gide himself did not like the vastly enlarged new work. In a letter to Simenon in September 1946, he says somewhat waspishly: "I have found in its pages hardly any of the extraordinary, irreplaceable qualities to which I attach so much of value in so great a number of your writings." Simenon, incidentally, would seem to agree with this view: "If I had to choose one of my books to live and not the others, I would never choose *Pedigree*," he told an American interviewer some years later.

Even so, it took Simenon longer to write than any of his other novels (nearly two years). It aroused great controversy when finally it appeared in the original French version in 1948 and landed him in several lawsuits brought by angry relatives and friends from Liège, who claimed to see themselves unflatteringly described in the text. "*Pedigree* was expensive for me," says Simenon. "Although I said at the time that 'Roger Mamelin', its main character whose story it tells up to the age of sixteen, was not really me and I coined the phrase in the interviews with Parinaud that in the 'novel' – for that is what it

139

is – 'everything is true while nothing is accurate,' that did not prevent everybody claiming that they could recognise themselves in it."

A local lawyer read the book, took down the names and addresses of the people referred to in it and, according to Simenon, then went to see them saying words to the effect: "Do you want to gain your own little house? Why don't you sue Simenon?" Several accepted the invitation. Simenon refuted the allegation of defamation and retained Maître Garçon, who had been successful earlier in the *Coup de Lune* litigation, to fight the first case. But, despite all Garçon's efforts, he lost. Other cases were pending, so prudently, in the next edition, Simenon left blank all possibly incriminating passages.

Even that was not enough. By the time of the third printing in 1957, the blanks themselves were removed and, as Simenon wrote in a new preface: "Not without a certain melancholy I have renounced even irony and pruned my book of everything which could appear suspicious or offensive."

Paradoxically, the one person whom Simenon was worried about offending and for whom he delayed the original publication for five years was, in the end, not at all concerned. That was his mother. As he later admitted in *Lettre à ma mère*, he had come subsequently to realise that his description of her in the novel (in the character of Elise) was unfair and overdrawn. Yet he need not have worried about hurting her feelings; the resilient Mme. Simenon was made of sterner stuff. As he told Brendan Gill, "At first, she was much offended. But *Pedigree* has made her famous in Europe, and she has got over being offended. People come from miles around to visit her. She likes to take them through the house and show them the table at which I wrote my first novel. But it is not really the same table. That table she sold." It is almost nice to know that the old lady did not change her spots.

In fact, back in the autumn of 1942 when Simenon was still writing *Pedigree*, Henriette was able to be of great service to her son. She saved his life by helping to prove that he was not Jewish.

At that time, whether in Occupied or Unoccupied France, the pressure upon the Jewish people who had not yet been sent to extermination camps in Germany, via the infamous transportation centre at Drancy in Paris, was being made even more acute. It was not so much the doing of the Germans but of the notorious "Office of Jewish Affairs" of the Vichy Government, which exercised theoretical control over the whole of France. By July 1944, the diligent anti-Semites of Vichy had sent to the German death camps 76,000 Jews, of whom only 2,500 survived. Even such co-operative people as Sacha

Guitry (allegedly surnamed Gutmann) and Serge Lifar (whose name, if spelled backwards, it was cunningly worked out, had the Jewish sound of Rafil) had to prove to the authorities' satisfaction that they were "unpolluted" Aryan back to three generations.

And it became Simenon's turn when "a cold and sinister" commissaire from Vichy knocked on his door one day. He began in abrupt style: "Well, Monsieur Simenon, you are Jewish, aren't you?" Simenon said: "No." "Come on, Simenon. *Shalom*! It's obvious you're Jewish. Your grandfather was called Brull with an *umlaut* over the 'u'. You're considered a Jew by our Service, and I have come to tell you that, unless you can prove you are not Jewish, you will be arrested and you know what that means."

Simenon asked what proof they wanted. He recalls that he even offered to show this man "with the face of a policeman" his penis so that he could see it was not circumcised, but the offer was rejected – "not all Jews have had it done." There was only one thing that would satisfy him: certificates of baptism and of birth that went back for three generations. "But how can I produce those?" said Simenon. "They are all in Belgium. I am not allowed to go there. How on earth can I get hold of them?" "You must know somebody in Belgium. I think your mother lives in Liège," was the reply. "Yes, but she is an old woman, you know." "It's all the same to me. She must go and dig out the documents – if they exist! I shall return in one month and, if they are not here, then you will be arrested." And with that he left.

In desperation, Simenon wrote to his mother and Henriette, then in her early sixties, scurried around by train and all manner of roundabout routes to unearth the documents from half-forgotten files in country churches and local town halls. She sent them to her son, and when his visitors returned he was able to present them with a flourish: "There you are! You can see for yourself that I am not Jewish. Even if my grandfather was a Brull, with an *umlaut*, he wasn't Jewish either. I've got his photograph and you'll see that he doesn't look a bit like a Semite." "I don't believe you," said the man, with obvious disappointment. "But there is nothing I can do about it."

Simenon's reasoning on the subject of his possible Jewishness is somewhat simplistic: "When that fellow arrived I was quite frightened because I had always wondered, in fact, whether my Grandfather Brull wasn't Jewish. I had always said to myself 'perhaps' but I shouldn't have minded. On the contrary. On the whole, Jews are a lot more intelligent than others. That's why they are looked on badly in some countries, because they occupy the important positions in the sciences as well as in the arts; in television, in radio, in cinema. So it's inevitable that the non-Jews who don't succeed try to kick out the Jews. Anti-Semitism comes from that."

Maurice Einhorn, writing in a somewhat Leftist publication called *Regards*, published in Brussels in early 1982 as a self-declared antidote to "the unanimous concert of eulogies" following the appearance in the previous autumn of *Mémoires intimes* and the launching of the highly successful Simenon Exhibition in Paris, states roundly: "In his works before, during and after the war, Simenon displays a profound anti-Semitism." To help support his claim, he cites passages from three of Simenon's books in which the author allegedly describes certain Jewish racial characteristics. The charge is groundless. As Harry Torczyner, born a Belgian Jew and now a leading international lawyer based in New York, and a friend of Simenon's since they did their military service together, declares: "The allegations in Einhorn's article contradict all I know of the personal views of George Simenon as expressed to me over the years."

Simenon may have many failings as a human being, but he is not a racist. The truth is that he has always been impressed by, and felt a particular sympathy for, the alien in society – whatever racial or religious characteristics set that person apart as a stranger. One has only to compare two of his less well-known novels to see, in interestingly contrasted fashion, that this is so.

In *Chez Krull* (written at Nieul in the autumn of 1938 and published in English under the same name some years after the war) the alien is a German; old Cornelius Krull, living with his family in a grocery store-cum-bar, on the lines of Simenon's Aunt Marie's establishment on the Quai de Coronmeuse at Liège. But the setting for the story is a small town bordering a canal in Northern France. The locals ostracise the German family because they are foreigners, and it is only the itinerant waterfaring folk on the canal who provide the Krulls' clientele and give them the wherewithal to eke out an existence.

Then the local slut is murdered, and everyone in the small town decides that the murderer must be a member of the Krull family. Passion rises feverishly, but it is suddenly discovered that the accusation is false. The Krulls look for the aged head of the family to tell him that all is now well, and find that he has hanged himself. "He had hanged himself," writes Simenon, "they didn't quite know why. But did they know why he, the wanderer, had settled here on the outskirts of the town, why, for years on end, he lived his life silently in this workshop, with his hunch-backed assistant?"

In *Le petit homme d'Arkangelsk* ("The Little Man from Archangel"), written at Cannes eighteen years later, the alien is a Jew, a little man born in Russia who has lived in a small provincial town in the heart of France near Bourges ever since he was a small child, brought there by his parents fleeing from the Russian Revolution. He is a modest bookseller with a secret passion for stamp collecting, who has learned to live happily within the cocoon of his own routine.

An Italian family living in the town foist their daughter on him, first to clean his house and then to occupy his bed as his wife. She is a tramp and has slept with everybody; but the little man, already in early middle age when he marries her, accepts this. When she runs off on occasion for a brief affair, he is always happy to take her back without a word of reproof, protecting her with what one might call – ironically – Christian charity.

The drama surfaces when she disappears one day with his stamp collection, by then extremely valuable. Out of pity for her, he delays telling the police about the theft and it is assumed by the whole town that he has killed her in jealousy – as a "real man" would – and has hidden her body. Feeling mounts against the Jew; not one of the people among whom he has lived so happily believes him. He is, after all, an alien. He is about to be arrested when a chambermaid from a Bourges hotel gives evidence that clears him completely. At home, free now to resume his life, he considers what has happened and, like the old German in *Chez Krull*, kills himself.

The man who could write these two novels cannot possibly be an anti-Semite or an anti-anyone in purely racist terms. To call Simenon anti-Semitic is like calling Shakespeare an anti-Semite because he created the character of Shylock – without taking into account that in the famous "I am a Jew" speech, in which he rounds upon his vilifiers, he puts into Shylock's mouth the greatest defence of a persecuted minority that has ever been penned by man. "If you prick us, do we not bleed? . . . if you wrong us, shall we not revenge?"

The encounter with the unsmiling *commissaire* from the Jewish Affairs Office soured Simenon's last days at Fontenay. But he had in any event decided to move on. The charm of the Château de Terre-Neuve had withered. He wanted his own house, not just part of someone else's, however splendid.

He wanted his own garden, like the one he and Annette de Bretagne (then living with her father in La Roche-sur-Yon, the nearest large town) had built almost with their own hands in the grounds of the old priory at Nieul. Perhaps above all, he wanted to get away from the sight of even the occasional German officer or soldier in the streets of Fontenay.

At first, he planned with the connivance of a local French-born friend to quit the Vendée altogether and drive with his family into Marshal Petain's Free Zone. All was arranged; as a foreigner, he could not get a pass to go into Vichy France, so he had fixed the numberplate of his friend's car over that of a truck he had rented expressly for the purpose. Its previous use had been to carry the dead from one city to the other, and Simenon had to disinfect it thoroughly before installing all their luggage.

He was sitting in the macabre truck-hearse at six o'clock one morning, ready to go and waiting for Régine and the others to come down, when the vehicle's radio crackled forth the news that the Germans had entered the Free Zone that very night. The date was November 11, 1942. Hitler had chosen the anniversary of the most triumphant moment in modern French history – the signing of the Armistice that ended the First World War with the defeat of Kaiser Wilhelm II's Germany – to push French faces even more into the mire and bring the whole of France under the jackboot of his armies.

Sadly, Simenon unpacked their luggage, handed back the car numberplate to his friend and returned the truck to the garage from where he had rented it. There was no point now in going to the one-time Free Zone. They would have to travel elsewhere to avoid the German presence.

In the event, they moved less than fifty miles away; to a small village, still in the Vendée, called St. Mesmin-le-Vieux. It was another rented home, the unoccupied property of a wealthy local friend who lived in Fontenay, but at least they had the run of the whole house, and there was not a German soldier within miles. The area was too remote, half lost amid the hills.

You could almost believe that life there would really be as it appeared in the novels that Simenon continued to write, with the war non-existent and no sinister officials arriving to arrest you because you were suspected of being Jewish.

CHAPTER 13

Occupation and Liberation

St. Mesmin-le Vieux is the same today as it was in the war years; no more than a small cluster of houses and a few shops grouped around crossroads on a minor D road amid the hilly terrain of the Northern Vendée. The house occupied by the Simenons is a big three-storey residence without much character: built in the late thirties in the style of a mock-Norman château with a gabled roof, large eaves, and with a separate barn-like building standing in its ample grounds.

André Caillaut, a farmer's son who still lives in the village, remembers the Simenon family staying there. For him, "It was almost a castle, not an ordinary villa. It stood out as being very different from the other houses." He remembers Marc as a little boy, going about the place in his small pony and trap, but "he had his own private tutor. He did not come to State school with us." He recalls one September picking a lot of wild mushrooms in the surrounding fields with his brother and, as they were walking home, meeting Simenon who offered to buy them. "He paid us with a ten franc note, which we were excessively pleased to bring home."

M. Constant Vaillant, a retired schoolmaster and an authoritative local historian, says that the neighbours can remember days on end when the shutters of Simenon's study were firmly closed, which meant that another book was being brought into existence. "He is remembered in the area as a man of charity," he says. For instance, he bought a cow and put it out to a local smallholder to rear for him with the sole aim of providing butter for the Simenon family; he paid for the butter and when at the end of war he left the village, he gave the cow to the smallholder. Every month he gave a sum of money to a young man whose father was a prisoner-of-war in Germany and whose mother did not have enough to feed and clothe them properly. When "jumble sales" were held to raise funds for parcels to be sent to prisoners-of-war, he freely gave all his manuscripts for auction

145

(Simenon himself confirms this: "That is why I have no original manuscripts of anything I wrote before 1945.") One gets the impression almost of an unofficial "squire of the manor", in the traditional English style; their principal friends were two local doctors and what M. Vaillant somewhat mysteriously calls "a few notables of the district."

It was a comfortable, contented kind of life; solid and peaceful. They even had with them their old ebony bookshelves, brought from the apartment on the Boulevard Richard-Wallace to the house at Nieul, where Régine went to fetch them in a hired lorry and was "politely received" by the German officers who were by then living there. Physically, they wanted for nothing; in the end, they had not one but three cows, which accounted for their entire dairy needs. They had pigs, chickens, geese and turkeys. They grew all their own fruit and vegetables. They had dogs, cats, horses. Simenon grew his own tobacco. The house was virtually a small farm, and he played the role of farmer. According to Annette de Bretagne, who no longer worked for Simenon but used to visit the house from her nearby home at La Roche-sur-Yon: "They led there a very simple rustic type of life. They had walks in the countryside and they worked on their little farm. It was a simple, healthy life."

In the just under two and a half years that they spent at St. Mesmin, Simenon wrote, in addition to the monumental (and time-consuming) *Pedigree*, five novels. Among them was *La Fuite de Monsieur Monde* ("Monsieur Monde Vanishes"), one of his most successful and certainly one of his most characteristic novels. "The profound sadness of your hero strikes me very much," Colette wrote to him from Paris.

Monsieur Monde has been described as Simenon's version of Everyman. He is a successful businessman who suddenly, on the morning of his forty-eighth birthday, as he is walking to his office, looks upwards and sees the buildings outlined against a pale blue sky in which a tiny white cloud is floating. From that moment on, he changes. He feels ill at ease in his office, with its usual routine, and realises that he must leave. "There was no inner debate . . . there was no decision to make, no decision at all." He shaves off his trim moustache, exchanges his finely tailored clothes for an ordinary, ill-fitting suit of the type worn by the man in the street. Then, almost automatically, he boards a bus for the Gare de Lyon. "He had not decided that he would do one thing or another. Once more he was following a programme that had been drawn up in advance, but not drawn up by him." Just as automatically, he takes a train to Marseilles. When he arrives at the seashore, he begins to cry:

> What streamed out from his being through his two eyes was all the fatigue accumulated for forty-eight years, and if those tears were sweet, it was because now the ordeal was over.
> He had given up. He no longer struggled. He had hastened from far off – the train did not exist, but only an immense movement of flight – he had rushed toward the sea which, vast and blue, more alive than any human being, soul of the earth, soul of the world, breathed peacefully near him . . . He spoke without opening his mouth because it was not necessary. He spoke of his infinite weariness which came not from his journey in the train but from his long journey as a man.

Thereafter, he takes on a new identity and leads an entirely new life until finally he realises that the time has come to return to Paris and renew his former existence. He does this and to those about him, even to his wife, it seems that he has not changed. But he knows that he has, and not even his closest business associate dares to ask him about where he has been or what he has done, "probably because like everyone else he was deeply impressed by this man who had laid all ghosts, who had lost all shadows, and who stared you in the eyes with cold serenity."

There was, indeed, a new serenity, mingled with joy, in Simenon himself when he wrote *La Fuite de Monsieur Monde*. He put a part of himself into the central character, for he too had just found his own personal deliverance. The book was written at St. Mesmin in March 1944; almost alone among his many works, it carries a dedication:

> *To Professors Lian and Giroire,*
> *To Doctor Eriau, in memory of February 1944*

These were the three doctors who in that month at last managed to convince him that the radiologist at Fontenay had made an apalling mistake. He was *not* facing the horror of an early death. He had lived those past three and a half years under the perpetual cloud of his own imminent demise; no women, no sex, nothing except the life of a literary gentleman farmer in his quiet country retreat. For all that he may enthuse about its wonders in *Mémoires intimes*, at the time he found it stifling. "I think, like you," he wrote to Gide later that year, "that my illness will have been salutary – and not only my illness but the long turning in upon myself of this war. You have not lived very much, you say. Me, I've not lived at all! For the most part of the time my hunger for life has been completely calmed. I have worked in my

147

little corner. I have written several novels, before and after *Pedigree*, which have not yet appeared and which I am keeping for after the War. Each time, I was thinking that at last I had freed myself of a great weight of obligation to the past (the phrase seems to me ill used, but I can find no other) that hung heavily upon my shoulders. And each time I realised that there remained still just a little bit of sludge that persisted.

"But, in March of this year, after having written *La Fuite de Monsieur Monde*, which is due to be published in three weeks, I had absolutely the impression, and I have it now, that I can write the word 'End', that a period of my life has finished and that another one has begun. What it will be, what it will give, I am still incapable of saying."

He had always had the somewhat romantic notion that, in literary terms, "life begins at forty". In an earlier letter to Gide, written in 1939, he had claimed that he had always known, ever since he was eighteen, "that the work of a novelist does not start until he is forty. I say a novelist and not a poet." But this new-found feeling of burgeoning fulfilment was something deeper than mere fancy. It had its basis in two solid physical facts: one was that he now knew that he was not going to die soon; the other was that at last he realised that his marriage to Régine could not endure. Both events flowed inexorably from the apparent miracle of the doctors' intervention in February 1944.

The story of his "cure", as told by Régine, is not without its funny side: "You know, I kept on trying to persuade Simenon that the radiologist in Fontenay had made a mistake, but he just would not have it. He would not believe me. Then at St. Mesmin-le-Vieux he started having aerophagia out of nerves, and aerophagia has much the same symptoms as angina – so he became even more convinced. He kept saying that his father had constantly been told that he had nothing serious but he died of angina!

"Our good friend Dr. Eriau at St. Mesmin never believed in Simenon's 'angina' and also kept trying to reassure him but with absolutely no success. If Simenon caught a cold or had a bad day, he thought he was dying. In the end, the only way that he was finally persuaded to go to Paris to get an expert second opinion – because you *could* go to Paris, if you wanted to, though there were fewer trains – was because another doctor, another friend, this time from Nantes, whose wife was staying at St. Mesmin at that time, did think he had angina and terrified him into going. He managed to persuade him to go and see Professor Lian, the greatest cardiologist in the country, who might at least be able to help him in some way. In fact, of course, what had happened was that those three years or so of living in a constant state of anxiety about his health had built up this nervous condition of aerophagia, whose symptoms were almost as bad as angina.

"This was proved as soon as they arrived in Paris, before they even had time to visit the cardiologist. For the doctor from Nantes, who went with Simenon, told me that when they started out Simenon behaved just like an invalid. He had to be pushed on to the train, he was dragging his feet so much. But when they arrived in Paris and got to their hotel they met by the purest chance Jean Cocteau and Marcel Pagnol, whom Simenon had not seen for years; and then the doctor could not control Simenon any more. He was at once like a new man. He and the other two galloped so fast all over the place – in and out of the night clubs – that the good doctor from Nantes could not keep up with them!

"In short, Simenon was already cured. That was the influence that the war had on Simenon in the years in the Vendée; he found himself oppressed and stifled, having to live in a small house and be a sort of amateur farmer."

In the morning Professor Lian, having checked some new X-ray plates taken by his colleague, Professor Giroire, revealed his diagnosis to Simenon: "You have a heart to live as long as you want. There is nothing wrong with you at all . . . I expect you've got a pipe with you still?" he asked. "Yes," said Simenon, "but I don't smoke it any more because of what the radiologist said." "But I'm sure you still carry some tobacco?" "Well, yes," conceded Simenon. "Well, light up your pipe then!" said Lian. "It'll do you good." He asked if Simenon had any friends waiting for him. "Yes," said Simenon, "Pagnol and Cocteau. They are waiting for me back at the Hotel Bristol and they are very worried about me." "Alright," said Lian. "You're going to invite them out to dinner tonight. You'll certainly find a black market restaurant where you can dine well. You'll have a superb meal, with lots of bottles of wine, and that is the only prescription I can give you."

Simenon returned to St. Mesmin literally a revitalized man. He was once again, in Boule's marvellous phrase, "like a mountain!" And it was through Boule that after nearly twenty years of illicit love-making, Simenon's marriage now turned irrevocably sour. For Simenon plunged back into sexual activity, after his long enforced abstinence, like a dolphin into the bounding waters of the sea. Perhaps in his newly restored vigour he was not quite so careful about concealing his daily assignations with Boule as he had been before. In any event, soon after

149

his return from Paris, Régine opened the door of his room where he was supposed to be having his siesta and found them together in the act of sex. Her horror and rage were instant: "Either you turn that girl out of this house at once or I shall go!" Quietly, in the garden a little while later, Simenon walked up and down with his wife and they talked. He said that Boule was not to be described as "that girl" (even today, nearly forty years later, he bridles at that description) and there was no question of his asking her to leave. "But neither can you leave," he told Régine. "Nor can I. Our son needs us both."

They made a solemn bargain, talking there quietly in their garden: they would stay together, for the sake of their child, "as husband and wife but really only as a pair of friends." Each rendered unto the other complete sexual freedom to do as they liked but, to the outside world, they would remain as married as before. They strolled up and down until night fell. All rancour was past. There was only tenderness. "I don't think I have ever so much appreciated the solid and faithful companion she had been to me for so long," Simenon says in his memoirs.

But for how long can a marriage totally without sex endure? Each was now going to live their own life, but what sort of life would that be?

The war in Europe was now entering its last stages. On June 6, 1944, the Allied Forces landed on the beaches of Normandy. There was fierce fighting in the northwest of France as they pressed on for Paris. In the southwest, there was no Allied invasion but Free French parachutists from Britain, dressed in the uniform of RAF airmen (so that, if captured, they would be imprisoned as prisoners–of–war and not shot as spies, which would happen if they were wearing civilian clothes) began to drop from the skies, to link up with local Resistance forces and help cause havoc to the German occupying armies in the less fortified areas of the hinterland. Simenon's own kind of "phoney war", preoccupied as he had been with his "illness" and his other introspections, was about to come to an end.

One night in July 1944 his house was ringed by alert men, dropped from the skies in British uniforms and with machine guns in their hands. They had heard from their local contacts that he had a car hidden beneath the straw in his stables: could they use it? "With the greatest of pleasure," he said. They uncovered his yellow Citroen,

of a successful writer: G.S. in the 1930s

Jean Cocteau (*left*) with Simenon's lawyer, Maurice Garçon,
1959

André Gide

le Terre-Neuve at Fontenay-le-Comte; the Simenon
d an apartment there during the War

G.S. with Marc at the Château de Terre-Neuve, 1942

Annette de Bretagne in 1939

illage of Cerizay, set fire to by the Germans in August 1945

Members of the FFI (French resistance fighters),
some of whom came to arrest Simenon in 1945

l drawing of G.S. by Régine Renchon,
Mme Simenon

Régine at Lakeville, Spring 1953

nenon home at Lakeville, Connecticut

G.S. and two-year-old John, March 1952

At the Venice Film Festival with Denise, August 1958

almost unused since he had bought it three months before the outbreak of war, and sped around the countryside on wide-ranging raids on Germans in the area. "They changed the colour every week," recalls Simenon. "When they had pulled off an important coup, they quickly changed the colour of the car. It finished up black, but it had been red, green, all the colours!" Marc Simenon, then only a small child, also remembers the parachutists: "I remember we had a yellow Citroen car – I remember the colour because it was unusual – that one day disappeared because it was given to the parachutists. I remember them coming to the house with their machine guns. You don't forget things like that, even if you're only five years old at the time."

Simenon says: "As I knew the countryside very well, they came to see me almost every evening. I had a large map of the Vendée and I would say, 'If you cut that railway line there, or block that little road at the vital spot, you can prevent the Germans moving their equipment through for quite a time.' And all this, with one of them on guard outside with his machine gun at the ready. It was really quite amusing."

The raids were highly successful. The parachutists made two openings in the back of the Citroen through which they could fire their machine guns. One of their number, a young baby-faced man in his early twenties who wore a priest's soutane over his uniform, was given the job of laying their small homemade plastic bombs; no one suspected the angelic-looking *curé* with the innocent eyes. Working mainly at night, they raided German camps and blew up stretches of railway line linking the German Army's sources of supply to the much vaunted "Atlantic Wall" along the coast.

They were not alone. Similar skirmishes were taking place through-out the area. The Germans remained at La Rochelle during the entire period (they were there until Unconditional Surrender was signed at Luneberg Heath in May 1945), but by mid–August 1944 their strength in the inland country areas of that corner of France was maggot-ridden like an apple, still bright-coloured on the surface but almost hollow on the inside.

On August 25, 1945, the day that Paris was liberated, Dr. Eriau came running into Simenon's house. "We must all flee, we must get away!" he cried. The Germans were falling back from the coast except for the obstinate pocket of resistance around La Rochelle. Streaming back from the area around La Roche-sur-Yon, their tanks, armoured cars and lorries were coming down the road along which stood the houses of both the Simenon and Eriau families. The Germans were burning and pillaging as they went, forcing the inhabitants out of their homes and then setting fire to the houses on either side of the roadway. In the neighbouring village of Cerizay, angered by the parachutists' successful ambush and the slaughter of a colonel and some of his men, they had taken fifteen hostages and set fire to the whole village in a holocaust in which 172 houses were razed to the ground and five hapless individuals were burned alive.

For nearly a week, Simenon, Régine, Boule and Marc – together with Dr. Eriau and his family – lived in the fields, sleeping on straw and obtaining only inadequate temporary shelter in leaking barns and the out-buildings of distant farms. The weather was atrocious and rain bucketed down from the skies in unseasonal fury. By the time that, weak and exhausted, the two families – together with many other inhabitants who had also fled to the fields – returned to their homes, they found the Germans mercifully gone. But Simenon was seriously ill. He had contracted pleurisy while living rough and for the next two months his life was in more danger than ever it had been in the long years of his so-called "illness".

Eventually recovered, thanks in no small measure to the dedicated care of his medical friend Eriau and the nursing of both Régine and Boule, he lived out the last few months of the European War in peace and quiet – except for one strange incident, the truth about which is not recorded in any of his writings.

In *Mémoires intimes* he tells the story of how, in the last stages of the German retreat, at about four o'clock one afternoon, Boule goes to the door of the house at St. Mesmin and a German officer is standing there, accompanied by the notorious *Mademoiselle Docteur*, a leading French collaborationist in the region. They ask where Simenon is. They have come to arrest him. Boule, thinking fast, says that he is not at home. He will be back in an hour or two for dinner. They always dine at six o'clock. "Alright. We will come back then," they say.

At once Boule runs out into the garden at the back of the house, where Simenon has all the time been working on some vegetable beds, to warn him. "I immediately telephoned a good friend of mine," he recalls, "who sold motor bikes and ran a café at the same time in the village. I knew he had a big motor bike and I asked him to come and fetch me quickly, in half an hour. I put some clothes, some tins of meat and things like that into a large bag, and asked him to advise me where he thought I should go and hide. He told me of a remote farm some seven kilometres away, which it would be almost impossible to find, and I went there and spent two whole days hiding in the straw, with the help of the farmer. Then I came back to my house and Boule told me everything was alright. The German officer had come back but she had simply told him I had not returned. I must have got wind of their arrival."

It is an interesting story and shows Simenon in an attractive light. At that time the retreating Germans *were* taking certain leading citizens with them as hostages, to barter with should they fall into Allied hands. The only untoward fact is that both Régine and Boule say that it was not the Germans who came to the door to arrest him – but the French! "It was the F.F.I., the *Forces Françaises de l'Interieur*," says Boule. "They were those people who in the last days of the war and afterwards used to shave the hair of all the women who had in one way or another helped the Germans. They would put these women with shaven heads in a cart and walk them all around the town. For example, poor old women who had washed the clothes of the Germans to earn a few coins – no more than that."

But she is loyal to Simenon: "Mind you, the F.F.I. may have only come to get information, I don't know. Maybe it was a matter of jealousy because Simenon had not fought in the war."

Says Régine: "The F.F.I. was a grouping of young men who wanted to make themselves important, I think. It was a sort of revolutionary movement that did not last long. I certainly do not know why they wanted to arrest Simenon."

Forces Françaises de l'Interieur was the name given in February 1944 by de Gaulle's Committee of National Liberation to all French units fighting on French territory against the German Occupation. In the following month, General Koenig, one of de Gaulle's top aides, was appointed their leader and entrusted with the co-ordination of their activities with the Allied Headquarters in London. It seems a thoroughly praiseworthy, if not heroic, operation but French people living in France at the time recall the F.F.I. with somewhat mixed feelings. "Of course, there were some very brave men among them," says Annette de Bretagne, "but there were also a lot of political extremists taking advantage of the situation for their own purposes and some straight-forward villians."

Says M. Pierre Chaigneau, Simenon's former card-playing companion at Fontenay: "When the Germans left, lots of people who had done nothing during the war, suddenly found themselves in the Resistance. Simenon, to my own personal knowledge during his time in Fontenay, had often been in touch with the German authorities. I know it was only to give a hand to some Belgians or French because he could speak German, but the F.F.I. didn't view these contacts with a benevolent eye. Many people during the war had to be in daily touch with the Germans, not because they liked them but on account of the circumstances. And many of them had their problems at the end of the war. Around Limoges, for instance, it was horrible. They shot a number of people who had had nothing to do with the Germans. And there were petty personal revenges, ransoms, murders, etc. That was all the work of the F.F.I. as well as their genuinely heroic deeds."

One accepts that this may be so. The F.F.I. – or men usurping that title – could well have wanted to arrest Simenon for their own ends; perhaps to hold him to ransom or exploit his presence in their midst in some other way. Nevertheless it is strange how he remembers the incident with the foreign invader cast as the villain of the piece and not his own adopted countrymen, fighting at least officially in the cause of their country.

Undoubtedly, an important question arises: Is the way in which Simenon treats the incident deliberate deception on his part, for whatever reason, or is it a perfect example of Dr. Pierre Rentchnick, the Swiss psychiatrist's, reading of him as a "fantasist"? It is a question to which Simenon himself may not know the answer.

CHAPTER 14

A New Life in the New World

Simenon came out of the war with a burning ambition to go and live in the United States. His often stated reason for doing so – a desire that his son should be educated and brought up there that he claims to have nurtured ever since a visit to New York during his world tour in the mid-thirties – does not have the ring of complete truth.

It is certainly ironic that the man who apparently gave no thought to escaping with his family across the Atlantic as the German Army marched into France, could not get there fast enough once the Occupation was over and the war at an end.

Could there be other reasons for this new "flight of Monsieur Monde"? France in the immediate post-war period was not an entirely happy country to live in, especially if one had somewhat questionable wartime activities to answer for. And there was no guarantee of its political stability. For all General de Gaulle's emotional appeal, no one could be sure that the Communists would not take over. As Simenon told a reporter in New York, through an interpreter, shortly after he had landed: "If 100 ships were to arrive in France laden with food, Communism would go down by half. But if this is to be a third winter without coal, anything can happen."

He could be forgiven for wanting to be out of all that.

Régine, as ever, is more honest: "I don't think the desire for Marc to be brought up in the United States, though genuine, was the entire truth," she says, "because we didn't go to America only for Marc's sake. There were other reasons, and I think that Simenon was influenced by the fact that France was threatened with Communism at that time. But I never thought we would stay there for ever. Neither did it occur to me that when we both returned permanently to live in Europe, I would be Simenon's *ex*-wife. It was just something that he wanted to do for the next few years or so." The house at Neuil was not sold. Their long-term home was still hopefully to be in France.

Yet in May 1945, almost as soon as Admiral Doenitz, the new

temporary Fuhrer, had signed the German capitulation papers at Luneberg Heath, Simenon and his family left St. Mesmin and returned to Paris. They were lucky enough to find their old apartment on the second floor at 21, Place des Vosges, available furnished on a short-term let. Simenon set about the arduous task of getting their papers in order, and obtaining the necessary visas, for their trans–Atlantic sailing.

It took some time and, while waiting, he knocked out two quick Maigret books: *Maigret se fâche* ("Maigret in Retirement") and *La Pipe de Maigret* ("Maigret's Pipe"), later to be published together in France under the title, *La Pipe de Maigret*. He had clearly lost none of his ability, for the combined book was to sell in the French language alone more than half a million copies. Nor was his dedication to the Paris of his memories undimmed. A chapter in *Maigret se fâche* begins:

> Paris was magnificently vast and empty. The cafés around the *gare de Lyon* gave off an aroma of beer and croissants dunked in coffee. In a barber shop on the Boulevard de la Bastille, there was a happy lightness in the air without any real reason but perhaps because this was Paris in the month of August, because it was in the morning and perhaps also because Maigret would soon enter to shake the hands of his comrades.
> – "One sees that you've just come back from holiday. You've certainly caught the sun!"
> ... [Later], his face freshly shaven, the back of his neck trimmed of hair, a slight trace of powder behind the ear, Maigret mounted the platform of a bus and, a few minutes later, he pushed open the door of Police Headquarters. Here too there was an atmosphere of the holiday season, with the deserted corridors where all the windows had been left open.

In the summer of 1946, with the war in the Far East not yet ended, an unchanged Maigret goes about his investigations in a Paris that is eternally peaceful but shows itself already preserved in the formalde-hyde of Simenon's imagination. "Maigret is essentially a nineteen-thirties figure," Maurice Richardson has observed. "He belongs to Paris before the war, and so do all the Maigret stories that Simenon has written since." "Many, if not most, of the places that Simenon loves to describe, especially in the books from the forties, will be gone in the not too distant future," an American critic, Lis Harris, has written in *The New Yorker*, "no cultural anthropologist could have better preserved such scenes for posterity." In fact, Simenon knew exactly what he was doing. Even as he wrote those two Maigret books, vacuum-wrapped in their own time capsule, he realised that the Paris of Maigret, the Paris of his own past life, was dead. "When I went back to

Paris after the war," he says, "I found a Paris that had been defeated but that claimed – or so, at least, de Gaulle would have us believe – that it had won the war. It was sad, and I hated it. My Paris no longer exists!"

On October 5, 1945, Simenon, Régine and Marc steamed into New York on a small Swedish cargo vessel that they had picked up at Southampton, after several patient weeks of waiting in London at Simenon's favourite hotel there, the Savoy. Boule, left behind with the concierge at 21, Place des Vosges, and with a weekly allowance from Simenon, was to follow as soon as her documents came through. It was originally envisaged that Annette de Bretagne would also go with them as, once again, Simenon's secretary, but it was not possible: "She could not speak three words together of English," explains Simenon, "and I had to have a completely bilingual secretary in my new life."

"I want to be a two-Continent writer," he told a newspaperman when leaving the offices of Harcourt, Brace & Co (now Harcourt Brace Jovanovich), his American publishers. "There is no longer a truly French or American writer. The tendency of writers now is toward internationalism. The war has brought us all very close. Writers no longer depend upon style, but upon the transference of their ideas. And a French idea is comparable to an American idea."

He appears to have made no reference to his desire to give his young son, described by the reporter as "a precisely polite blond child of six", an American upbringing. One would have thought that so astute a self-publicist as Simenon would have realised the public relations value of such a pronouncement, if such a thought was in his mind at the time.

To another reporter – this time in Montreal, where soon afterwards he took his wife and child to find their feet for a while, in the more familiar French-speaking ambience of that Canadian city – he said that he needed, as his first priorities, "a car and a secretary." It was his search for a secretary that, within a month of his arrival in the New World, was to change irrevocably his life and that of all those around him.

In, as Americans say, the fall of 1945, Denise Ouimet (a later conceit is to write her first name as "Denyse") was an attractive, svelte French-Canadian woman of twenty-five. The daughter of a French-speaking Government official in Ottawa, she had for the past two years been working for the British information services in Philadelphia as part of the war effort.

Even today, in her early sixties, after a life of many vicissitudes and, in the last two decades, years of mental illness, a successful battle with cancer and the aftermath of an appalling car accident, she still gives off an aura of smouldering sexuality. In her mid-twenties, she must have been stunning. According to Simenon, she claimed to have had twenty-five previous lovers. "In many ways, I was ahead of my time," she says. "I had decided to live my life according to my own ideas. I didn't want to get married – I hated marriage. I'm not at all 'Women's Lib' but my friends had one goal, 'get married', and to me that was not the only way to fulfil one. It was up to me, if I had a child, whether to keep it or not – but I never had to make the choice. I was lucky because I was taking no contraceptive measures.

"I was the black sheep of my family and very proud of it."

Today, still in law Simenon's second wife, although they have not lived together for nearly twenty years, she is undoubtedly "the black sheep" of her present family. Of her three children by Simenon, their daughter, Marie-Jo, has killed herself (according to Simenon and his eldest son, Marc) because of Denise's alleged lies to the girl about her father, and her two sons, John and Pierre, do not see her and do not appear to want to see her. Says John, in words that seem cruel on the printed page but are spoken with quiet sincerity: "My mother is a natural entity that I neither hate nor love – she doesn't exist. If I were to discover all the lies and become clearly aware of everything that has happened – things that she has done to my father – I would start hating her. My 'little brother', Pierre, [he is in his early twenties] doesn't really care and doesn't want to know either."

As for Simenon himself, there is a bitterness between these two human beings that is almost searing to encounter. Although in recent years he has written about her copiously, he cannot bring himself to mention her name in conversation and either calls her *La locataire* ("the lodger"), because he regards her as someone to whom he pays monthly rent by way of allowance, or simply "my second wife"; in print, he merely refers to her as "D". Someone who boasts that, like Maigret, he never judges has judged her and found her beyond redemption – which is the measure of his hurt, his contempt, and perhaps also his unacknowledged subconscious feeling of shared guilt.

In 1978, Denise published a biography with the title, *Un oiseau pour le chat*, which means "A Bird for the Cat" – because, she says, Simenon played with her like a cat with its prey. She proclaimed to the world her version of the secrets of their marriage bed, seeking to expose him as a veritable monster, not with merely a healthy, if somewhat excessive, interest in sex but as an insatiable womaniser with an almost repulsive obsession with sexual matters. And that was not his only vice. He appeared in her pages as a whisky-drinking alcoholic, who screamed and ranted and wanted the whole world, and in particular her, to dance to his own tune.

Simenon promptly dismissed the book to the media as "fit only for the psychiatrists" and said he would not read it; only later in *Mémoires intimes*, published three years afterwards, to devote much time to refuting some of her charges. He hates her with a slow-burning, incandescent hatred. Yet he says: "Go and see her. You must judge for yourself."

"You say you want the facts and I will tell you the truth," Denise says. "There may be times when my truth is different from Simenon's truth, and yours may be different again." On checking what she has said against what others have said or against the occasional documentary evidence, there have been what can, to my mind, only be described as misstatements of fact that go beyond the mere frailty of human memory. Even so, some of what she says seems to be the truth, even when it contradicts Simenon himself. Her son, John, has only read the first fifty pages of her book: "I just couldn't go any further," he says. "It was not a strong emotional thing. It was pure boredom and lack of interest, but I accept that there is a lot of truth in what she says."

Denise has not been content to attack Simenon in just factual terms. In what was clearly a deliberate (but, as it turned out, unsuccessful) attempt to steal the thunder of *Mémoires intimes*, she brought out, shortly before the book's publication, her first novel, written under the name of "Odile Dissane" and called *Le Phallus d'Or* ("The Golden Phallus", although, like her biography, it has not been translated into English). Its central character, "The Old Man", sleeps with every woman in sight, hoards his money in golden phallic objects and creates such a claustrophobic atmosphere of hatred and domestic tensions that, when he dies, a devastating row breaks out over the disposal of his immense estate. Mistresses, secretaries, prostitutes, the Italian maid who takes his wife's place, his daughter who committed suicide, all swirl around in the vortex of the story. In the preface, Denise claims that any resemblance to living persons is entirely coincidental, but there can be little doubt who is the real-life model of "The Old Man".

When the novel appeared, she saw fit to tell an interviewer that

THE MYSTERY OF GEORGES SIMENON

Simenon is not the great lover of women that he professes to be. "He was a true misogynist," she said. "He was possessive and jealous. He wanted women under his thumb."

"I asked Simenon once, 'How could you choose such a person?' " says Annette de Bretagne. "And he answered me, 'Annette, it was passion and passion is a disease!' "

This then is the woman who Simenon, slightly out of breath from hurrying through the streets because he could not get a cab, found waiting for him when he arrived fifteen minutes late for lunch at the Brussels Restaurant in mid-town Manhattan on November 4, 1945. He had left Régine and Marc in Montreal and was in New York to set up his detailed working arrangements for life in the United States. A mutual friend had told him that this good-looking, bilingual French-Canadian girl could make him an ideal secretary.

The impact was instant on both sides. Although she had hardly heard of him and knew nothing of his fame in Europe, she accepted the job. That same night, naked in the thick-carpeted luxury of his room in the Hotel Drake, they became lovers. "I threw myself upon her," recounts Simenon in his memoirs with his typical attention to sexual detail, "and I had hardly penetrated her when she began to moan, trembling throughout her body. The moaning became a cry which they must surely have heard in the next room. At last came a tremendous spasm which almost turned her eyes in upon themselves so that I was afraid I could see only their whites. I have known many women but I have never seen such a complete surrender to the ecstasies of sex."

He was forty-two, Denise was twenty-five; Régine was a sexually disinterested forty-five. From that moment on, the marriage survived only under sentence of death.

Simenon was in love as he had never been before. In purely sexual terms, it would seem that he has never found such a perfect partner as Denise Ouimet. In one night alone, soon after their meeting, she claims that they made love seventeen times and, even if that is exaggeration, there can be no doubt of their absolute compatibility. In comparison, the solid, sincere and resolutely plain Régine must have seemed a woeful also-ran; but she still remained not only his wife but a good friend too. "This time I am really in love," he told her when he returned to Canada a short while later. "A young girl in New York?"

she asked. "Yes," he replied, but he did not want to tell her any more; out of superstition, in case this magnificent new affair did not last.

But it did. When he came to write his first novel on North American soil two months later, in January 1946, he produced, in *Trois chambres à Manhattan* ("Three Beds in Manhattan"), an absolutely untypical love story full of tenderness and delight, with that supreme rarity in a Simenon work: a happy ending that looked forward to an even more joyous future.

For once, Simenon incorporated into an almost contemporaneous novel a major event from his own life without the usual gestation period of several months, if not years. The book recounts how a French actor, François Combe, newly arrived in New York to try his luck in the United States, meets by chance a lonely, world-weary woman named Kay, also French, with whom, as two aliens in a distant land, he converses (as did Simenon and Denise) in his native tongue. As with Simenon and Denise, they spend their first night in an aimless, rambling nocturnal walk through the empty streets of the city before, as dawn approaches, their passion culminates in frenzied coupling in a hotel room.

Combe describes Kay as "the three o'clock in the morning type of woman, the one who cannot make up her mind to go to bed, who needs to keep up her state of excitement, to drink, to smoke, to speak, to finally fall into a man's arms when her nerves are frayed out." They part briefly, they come together again. He understands that the past of neither of them matters. "To begin a life from scratch. Two lives. Two lives from scratch." Theirs is a love that transcends physical sex:

> He felt her go limp in his arms. He was just as weak and clumsy as she was as the result of this wonderful thing that had happened to them, but he tried to lead her to the bed before she collapsed. She protested feebly: "No".
>
> The bed was not their place that night. The two of them were wedged into the big, threadbare armchair, so close that their pulses pounded in unison and each could feel the other's breath upon his cheek.
>
> "Don't say a word, François. Tomorrow . . ."
>
> Tomorrow with the dawn they would enter into their new life forever. Tomorrow they would be lonely no longer, they would never be lonely again. He felt her shiver, and at the same moment he felt a tightening in his throat like some old, forgotten affliction. At the same instant they had both looked back for the last time at their past solitude. And both wondered how they had managed to live through it.

Trois chambres à Manhattan, although one of Simenon's very few books without a corpse, proved a runaway best-seller. In 1965, it was made into a film, directed by Marcel Carné and starring Maurice Ronet and Annie Girardot as the two lovers.

There is no doubt at all that Simenon is François Combe and Denise is Kay. Both Denise and her son John have said as much. As for Simenon, he told an interviewer in the French review, *Réalités*, some years later: "You may perhaps have noticed that from the time of *Trois chambres à Manhattan* onward my female characters have become less two-dimensional, less hard and less ruthless than before . . . I have the impression that at the age of forty . . . I was suddenly seized with a wish to understand women; till then I had only wanted to make use of them, in my novels, I mean. I made use of them as companions for the male character and to round off a story, but basically I suppose that, up to that time, I had known only one kind of woman. Suddenly, I discovered that there were other kinds."

On the morning of January 4, 1946, Marc came running excitedly into Simenon's study in a chalet that he had taken for his family in the snow-covered Canadian ski resort of Ste. Marguerite on Lake Masson: "Dad, come quickly. Your new secretary is downstairs. She has just arrived!" Nearly forty years later, Marc still remembers the occasion: "I think I knew at once on that very first day that something had happened between my father and that woman. A child *feels* things. He knows by intuition. I think if you bring a woman into your house and you are in love with her, your child – even if he is only six years old, as I was – will know at once. It's because of the way you act, because of the way she acts. I knew. I knew immediately."

Unlike her son, Régine took longer to light upon the truth. At first she contrived to reassure herself that all was well. In a somewhat bizarre gesture of friendship to the beautiful new secretary, she offered to paint her – in the nude. Denise accepted, and a few days later Régine told her husband: "I know she cannot be the young woman you told me about in New York. She has an operation scar on her tummy, and you've always said you cannot stand women with scars on their body."

Alas for Régine, passion makes new rules. Even the scar did not suffice to cool Simenon's ardour. Instead, he set about remoulding Denise to his own image of her – just as he had done, in years gone by, with Régine herself and Boule. He made his new love call him "Jo" and not "Georges" because she confessed to having had a previous lover with that name. He insisted that she grow her hair long, with a chignon piled high on top of her head. She had to put on weight to make her body more comely, wipe off her make-up and no longer paint her fingernails. He wanted her to have "the natural look"; that was both his caprice and his dictate.

It was this all-too-familiar pattern unfolding before her eyes that finally spelled out to Régine that this really *was* "the young woman from New York" of whom he had spoken so rapturously. "It is my husband who asked you not to wear make-up any more and to let your hair grow?" she asked Denise one day. "I love him," was the candid reply. "That is your affair," said Régine, with a shrug of her shoulders. "I simply warn you that you won't remain for long the only one." "I am not jealous," said Denise pertly, knowing the older woman's weakest point.

Denise claims in her biography that there was a further conversation between them. By now, Simenon was sneaking out at night to spend time with her in her log cabin in the grounds of the family chalet. She felt her position was secure and says that she and Régine reached a "gentleman's agreement" (she actually uses that English expression in the French text of her book) whereby, as she quotes Régine: "The husband, he is yours. The child you love and I give him into your care. But be careful, the name and the money I keep!"

I find it impossible to accept that any such conversation took place. Régine adores her son; even in her eighties she still keeps a bed made up for him in the house at Neuil in Simenon's old study in case he should arrive. She has suffered much in her life for her child. It is beyond belief that she would have been prepared to surrender him in such cavalier fashion. When confronted with the passage in Denise's book, she denies it emphatically.

In fact, what seems to have happened is that there was no great confrontation, no great declaration on either side of what the precise position was or what the future would turn out to be. Régine was content just to let the whole thing work its way through; ever since the incident with Boule back at St. Mesmin, she had learned to curb her jealousy. She had her son, whom, however reluctantly she had conceived him, she still regarded as the centre of her world. She had her painting. She did not really like America and never mastered the language, but that did not bother her too much, for Simenon was happy to let her pay frequent visits to France – where, incidentally, she restored the house at Neuil, laid waste by years of German officers' occupation followed by French requisitioning for homeless families, to something like its former splendour. If Simenon no longer came to her bed, well – pouf! – what did that matter? That had been no great joy for her anyway.

Régine coped stoically with her new role, with the same calm strength that she has displayed throughout her long life. It is difficult not to like, and admire, her.

As for Simenon, John says shrewdly: "He was really longing to fall in love – and it happened! It was probably 100 per cent and he made it 5,000 per cent." Despite the cynicism of this comment, there can be no denying that Simenon was idyllically happy with the new situation in his life; and his work as a novelist flourished in the golden glow of his inner contentment. "It is very pleasant to discover 'Love' at your age," Gide wrote to him, "and it is reflected in the new ease and mastery of your work." In just over a year, Simenon wrote no less than eight novels – all of them for a new Parisian publishing house, *Presses de la Cité*, which, masterminded by a brilliant young man of Danish origin called Sven Neilsen, had taken over from Gallimard as his publisher. As has been stated earlier, some French critics maintain that the style and content of Simenon's works have varied with his publisher: but Gilbert Sigaux, the doyen of them all, is surely right in his view that there is no aesthetic difference between the works published by one publisher and another. Nevertheless, it was the shrewd Nielsen's idea that henceforth all the Maigret novels were to have the name "Maigret" in the title, and Simenon's first book written in the United States was, appropriately, *Maigret à New York* ("Inspector Maigret in New York's Underworld").

He wrote in many different kinds of setting: from that first Maigret, written with the snow still on the ground at Ste. Marguerite, to *Le Passager clandestin* ("The Stowaway"), which came into the world at Bradenton Beach in Florida, with the sun beating down out of a near-tropical blue sky and Simenon naked at his typewriter with handkerchiefs tied around his wrists to stop his sweat falling on to the paper.

In all, during his ten years in the United States, he wrote twenty-six Maigrets and twenty-seven other novels. Two of the Maigrets were set in America, with the Parisian policeman somewhat incongruously in the country on a sort of working holiday, and seven of the non-Maigrets also had an American locale. As Brendan Gill has observed, an English or American reader cannot help being startled when he first comes across dialogue such as this, in *Les Frères Rico* ("The Brothers Rico"), when one gangster brother telephones another: "– *Eddie?* –

Oui. – Ici, Phil." Even so, the skill with which he sketches American scenes is as deft as that displayed in his novels with a European setting. There is, for example, the parched Arizona landscape and the "luminous mist that rose from the desert of sand . . . the ever-changing colours on the mountains that seemed, far off, to close in the world on all sides" in *La Jument perdu* ("The Lost Mare", not as yet published in English). There is the swollen Santa Cruz river, the real protagonist of *Le Fond de la bouteille* ("The Bottom of the Bottle"), during the rainy season where it was "high, already higher than during the night. It formed a dark yellow mass, flowing slimy and thick, heaving in places, breathing like a beast, carrying along tree trunks, empty cans, all kinds of filth."

And there is this vivid description of the sea at sunrise off the Florida coast as Eddie Rico wakes early one morning: "The sea was calm. All he heard was one small wave, the one which, forming not far offshore in a barely perceptible undulation, rolled onto the sand, in a sparkling curl and churned up thousands of shells."

Yet the most impressive thing about Simenon's working decade in the United States is the way in which, writing over three thousand miles away, he can recreate a France, and above all a Paris, where you can almost smell the garlic and feel the warmth of the freshly baked *croissants*. It is impossible to better this kaleidoscopic setting of the scene beside the Seine in the heart of Paris, as an old quayside bookseller is about to die. It comes from *L'Enterrement de Monsieur Bouvet* ("Inquest on Bouvet") and was written in a sun-drenched house overlooking the Pacific Ocean at Carmel in Southern California in February 1950:

> The street sprinkler went past and, as its rasping rotory broom spread water over the tarmac, half the pavement looked as if it had been painted in dark colours. A big yellow dog had mounted a tiny white bitch who stood quite still.
>
> In the fashion of colonials the old gentleman wore a light jacket, almost white, and a straw hat.
>
> Everything held its position in space as if prepared for an apotheosis. In the sky the towers of Notre Dame gathered about themselves a nimbus of heat and the sparrows – minor actors almost invisible from the street – made themselves at home high up among the gargoyles. A string of barges drawn by a tug with a white and red pennant had crossed the breadth of Paris and the tug lowered its funnel, either in a salute or to pass beneath the Pont Saint-Louis.
>
> Sunlight poured down rich and luxuriant, fluid and gilded as oil, picking out highlights on the Seine, on the pavement dampened by the sprinkler, on a dormer window and on a tile roof, on the Ile Saint-Louis. A mute, overbrimming life flowed from each inanimate thing, shadows

were violet as in impressionist canvasses, taxi redder on the white bridge, buses greener.

A faint breeze set the leaves of a chestnut tree trembling, and all down the length of the quai there was a palpitation which drew voluptuously nearer and nearer to become a refreshing breath fluttering the engravings pinned to the booksellers' stalls.

People had come from far away, from the four corners of the earth, to live that one moment. Sight-seeing cars were lined up on the *parvis* of Notre Dame, and an agitated little man was talking through a megaphone.

Nearer to the old gentleman, to the fat bookseller dressed in black, an American student contemplated the universe through the view-finder of his Leica.

Paris was immense and calm, almost silent, with her sheaves of light, her expanses of shadow in just the right places, her sounds which penetrated the silence at just the right moment.

The old gentleman with the light-coloured jacket had opened a portfolio filled with coloured prints and, the better to look at them, propped up the portfolio on the stone parapet.

The American student wore a red checked shirt and was coatless.

The bookseller on her folding chair moved her lips without looking at her customer to whom she was speaking in an endless stream. That was doubtless all part of the symphony. She was knitting. Red wood slipped through her fingers.

The white bitch's spine sagged beneath the weight of the big male, whose tongue was hanging out.

And then when everything was in its place, when the perfection of that particular morning reached an almost frightening point, the old gentleman died without saying a word, without a cry, without a contortion while he was looking at his coloured prints, listening to the voice of the bookseller as it ran on and on, to the cheeping of the sparrows, the occasional horns of the taxis.

This is Canaletto in print; painting in words a picture of such complexity and detail that one feels as if Simenon is sitting in a helicopter poised high in the sky above Paris, all-seeing, all-comprehending. He has gone beyond the stage of being what British critic Raymond Mortimer once called "the poet of the sordid". This is descriptive writing of the highest calibre. Yet, as Gide wrote to him when he was in the United States: "Nothing is more difficult than making the public go back on a too hasty first impression. You are still the slave of your first successes and the reader's idleness would like to put a stop to your triumphs there. . . . You are much more important than is commonly supposed."

As Simenon thickened and matured into middle age, the words he had put years earlier into the mouth of a fictitious character, the murderer Kees Popinga in *L'Homme qui regardait passer les trains* ("The

Man who Watched the Trains Go By"), became triumphantly true of himself: "For forty years, I looked at life like the poor little boy who presses his nose against the window of a pastry shop and watches others eat the pastries. Now I know that the pastries belong to those who bother to take them."

CHAPTER 15

Happiness in New England

It would be wrong to describe the Simenon household in those last years of the forties as a *ménage à trois*, with Simenon cosily ensconced between his wife and his mistress on a day-to-day domestic basis; although people could be forgiven for thinking this was the situation because their invitation cards, on formal occasions, would read:

> *Mr. and Mrs. Georges Simenon*
> *and Miss Denise Ouimet*
> *have the honour of inviting you to . . .*

But, in fact, there was no single household under the one roof for any significant length of time. "Simenon never went from one woman's bed to another," says Denise. Indeed, he never went to Régine's bed again. It was only for a few months in Canada, after they left St. Marguerite for nearby St. Andrew's-by-the-Sea, and later briefly, at Tucson in Arizona, that all three occupied the same house together – with Simenon and Denise in the main bedroom and Régine relegated to a guest room. From September 1946 to June 1950, Simenon and Denise wandered across the face of the United States: a few months in Florida, over two years in three different homes in Arizona, nearly a year in Carmel in Southern California. During all that time, when she was in the country and not back home in France (except in Tucson in 1947), Régine, with Marc, lived in a house nearby, merely taking her meals with Simenon and Denise. When she was in France, Marc stayed with his father.

When eventually Boule arrived from France in 1948, after many problems clearing her passport and visa, she moved in with Régine and helped look after Marc. The days of her daily couplings with her *petit monsieur joli* were over.

For Simenon and Denise, life was exhilarating and (whatever he may say now) hugely enjoyable. "I had no idea who Simenon was

168

when I fell in love with him," says Denise. "I fell in love with the man not the writer, and it happened on that first day. In his whirlwind fashion, he swept me up. I've only had one love like him: together, there was everything in the sense of physical compatibility. One just wouldn't believe it!"

In her biography, she tells the story, in lurid detail, of how one evening, in a hotel suite, Simenon insisted on her sitting in a black see-through negligee with a very low neckline that he had just bought her, while a young waiter served the first two courses of their dinner. Then while the young man was out of the room, fetching her dessert, he slid the negligee completely off her shoulders so that she sat naked to the waist. He made her sit like that while the waiter served the rest of their meal; then, when he had finally departed, Simenon threw himself on her, stripped off her garment and carried her, naked in his arms, to their bed.

Some months later she claims there was an incident, during a visit to Cuba, when they were staying in a hotel which they suddenly realised was a brothel. Some of the "girls" invited them to a "private show", which ended up with Simenon tearing off his clothes and diving in among their naked bodies before calling her to join him; whereupon the two had sex together with the others caressing and mauling their pumping forms.

"I wasn't a slave," she now maintains. "I just wanted to please him in every way I could. For once in my life, all my sacred principles and convictions were swept away. I tried to do everything that he wanted me to do. I tried to be the woman that he wanted me to be." To prove her utter and unique dedication to him, she even destroyed, at his command, the letters she had always kept from her father, whom she had adored and who had died before she met Simenon.

For his part – arrogant, cruel, self-centred though he may have been in his passion – he was genuinely happier than he had ever been in his life. Years later, as he records in *Quand j'étais vieux*, he was to think of her as "a real woman" and to relive in his memory nights of ecstasy – such as in the moonlight at Tumacacori in Arizona, when, after crossing a flooded arroyo, they undressed to ford the water and there was not another human being for miles around. "That was the nearest we came to nature. We were like a pair of coyotes, and real coyotes must have been watching us."

It was all undoubtedly splendid for the two lovers, delighting in the joys of their bodies like two wild animals; but Marc remembers those years differently. "A child can feel lots of things, and I think I sensed

169

there was something wrong about the whole situation. It was all false. All the outbursts of love that Denise had for me I never really felt to be genuine. And perhaps there was some sort of jealousy on my part because my father was living through a period of real passion for her. It was a passion he was feeling for her – and not for me.

"Early on, I decided to get away from my family as much as I could, and as quickly as I could – to boarding school or whatever. As soon as I was able to, I lived my life very much out of the family."

Parents are fond of saying what a happy burden it is to have children; children can at least as often be forgiven for thinking what a burden it is to have parents.

One morning in November 1947, with Simenon sitting in the study of their rented home at Tucson in Arizona working on *Les Vacances de Maigret* ("No Vacation for Maigret"), the telephone rings and Denise answers it to be asked "Is it true that Simenon is dead?" She goes into a fury: "How dare you? Who are you?" It is a reporter calling from Paris where the word is that Simenon has died. "No, he isn't!" she screams down the line. "At this moment, he is in his study writing a novel. But you have no right to phone up like this. He could have been away and I could have answered the telephone, and I might genuinely have thought he had died. You have been wantonly irresponsible!"

"But I was still so shocked," she says, "that when I put the telephone down, I tiptoed downstairs and stood outside his door to reassure myself by the sound of his typewriter." She could not understand it. But then two days later a telegram arrived from Simenon's mother: *Christian mort* ("Christian is dead").

One will read nothing of this incident in all the books and dictated memoirs that have flowed from Simenon. In fact, he is strangely silent as to what actually did happen to his younger brother. We know, from *Lettre à ma mère*, that his mother once said to Simenon the appalling line: "What a pity, Georges, that it's Christian who had to die." But nowhere does Simenon tell us where, how or when he died.

There is a mystery here. Régine, who by the last months of 1947 had largely gone out of Simenon's life, claims not to know the exact circumstances of her brother-in-law's death: "He died during the war. He was killed by the Germans. I'm not sure if it was in Belgium. It would be better if you asked Simenon directly. He did not die of illness. He died rather young – around his forties."

170

But Simenon says: "I do not know the date of my brother's death. He was killed in combat in Vietnam, but I do not know the year." He suggested that perhaps the authorities in Liège might help.

Vietnam? "In combat" and not by the Germans during the war? Why all this uncertainty? Professor Maurice Piron of the Simenon Centre at Liège University reports that the local authorities say: "Christian Simenon, who served in the French Foreign Legion, was killed in Indo-China [Vietnam] at That Khe on October 31, 1947."

It becomes more bizarre. Why the French Foreign Legion? One wonders who is hiding what from whom – and with what motive. The simple truth is that Christian is the skeleton in the Simenon family cupboard. Undoubtedly, Georges Simenon feels some shame over the facts, but it will be seen that he himself comes out of the sad story with honour and compassion. In any event, the story is part of Simenon's own life and must be told.

In the summer of 1940, when Simenon was engaged in looking after the Belgian refugees in La Rochelle, Christian suddenly turned up by boat from the port of Matadi in the Belgian Congo. He had managed to get away with a great deal of local gold. It belonged back in Belgium and that is where Christian was heading, together with his valuable load. Simenon did not see him again until five years later. It was in the early summer of 1945. The war in Europe was over and Simenon, with Régine and Marc, had returned from St. Mesmin and was staying temporarily in his old apartment on the Place des Vosges in Paris. He got word that his brother was waiting to see him. Christian was sitting on a bench in the Place. He did not want to come up to Simenon's apartment.

Simenon hastened down to greet him – and was appalled to hear his story. He was on the run from the police! Apparently, his had not been a glorious war. He had got himself involved with the collaborationist Rexist Movement in his native country and the climax had come one dramatic night when, a little drunk (because Christian had what they call "a drink problem"), he had agreed to drive a car for some Rexists mounting a raid against Belgian Resistance fighters. He swore he had not killed anyone: when the machine guns began to spit out their message of death, all he did was vomit. Yet now he was fleeing for his life. In the angry mood of those first months after the liberation of Belgium, many men had been put against the wall and shot by the returning authorities for less than he had done. He pleaded with his illustrious brother for help.

He would not visit Simenon's home – that would be too dangerous

171

for both of them – but they met furtively a few more times in public places like bars and parks. Simenon asked his most famous contact, André Gide, for help, and Gide came up with the idea that Christian should take the classic way out for all such fugitives from the law: join the French Foreign Legion. And that is exactly what Christian Simenon did.

He became Private Christian Renault in the French Foreign Legion, stationed in North Africa; to where his brother assisted his passage. Denise remembers Simenon receiving letters from "Christian Renault" when they were living together.

He did well. He worked his way up from private to sergeant, which was not easy in the tough regime of the Legion, only to be killed in one of the first battles of the long, grim French rearguard action in Indo-China. That was a conflict which lasted until 1954, with the eventual triumph of Ho Chi Minh's Vietnamese forces at Dien-Bien-Phu and the final snuffing out of French colonial power in Southeast Asia.

Yet despite his valiant death, Christian's name remained for several years in the shadows, until finally there was an amnesty and he was rehabilitated. For a long while, Simenon felt remorseful for his brother's death: "How could I have known there would be a war in Indo-China," he kept saying, "and that the Legion would be sent to fight there?" "That's right," Denise would try and console him. "You were saving his life when you helped get him into the Legion. Do not grieve."

But that implacable person, Simenon's mother, never forgave him for Christian's death. Even when she visited him at Lakeville, Connecticut, several years later, and was an honoured guest at his house, Denise overheard her say to Georges: "If it were not for you, Christian would still be alive." "It was chilling, it was awful," she recalls. For years, Simenon would not talk about his brother or his role in his fate. It was kept a family secret. But there are far more iniquitous crimes than helping an only brother, who was not a murderer, to escape from the sometimes wild justice of those early post-war months in Europe.

In late January 1949, when they were living on a ranch called "Stud Barn" near Tumacacori in Arizona on the Mexican border, Denise became pregnant. The wonder is that it had not happened long before; since the first three months of their liaison, Simenon had taken no contraceptive precautions. The child was almost certainly conceived in Denise's hospital bed, where she was recuperating from a bad fall after her horse had thrown her while they were out riding on the Arizona back-bush. Simenon could not wait until she was allowed home by the doctors to resume their sexual relations.

"He will be beautiful, Jo," Denise told him. "Love children always are the most beautiful."

And it was a healthy, lusty baby – to be named Jean ("John") Dennis Chrétien Simenon – that was born in the early hours of September 29, 1949. Simenon was in raptures at the arrival of his second son, but it created immense problems for him. "We are in danger of being shipped back to France by the Immigration people as undesirable aliens," he told Régine. Technically the child was not illegitimate by the state law of Arizona – "but I cannot stay in Arizona for the rest of my life!" he said.

There was only one remedy. Although neither he nor Régine had talked before of divorce and, for his part, he still insisted that he did not really want one, there would have to be a dissolution of their marriage and he would have to marry the newborn child's mother. Says Simenon now: "Without Johnny*, I would never have married. I didn't want to marry my second wife at all. I didn't want to leave Tigy and my son [Marc]." It was not a particularly promising start to a new "life-long" union.

In *Mémoires intimes*, Simenon represents Régine as easily giving way to his request for a divorce: "Yes, I understand," he quotes her as saying. In reality, she fought bitterly against the idea of giving formal expression to the loss of her husband, a loss that had now endured for nearly five years. He was, and is, the only man who has shared her life. She had to be persuaded, and Simenon hit upon a neat Machiavellian way of doing so that would have done credit to one of the less attractive characters in one of his novels. "He asked me to intervene with Régine on his behalf," says Harry Torczyner, his old attorney friend from the days of their youth in Liège. "I looked like one of her childhood sweethearts from the old days and he thought that would help soften her heart." It did – plus rigorous financial conditions, including an outright gift of the house at Nieul, that left Simenon "almost penniless", to use Denise's not disinterested expression.

But he too knew how to exact his own emotional pound of flesh. The divorce agreement, negotiated on Régine's behalf by an attorney,

---

* Simenon has always called his son "Johnny", although he is "John" to most other people.

paid for by Simenon and found for her by Torczyner (who acted for Simenon), contained a clause stating that until Marc was eighteen years of age she would have to live with the boy "within six miles" of wherever Simenon himself was residing at the time. Her own preference would probably have been to return with her son to France, once the divorce had gone through. So how could she bear to stay on in a foreign country, where she never really felt at home, obliged for the next seven years to trail around after an ex-husband, whom she still loved, like a dog tied to the back of a cart on a Mexican dust-road? Her reply is characteristic: "Because there is a child who would have suffered. Marc was very upset. At least, in this way he would still be physically close to both his parents."

Yet at the time the bitterness was there. Meeting Denise in the street in Carmel, where both households were then living, Régine cut her dead and has not spoken to her since. Boule, as ever more volatile in defence of those whom she loved, told Denise outright that she despised her for what she was doing to Marc. "When I learned through the newspapers that Simenon was divorcing, I was bewildered," says Annette de Bretagne. "When a man has spent over twenty-five years with a wife, he does not divorce her even if he has an affair. Perhaps the marriage would never have ended if Régine had been more sensual – as sensual as Denise."

It took Harry Torczyner nearly two months to find grounds for divorce that would be acceptable to Régine as well as valid in American law, French law and Belgian law (for, of course, both parties were still Belgian nationals), and yet would not be too dishonourable for Simenon. Régine was to be the petitioner but, if at all possible, there was to be no question of Simenon's adultery as the basis for the decree. In the end, Torczyner lighted upon the fact that in the state of Nevada divorce was possible on the grounds of refusal of conjugal rights for at least three years. That fitted the bill admirably: Simenon and his wife had not shared the same bed for the past six years.

On June 21, 1950, having established the necessary six weeks' residence in Nevada's capital city of Reno, Régine obtained her divorce at the hands of a six-foot-ten-inch judge wearing a ten-gallon hat. She flew at once to Carmel. As she did so, Simenon and Denise flew into Reno and on the following day the same judge, still wearing his ten-gallon hat and now even more resplendent in a blue turquoise suit, pronounced them man and wife.

If only he had been able to appreciate it, Simenon's new wife had already given him an inkling of what he might be letting himself in for.

During the protracted divorce negotiations, Régine had requested the right to remain legally "Mme. Georges Simenon". "No," said Denise. "*I* shall be the only 'Mme. Georges Simenon'. At least, the only one who is the wife of the writer, Georges Simenon. She can only be 'Mme. Régine Simenon'." No doubt, Régine accepted her fate with a shrug of her shoulders and her sad smile. But should not Simenon, even at that early stage, have realised that passion, always a marvellous basis for an affair, is not necessarily the best grounding for a marriage?

As it was, he was far too involved with Denise and the extra dimension to his happiness caused by the birth of John to heed the warning.

Lakeville, Connecticut is a small country town of some 25,000 inhabitants in the heart of New England, hemmed in by trees with seven lakes in the area, one of them in the centre of the town itself. It is the last place in the world that one would expect Simenon to have lived possibly the happiest five years of his life.

Even today, none of the local inhabitants who knew the Simenon family there from July 1950 to March 1955 know why this celebrated French writer, with his strange ways, burst upon their small town or why, with equal abruptness, he left them without even a farewell party for his friends to mark the occasion.

But even Simenon's two older sons look back on their childhood in Lakeville with affection. Marc has taken his own young family there on a sentimental trip to see the places that he at one time knew so well. The memory of his "idyllic" years there is so intense for John that he does not want to return until he can go back with someone who is very special to him. "For me," he says, "it is the ideal place that I remember from my childhood. Perhaps I tend to make more of it than it really was, but that is the way I feel about it. Probably it has to do with the fact that I remember it as a time when my father and mother were getting on very well with each other; it's also the time when my mother did care about me as a child. So I was being pampered – but that didn't last very long!"

How did Simenon choose this place? His first idea, after the divorce and his marriage to Denise, was to take his new wife and their small child on a long journey to Europe; but, according to him, the Belgian Consul-General in New York talked him out of it because of the political situation there, the Korean War having sparked off a near-panic about the possible outbreak of a Third World War. "Many Frenchmen, frightened of a war, have applied for visas to come to the United States," he said. "So why don't you stay on this side of the Atlantic for a while? Now is surely not the time to visit France."

He suggested that Simenon might like to consider finding a home in Connecticut, where so many wealthy or influential New Yorkers lived and commuted into the city. "So I took my car and we drove up into Connecticut," says Simenon. "But I was disgusted by the commuter part of the south of the state, with all those cars parked at the railway stations. So we carried on northwards and then, at about lunchtime, we got to this place with a little restaurant by a small lake in the middle of the town, and I asked the name of it and they said: 'Lakeville'. I asked if there was a good local school for Marc, and they said 'Hotchkiss School' [one of the finest private boys' schools in the United States]; so within three days we had returned to the town and settled into a hotel, while I looked around for somewhere to live." It was a typical instant decision.

Within ten days, Cap Robinson, a local estate agent, had found him an ideal home: Shadow Rock Farm, an old white New England farmhouse, extended to comprise over a dozen rooms and four bathrooms. It was close to the town but remarkably secluded, set in thirty-one acres of fields, woods, cliffs and swamp. Near the house, built on a base of natural rocks, was a small swimming pool and beyond that a brook and the remains of a stone dam and millrace. There were three barns on the property. It was Simenon's wartime farmhouse at St. Mesmin writ large and transported to the American scene. Almost as soon as he saw it, Simenon said: "Yes, we'll have it!"

The owner of the house was himself no literary novice. Ralph McAllister Ingersoll had been the managing editor of *The New Yorker* in its early days and was later editor of Henry Luce's *Fortune* magazine, before becoming the publisher of a highly successful chain of local newspapers. He was a very wealthy man and loved Shadow Rock Farm, which he had modernised, but his new wife (one of four in total) did not like the place and, without too much enthusiasm, he was selling it. He still remembers Cap Robinson telephoning him and saying: "I've got a crazy Frenchman here who wants to buy your place, but he says he's got no money." "What's his name?" asked Ingersoll. "Georges Simenon," was the reply. "Jesus Christ, I'm a great fan of his!" said Ingersoll. "For Christ's sake, hold him there until I get over!"

He drove over and the three of them – Ingersoll, Simenon and

Denise – had a splendid lunch that lasted for three hours and in which a deal was struck. "He said he didn't have the money because it was all tied up in France," says Ingersoll. (Or was the real reason, as Denise claims, that Régine's divorce settlement had left Simenon "penniless"?) "But I told him not to worry about that. I was just so pleased for him to have the place. We agreed a price of 60,000 dollars and I gave him a private mortgage to pay it off over twenty years – on condition that if ever he wanted to get rid of the property, he would sell it back to me at the same price. But then what does the so-and-so do? When eventually he sells the place, he does not even tell me and gets the highest price he can!" (Simenon denies this charge of bad faith and says that he never agreed to sell it back to Ingersoll for its original purchase price. Whatever is the truth, Ingersoll has remained very bitter.)

As soon as possible, Simenon and Denise, together with baby John and now joined by Boule, moved into Shadow Rock Farm. Of course, within a short while, Régine and Marc had to follow suit; installed in a small house at Lime Rock, a nearby village. Simenon soon fitted into the local scene. "The town has a big summer colony," he later told Brendan Gill. "When I came here, the townspeople asked me one thing – 'Will you be summer or year round?' I said, 'Year round'. They said, '*C'est bon, Simenon!*' It is not for my books that they accept me. It is that I am 'year round'."

But Régine never enjoyed life in the area and made only one close friend: Maxine Mallach, a homely sort of person whose father owned the property in the grounds of which stood Régine's small house. "She was very unhappy here," says Miss Mallach, who still lives in the same house overlooking Régine's former home. "She is the most talented person I have ever met, who could do everything – except speak English! I had to speak in a sort of broken English for her to understand me.

"I think she was still in love with Simenon, and she was very bitter about Denise. She told me that she felt 'that woman' had stolen her husband from her in devious ways. She said she had seen her working to that end.

"To my mind, Simenon was so cruel to her in so many ways. She had to share her child with him. Simenon had Marc at weekends and she had him during the week, but especially towards the end of her stay here Simenon was continually encroaching upon her time with her son, tempting the boy to be with him. It was terrible to see."

When later this charge is put to Simenon, he angrily protests: "Not

177

at all! I had to do it! I had to take over in some respects from the boy's mother. She was not doing what she could have done, and what I was very happy to do." It is impossible to say if this is fair comment. Whenever children are used as pawns by parents, such disputes always take place. In this respect, Simenon is sadly a man like any other. Miss Mallach does, in fact, admit: "Simenon was exceptionally good with children. Undoubtedly, Marc had a happy time with his father as a youngster. Tigy could not provide that same kind of fun. She did her best but she just could not compete.

"She was pleased nevertheless that Simenon got on so well with Marc because it was a male influence on the boy, which she considered he needed. But I always had a feeling of sadness for her. She was a sad person."

All that Régine says is: "No, those years in Lakeville were not a happy time for me."

For his part, Simenon, whose command of the English language by then has been described as "just like Maurice Chevalier with that same lovely accent", really entered into the spirit of the town. Elise Becket, who is every Englishman's idea of a white-haired, elegant New England lady of good breeding, remembers once going to buy meat in a local market and seeing Simenon standing in line with other shoppers, with little John, then aged about three, holding his father's hand, a toy pipe clenched firmly between his teeth. Mrs. Becket, whose husband Campbell became Simenon's local lawyer and one of his closest friends in the town, says: "Every single thing that I saw about Georges – and I didn't have any feeling that he was putting on an act or being in any way unnatural – was warm, genuine, friendly. He was a devoted man, loved his children. Awfully nice with the neighbours. Talked to everybody of all different social strata in exactly the same natural way and with a twinkle in his eye."

Says "Cam" Becket, a sprightly veteran of remarkable vigour still playing squash at eighty: "Anyone coming to a place like this would have to work his passage in any event, even if he wasn't a Frenchman. But I would say that he was very popular in an abstract way. People respected his privacy. I would ask, 'Do you know Georges Simenon?' and they would say, 'Well, I have never visited him but I hear the best things about him. He's an awfully good fellow!' "

Brendan Gill gives this acount of Simenon, when a novel is finished, "slowly coming back into the life of the village. . . . His blood pressure, which has mounted steadily during the writing of the novel, returns to normal. His trips to the village are marked by jaunty cries of

'Good *morning*! Good *morning*!' He joins a friend for a glass of beer in the tavern next to the post office. They swap prophecies about the next day's weather. There is snow in the air. Well, but what can you expect at this time of year?"

The local inhabitants, even if not very many of them actually read his books, knew of his fame and, like the worthy citizens of Fontenay-le-Comte ten years earler, were quite proud of the celebrated stranger incongruously in their midst. When in the summer of 1978, twenty-three years after Simenon and his family had left the area, a German film unit arrived to shoot scenes for a television film of *La Mort de Belle* ("Belle"), a non-Maigret novel set in the town, the *Lakeville Journal* sent out a reporter to talk to Mrs. Dolores James, a local resident who had worked, as a young woman, in the Simenon household as John's nanny. It carried the story on its front page, and Mrs. James, an attractive black woman, told the newspaper's readers of Simenon's "obsession" with Josephine Baker, whom in her younger days she resembled. She "vividly" remembered him, in a tweed cloak, smoking his pipe and wearing a deerstalker hat, and looking just like Sherlock Holmes, trudging around the local lanes for hours at a time when he was "stumped" for ideas. No one seems to have minded that Simenon had chosen their delightfully quiet corner of Connecticut as the setting for a particularly unpleasant murder – exactly the same reaction as that of the inhabitants of Fontenay to the series of murders set in *their* peaceful town in *Maigret a peur*.

Yet at no time did Simenon pretend to live an "American" kind of life. "Shadow Rock Farm was the home of a Frenchman who happened to be living in Connecticut," says Elise Becket. "Georges and Denise spoke French between themselves and with the children. When Georges said he wanted 'Cam' to be his local lawyer, he made quite a ceremony about it. It was really rather sweet, but no one born around here would have thought of doing anything like that." In truth, the townsfolk found his foreign eccentricity charming; though estate agent Cap Robinson's young daughter and her friends were somewhat shocked when Simenon came down to swim at one of the nearby lakes and took off his beach wrap to reveal a minute bikini. Even young men, let alone middle-aged authors, were supposed to wear bathing trunks in New England in those days.

A local doctor friend never knew when Simenon, stuck for some medical detail for a book, would telephone him and insist on being put through at once, no matter whom he might have with him. He recalls how once he was in consultation with a highly nervous patient and

Simenon called to ask about the quickest way to kill someone through poisoning. "Well, you could do it with digitalis," the doctor said. "But two tablets wouldn't be enough. You'd have to use a bigger dose to make a good job of it." The patient turned pale, left the room and never came back.

Writing on an American typewriter with a French keyboard, Simenon produced twenty-six novels in the nearly five years that he lived in Lakeville. They are equally divided between Maigrets and non-Maigrets. In all his career, he has never been more prolific. When Brendan Gill visited him in the autumn of 1952 for *The New Yorker*, he found a man "whose predicament has never been more agreeable. It is so agreeable, indeed, that he dares not speak of it without knocking wood and lowering his voice to a propitiatory baritone whisper.

" 'Look! I am happy!' he says, rolling his eyes in wonder about the living room of his white farmhouse. 'After thirty years of travel, travel, travel, I have settled down. I am taking root!' He attempts to lift one foot from the pine floor. Impossible – it has taken root."

CHAPTER 16

But it does not last . . .

Simenon's attitude to academic acclaim is ambiguous, to say the least. He purports not to be bothered by it, one way or the other. Ralph McAllister Ingersoll says: "I tried to get American publishers to take him seriously. He has never been taken seriously in the United States as the great writer that he is. He wrote too many books for American publishers. Being so prolific ran against him violently in America."

Gilbert Sigaux says much the same thing has happened in France. "He writes far too much for any of it to be really good", seems to be the attitude of the Literary Establishment on both sides of the Atlantic. It is all very well for André Gide to tell him that he is "much more important than is commonly supposed", for Dashiell Hammett to say "there is something of the Edgar Allan Poe about him". It still remains the case that, in Brendan Gill's words, "Simenon, though popular, is not fashionable. Reviewers (at least, when writing of his works in English translation) generally ignore him or list him, willy-nilly, under 'Mystery'."

Understandably, Simenon's reaction to all this has been somewhat contemptuous. When writing about the Nobel Prize for literature in *Quand j'étais vieux*, he says: "The papers have me considered for it again. This is beginning to exasperate me. One year I'm called the favourite, another an outside chance. And this has gone on for more than six years. I've asked nothing. I don't ask for anything. Let them f . . . off and leave me in peace. The Nobel would have given me pleasure a few years ago. Now I'm not sure I would accept it."

In later life, he claimed to have made up his mind on the subject. In February 1978, on his seventy-fifth birthday, he told an interviewer, "I have already decided to refuse the Nobel Prize even if they offer it to me. I know I am regularly on their lists. I haven't a single literary prize and I don't want one. Prizes, medals and ribbons evoke for me only those pictures of the 'best cow of the year' award at country fairs." He said that two distinguished French writers had told him they wanted to ask the Belgian Government to accord him dual nationality with France so that he could be put up for the French Academy, but he had talked them out of the idea. "I would look ridiculous in a green uniform and a funny hat with a sword at my side."

Yet, for all this, Simenon did accept his selection to the Belgian Royal Academy in 1952 and travelled specially to Europe, with Denise, for the occasion. Why accept *this* honour? "Well, you don't have to wear a uniform in that particular Academy," he says in his memoirs.

Be that as it may, the trip to Europe was an immense success. When the *Ile-de-France* docked at Le Havre, not only were his three French publishers – Jean Fayard (son of Arthème), Gaston Gallimard and Sven Nielsen – waiting for him, but also thousands of fans who roared out a greeting from the quayside: "Sim-e-non! Sim-e-non! Sim-e-non!" And that set the tone of a triumphal journey which took them to Paris, Milan, Rome, Brussels and Liège.

Yet even on this splendid sort of occasion, the dark side of Simenon's sexuality could not be prevented from asserting itself. On their trans-atlantic crossing, Simenon picks up an attractive blonde passenger (whom he calls in *Mémoires intimes* "the little countess" but whom Denise, in *Un oiseau pour le chat*, for once less pretentious than her husband, down-grades in the peerage to "the little baroness"). She is bored out of her mind with a husband who hardly comes out of his cabin. So Simenon invites her back to theirs. It is interesting to see the contrasting way in which husband and wife, in their subsequent memoirs, describe what then took place:

> *Simenon*: She arrives, making a sensational entry – letting fall at once her dress to reveal her plump, pink body. I do not delay in penetrating her and she has an orgasm once, twice while, in her turn, D. takes off her clothes. At the moment when the countess senses that I am going to ejaculate, she pushes me back gently: "No! for her . . ." D. is ready. That is all.

> *Denise*: Her silk dress fell to her feet. I went into the bathroom. Almost immediately Jo called me: I came back. They were already engaged in the preliminaries. The "little baroness" smiled towards me: "Come, let us all three make love. It is extremely agreeable!" That was direct . . . I found it rather droll and at the same time I was troubled. Jo encouraged me: "Come on! Take off your bath-robe . . ." I sat down on the bed; he got up and made me lie down on the other side of him. He passed from one of us to the other. Suddenly, in a hoarse voice, the baroness exclaimed: "No, give it to her!" – and he threw himself back on to me. Jo always claimed afterwards that "the little baroness" had given there an example of generosity without equal . . . I contented myself to smile.

With a couple like that, who is the kettle to call the pot black? Simenon's account, less sanctimonious and more bluntly factual, is not quite so unpalatable as Denise's cloying version. Even so, with a husband and wife who can both perform like that, and write about it afterwards for the delectation of their readers, the only person who comes out of the affair with anything like a sort of tattered honour is the "little countess" or "little baroness", or whatever she was.

There was one other person on that garland-strewn journey to Europe who showed herself, in her own very different fashion, in no way to have changed character: Mme. Simenon, Georges' mother, now in her early seventies. The incident occurred in Liège, where her son's ex-colleagues on the *Gazette de Liège* had invited him to an informal dinner at one of the city's big beer halls. Mme. Simenon, as befitted the homecoming hero's mother, had been invited to the many functions in his honour and a large car was always sent to her small terraced house to collect her; but this time Simenon tactfully explained to her that perhaps this beer-drinking occasion for a group of journalists and ex-journalists was not exactly suitable for a respectable old lady. "Good heavens, Georges!" she said, disapproval in her voice. "Be careful what you do. You'll see, they're going to drag you into an orgy!" He was then nearly fifty years of age.

In the following year, she showed again that she had lost none of her staunchly independent characteristics with the passage of time.

Simenon had invited his mother to visit his home at Shadow Rock Farm for as long as she liked. He picked her up by car at the airport in New York and, to his amazement, she was dressed "like a beggar-woman", although he knew for a fact that a relation who owned a number of dress shops in Liège and elsewhere had provided her with an ample wardrobe. When they got to Lakeville, he asked if she had anything else to wear. "No," she said defiantly. She had deliberately left all her new clothes at home. Nor was that all. Denise, going through her mother-in-law's things, discovered that she had with her only one old corset, frayed and out of shape. Denise promptly went out and bought another. Without saying anything, she threw the old one in a garbage can.

Next morning, Denise went to the garbage can – and the corset had gone! The old lady had got up in the middle of the night, found her way along the deserted corridors of the unfamiliar house to the garbage cans, and retrieved her tattered undergarment. She never said a word. Nobody said a word. The same night Denise, not to be outdone, put the old corset back in the garbage can. And once again in the morning, it was missing. Mme. Simenon had reclaimed it.

It got to be a battle between the two women, between the two wills. On the one side, Denise–"haughty, aggressive, merciless," as Simenon calls her in *Lettre à ma mère*, where he recounts the story – and on the other the little old lady who had come all the way from Liège wearing the oldest clothes she had, as if to proclaim: "You invited me. You insisted on my coming. Well, you'll have to take me as I am, because you can't impress me with your fancy ways."

During that visit, Simenon and Denise were almost like joint conspirators in the silent conflict with his mother. The sad thing is that when, eighteen years later, the old lady died, Simenon did not tell his by-then estranged wife and she had to read about it in the newspapers.

Despite John's euphoria about Lakeville where he remembers his father and mother getting on so very well with each other, and for all Simenon's rapturising in print about the great happiness of his time there, even in those early years of his second marriage a small black cloud was beginning to form in the clear blue sky of his much vaunted contentment.

Denise ran a very different sort of home from that of the more easy going Régine, who had been content to leave all matters of detail (and the cooking) to Boule. Denise was herself a fine cook, and she organised her home rather as an admiral does his flagship. "Everything was in order, everything had its place," remembers Dorothy James of her days as John's nanny. "Mrs. Simenon was absolutely in command of the household down to the smallest thing."

As well as wife and secretary, Denise virtually became Simenon's business manager. "My wife is the equal of two agents and six lawyers," Simenon told Brendan Gill. "She manages everything." "He used to say I was five people in one," Denise wistfully recalls. "His wife, his mistress, the mother of his children, the keeper of his house and his agent." Simenon nowadays prefers to say that she gave herself status that was not rightfully hers. That she made herself more important than she was or needed to be.

There may be some truth in that; but it also seems undeniable that in the aftermath of the divorce settlement, Denise did her best to remedy her husband's somewhat impoverished financial condition. She was of undoubted assistance to him.

But she *did* give herself airs and graces. She *did* enjoy being the wife of a famous literary figure. Simenon noticed with misgiving that at a ceremonial luncheon during their visit to Liège for his election to the Belgian Royal Academy, Denise spotted her mother-in-law's name card placed immediately on the right of Simenon, as guest of honour. She at once picked it up, saying in a peremptory tone, "Over here, Mama!" and led the old lady to the less prestigious place that had been allotted to herself. "I didn't have the gumption to intervene," he has written, "but I was so ashamed of myself that during the meal I paid no attention to the music nor to the speeches afterwards."

Why did he say nothing? One obvious explanation is that he was still besotted with Denise. At the beginning of their time in Lakeville, he was so jealous of her that it was almost ugly to see. "When they came to live here, I suggested that she might like to go to my hairdresser because she had such lovely long black hair and he was French, so I thought they might have something in common," says Orpha Robinson, Cap Robinson's widow. "But Simenon would not let her go because he would not let another man touch his wife's hair."

Mrs. Robinson remembers another occasion, in their early days at Lakeville, when the two couples went to a dance that was supposed to be part of the newcomers' introduction to the local community and Simenon almost caused a fight because he would not let his wife dance with anyone else.

But the white heat of passion did not last. Soon it became local gossip that Simenon had more than just an employer's interest in some members of his domestic staff. Dolores James, who was fifteen when she first went to work for the household, remembers Simenon's freedom of outlook in sexual matters. "I was a little afraid of it but he tried to explain it in his own way," she says, with an embarrassed laugh. "Now I think more about it than I did then. I tried to erase it from my mind. That was not my kind of upbringing so it was very hard to accept. Now when I look back I wish I had had more of an education and been less frightened of myself."

As Simenon's passion for Denise cooled, so his sexual need for contact with other women reasserted itself. With Dolores James, it was of the fatherly kind. "He was a very special friend," she says. "He got involved with his employees, sort of included them, and tried to get me aware of myself as a person. I was very young then, in my teens. At that time, I didn't know what I wanted to do. It was a very exciting experience being in a famous author's home.

"Josephine Baker was a very big part of his life, and he talked about

185

her a lot. I guess I resembled her. Then I got a chance to meet her. She visited the house with her husband and she talked to me. She told me to stay with the family because they could do a lot for me." Long after she left "Mr. Simenon's" employ, they were still writing letters to each other and he was concerned to know how her life was progressing.

But, as ever with Simenon, sex was primarily of the purely functional kind. Says Mrs. Ralph McAllister Ingersoll: "We had a French woman friend, who, with her husband, used to go and visit the Simenons before coming on to spend a few days with Ralph and myself, and the stories she told about him were fantastic – that he was sleeping with anybody who walked in. Not only that, he would describe this all to Denise. He would tell his wife all about it! From everybody's description around town, he seemed to me like a different human."

Denise was finding out the hard way that her husband could not for long remain wholly faithful to any one woman; but at least he was honest with her. "My second wife was never jealous," he says. "I never had to indulge in all the lies and subterfuges of my years with Tigy."

Soon Lakeville became too small for this reawakening of his sexual impulses. He began to look outside the town for more extensive opportunities for enjoying what Annette de Bretagne has called his "women of recreation". He often went to New York ostensibly to see his publishers. Brendan Gill remembers getting a phone call from him in the spring of 1953, shortly before Marc's fourteenth birthday, "because he wanted to arrange properly his son entering manhood." He asked Gill to recommend the best brothel in New York for this purpose – "and then went along first to sample the wares for himself." "Yes, that's right!" recalls Simenon happily. "But, although it was undeniably pleasurable, I need not really have bothered. Marc later told me that he had acquired his manhood a few weeks before his birthday without my help."

Denise, despite the many pleasures of her sensuous body, was falling back into the almost inevitable place (given Simenon's sexual temperament) of being just one of his women. And with this realignment of her sexual role, came another development: nearly every month she fell ill, she would take herself to bed and not get up. "It was more psychosomatic than real," says Simenon. Their local doctor told him there was only cure: "Take her out of the house more. Away from Lakeville. Spend at least one week a month in New York or Boston or

Chicago, or some other large city. She wants to be taken out of herself, away from the children and daily routine."

Looking back over the years, it seems quite clear that two things were wrong. One was that for the first time in her highly charged existence, Denise was experiencing a form of sexual rejection; unable any longer, by the sheer force of passion, to keep her man exclusively in thrall. That was not easy to bear, with or without Simenon's "honesty" in telling her about his exploits.

The second was that her position as the wife of a famous international author had by now gone completely to her head. She had never recovered from the absolute eye-opener of their European grand tour in the spring of 1952. The two of them had been fêted on all sides. Brought up in North America, she had not really appreciated just *how* famous Simenon was, and how many important people he knew intimately as friends. Maurice Chevalier, Jean Gabin, Charles Boyer, Jean Renoir, Jean Cocteau, Marcel Pagnol, Michel Simon . . . in Paris, it must have seemed to her that nearly all the great names of French literature, stage and screen called her husband *tu* instead of the formal *vous*. As a French-Canadian, looking at Paris through the rose-tinted glasses of a transatlantic provincial, all this seemed even more exciting.

It must be remembered that this was a woman who, even before she met Simenon, had been so star-struck that she had commissioned Karsh of Ottawa, one of the most famous photographers in the world, to take her photograph – even though she had to ask him to accept payment by instalments. Furthermore, her volatile nature was such that, shortly before meeting Simenon, she had decided in a bout of depression to kill herself. She felt so "unfulfilled".

Knowing all this, and still genuinely loving his wife, Simenon accepted their Lakeville doctor's advice. One week out of every four he transported Denise away from the humdrum life of the small Connecticut town to the bright lights of Manhattan. Against his own personal taste, he found himself once again plunged into the same kind of hectic social life that he had known for a while in Paris in the mid-thirties: "We went to New York, always to the Plaza Hotel, always to the same suite and we always did the same thing. . . . We came alive at night and slept during the day, which I did not enjoy one little bit. I thought I had put that sort of life behind me when I had left Paris to go and live in the 'old grandmother's house' at Nieul."

It did not do any good. Simenon dates the first manifestation of

Denise's subsequent psychiatric condition, for which later she was to be treated in a Swiss clinic, one evening in the Plaza Hotel at about that time: "Earlier, she had asked me to buy her a small portable vacuum cleaner, and I wondered why. Then I came into the suite and found her, completely naked, opening all the wardrobes and drawers. She took out the lining paper and vacuum-cleaned the whole thing right through before putting in a new roll of paper she had brought with her. But that wasn't all. She then went on to disinfect the bath, the handbasin and all the telephones." In the years that followed, that was to become a ritual whenever they went to stay in a hotel, even in the George V in Paris or the Savoy in London.

A cry for help – or the onset of illness? It was probably something of the two.

The birth of Marie-Jo in February 1953, a few days after his fiftieth birthday, was one of the supreme moments of Simenon's life. "When Tigy was pregnant with my first child, I hoped it would be a girl," he says. "I sent for all the best catalogues of baby clothes. I *wanted* a girl. I wanted to dress her, both as a baby and later as a young woman – as, in fact, I did with Marie-Jo until she was fifteen years of age.

"When at last my third child was a daughter, for me that was the fulfilment of a dream."

As for his work, that blossomed amid the gentle hills and tree-covered terrain of Connecticut. "He pretended to a lot of people in Lakeville that he couldn't speak English," says Ralph McAllister Ingersoll, "and yet he absorbed and felt the character of a number of people that I know well." "Even his pipe," according to Brendan Gill, "rocking constantly in a corner of his mouth, was, one would swear, peering about and sizing things up." When some years later "Belle", the novel set in Lakeville, appeared in the United States, the local townsfolk recognised with glee some of the characters.

"I'm very glad I went to New York," Simenon states in *Quand j'étais vieux*. "If I hadn't gone, how long could I have continued to have anything to write about?" Allowing for his natural tendency on occasion to exaggerate, even to romanticise, there is still a modicum of truth in this. Fifteen of his novels are set in the United States, all but two of them written while he was there.

Yet as early as the autumn of 1952, when Brendan Gill visited him, a false element was stealing into the rosy picture. "It is a snug, sunny and affectionate-seeming house," Gill reported. But, although there was lyrical mention of "his young and pretty wife, French-Canadian whom he met soon after landing in the United States and who has since taken over the far-flung business operations of Simenon, Inc.," there is not a single reference in Gill's long article to any first wife or the fact that she was living, by Simenon's own demand, within a mile or so of her ex-husband. "He expressly asked me not to mention her," explains Gill. "That was the only condition he imposed on me."

Such a strained existence could not last indefinitely. In the spring of 1955, Hamish Hamilton, his British publisher, came to stay with him for a few days. On his last night, the two men sat up late talking: "Georges," said Hamilton, "frankly what keeps you in America?" "I was surprised by the question," says Simenon now. "But I trotted out at least ten good reasons for staying. Hamish listened politely and said, 'Yes, yes, yes.' But he did not seem very convinced."

The next day, after Hamilton's departure, Simenon, without any previous discussion with her whatsoever, turned to Denise and said: "How long will it take to pack?" She asked how long they were going for. Was it to New York? "No, for a very, very long trip – we're going to France!" Just the two of them? "No, we're all going!"

Simenon says she was delighted with the extraordinary news.

"I deeply believe that it was because of her I was going back to Europe. I had meant to end my days in Lakeville. You know what they call the 'goute d'eau' (the drop of water), when it goes drip, drip, drip and ends up making a hole in the stone after years and years? Subconsciously, I had been subjected to that. Deep down, in marrying me, she hoped to live in Paris – to live in France. All her life, like most French-Canadians, she had wanted to come and live in France. It was her Mecca.

"After we came back from Paris on our Belgium trip, it became much worse. Two days did not go by without her talking about Paris, etc. It was 'goute d'eau' technique!"

In typical fashion, he wasted no time. The decision to return to Europe was taken in February 1955; within a few weeks, on March 19, they set sail from New York on the Ile de France. "We left everything behind," says Simenon. "I told Cap Robinson to sell everything that was in the house." To this day, his friends in Lakeville do not know why he left them. Ralph McAllister Ingersoll, who says they had become close friends over the previous five years, claims to remember some excuse about Simenon's mother dying (in fact, she lived on for another sixteen years). "Cam" Becket says: "I think we all had the impression that he was not going for good. That he would be back one day."

But he never has returned. He has irrevocably closed the door on the American part of his life. Now he was returning home. But where was "home"? Paris, on which his fame was primarily based but where he had not lived, for any length of time, for some twenty-odd years? Nieul, where the old priory that he had so lovingly re-built was now Régine's home, with the gate firmly bolted against him – at least, so long as he was still with Denise?

He determined to give himself time to decide. This was going to be a major event in his life. As he had told Brendan Gill only a few years earlier at Shadow Rock Farm, "This is the twenty-sixth house I have lived in. I think maybe twenty-six houses is enough for one fifty-year-old man."

Paris was impossible for him, despite all Denise's longings; he could not abide the "cock-a-doodle-do" Paris of the post-war years. Where else then as a temporary staging-post while they looked around for something more permanent? There was only one area of France that would have sufficient "animation" for the starstruck Denise: the *Côte d'Azur*.

Within a month of their arrival at Le Havre, they had installed themselves in a splendid villa at Mougins, a picturesque village in the hills behind Cannes, where they stayed for the next six months and where Simenon, with his normal ability to block out his outside life from his inner existence, wrote no less than three novels. His last novel written at Lakeville, amid the January snows and ice-covered lakes of Connecticut, was a particularly gruesome Maigret story, called *Maigret et le corps sans tête* ("Maigret and the Headless Corpse"), dealing with a headless body picked up out of a canal in a dreary dock area of Paris. His first novel in the South of France, written in the jasmine-scented, July sunshine of Mougins, was *Maigret tend un piège* ("Maigret Sets a Trap"), in which the detective has to solve the mystery of six horrific murders in Montmartre, where the killer stabs to death his unknown women victims in the street because he needs to make "some furious, violent gesture". No one reading these two consecutive works would guess for a moment that three thousand miles and, in a sense, a completely different lifestyle separated the writing of them.

In October 1955, Simenon moved down from Mougins (his rented villa was then taken for a while by Maurice Thorez, the French Communist leader, who obviously saw nothing incongruous in also enjoying the pleasures of capitalist existence) to an even more magnificent villa called "Golden Gate", situated in probably the most affluent residential area of Cannes, which also has an American name – "California". The house was "sumptuous", Simenon's own word, and it was to be his home for nearly two years. But despite the glamour of illuminated water fountains lighting up the extensive grounds at night and the heated swimming pool built into rocks, it was to be a setting for only partial joy. "The first memory that I have of something really wrong between my mother and father is in Cannes," says John Simenon.

CHAPTER 17

Return to Europe

Simenon brought back to Europe one legacy of his years in the United States, about which he is, perhaps quite understandably, something less than frank in his printed work. "I just missed being an alcoholic," he says in *Quand j'étais vieux* – which seems soul-baring enough, until one looks into more of the facts.

Undoubtedly, he drank only moderately until he began the first Maigrets. At that time he developed the habit of drinking wine, reaching a daily average in the days just before the Second World War of no less than three bottles of claret. Yet – "I was rarely drunk," he claims. "I needed, as early as the morning, especially to write, a pick-me-up. I was persuaded in good faith that it was impossible to write otherwise. And, away from work, I drank anything, aperitif, cognac, calvados, marc, champagne."

It was always the product of the grape. But when he went to live in the United States, he acquired the taste for American-style, gin-based cocktails, and, above all, Scotch Whisky. It was then that he entered into a world of:

> a particular, almost permanent state, in which one is dominated by alcohol, whether during the hours one is drinking or during the hours when one is impatiently waiting to drink, almost as painfully as a drug addict waits for his injection or his fix. If one has never known this experience it is difficult to understand American life. Not everyone drinks, but . . . the crowds cease to be anonymous, the bars cease to be ordinary ill-lit places, the taxi drivers complaining or menacing people.

He did not drink alone. "We knew that state, D. and I, only intermittently, and I admit that alcoholism for two, accompanied by love, by passion, by exacerbated sexuality, is not at all disagreeable, quite the contrary." He claims that they both put it all behind them "one sunny day in Arizona in 1949, when we decided to put ourselves on the wagon (complete abstinence). Not out of virtue. Only because we knew that we were, both of us, incapable of stopping in time."

But they *were* both "incapable of stopping in time" – and they did not stop.

It has always to be remembered that *Quand j'étais vieux* was read every day, in manuscript by Denise, as it was written. "I could only put into the notebooks what I knew she would like to read," says Simenon (although nowhere in the text, when it eventually appeared, first in French in 1970 and then in English a year later, is this made clear). In fact, neither Denise nor Simenon went permanently on the wagon in 1949 or, indeed, at all. When Annette de Bretagne went to see Denise at the Hôtel George V in Paris in 1963, to discuss something to do with the impending publication of Simenon's latest novel, *Les Anneaux de Bicêtre* ("The Patient"), she found her at 9.30 in the morning already drinking whisky. "I used to see her sometimes during her visits to Paris at that time," says Annette, "because I was already working for *Presses de la Cité* [Simenon's French publishers] and M. Neilsen would ask me to go over and see her in case I could help her at all. It was an unusual pleasure, like a game – we used to drink a lot. I don't believe it was through M. Simenon that she drank so much. She probably began very young."

Marc Simenon is even more blunt: "I am not an analyst of my father's life," he says, "and I don't want to be. But I do know that by the time that Marie-Jo was six or seven – which would put it at about 1959 or 1960 – Denise was drinking and so was my father. He can be a heavy drinker."

John Simenon is even more dismissive of the myth of "going on the wagon" in Arizona in 1949, the year that he was born. "As far as I can remember, my father has always had a very special relationship with alcohol. I would not say that he is an alcoholic, but later on, in Switzerland, in the early sixties, I have memories of my father being drunk often. I learned to hate him for a while because of that, and because my mother was also saying awful things about him. Painting him as a drunk and saying, 'Look how bad your father is' and so on.

"He would mostly start after lunch and then it would build up. There would be times when he was not drinking for as long as two months, but then I would come back from school in the afternoon and find him not himself. I have memories of specific scenes – of my father being very drunk and throwing glasses and my mother having hysterics."

So far as John can tell, it all began very early; soon after their return from the United States. "The first memory of something really wrong between my mother and father was in Cannes. I heard an enormous crash and I went down to the dining room, and there on a green wall was a bunch of spaghetti dripping down. My father – who could be very violent – had thrown his plate against the wall, and for ever afterwards you could see the remnants of the spaghetti sauce on it."

The evidence as to Simenon's having put excessive consumption of alcohol permanently behind him back in 1949 is all one way – and that is, against his claim to have done so. For consider the further testimony of two medical men outside the family:

Dr. Pierre Rentchnick, the Swiss psychiatrist, says: "Of course, he drank excessive quantities! But he was not an alcoholic in the medical sense of the word. Beethoven was not an alcoholic even though he died of it; today he would have taken tranquillisers – and Simenon is the same type. For the obsessional compulsive, it helps him to live better. It is an alcoholism, if you like, of tranquillisers, an alcoholism of medical necessity.

"The difference is subtle. We have patients who are alcoholic but they are not creative people; they sink into it, they are committing suicide. Simenon, I think, was looking for his creative impulse with alcohol."

Dr. Jean Martinon is one of Simenon's few close male friends still living. He is a paediatrician and lives in Cannes. Although he and his wife had first seen Simenon, then with Régine, on the island of Porquerolles on holiday in the thirties, they only got to know the writer, then with Denise, twenty year later, when Dr. Martinon was called to the house to treat the young Marie-Jo for some childhood ailment. Thereafter, he became the regular medical consultant for all the children.

He and Mme. Martinon regard Simenon with genuine warmth and affection, but he admits: "Johnny, Marie-Jo and Marc have all been struck by their father's sudden outbursts of violence. He could be extremely violent, but most of the time he was gentle and courteous. You have to remember that both he and Denise drank a lot. One said, 'I drink so that the other doesn't feel ashamed of drinking'; and the other said, 'I drink to accompany the other.' Then they would stop for months. They always used to say, 'It doesn't matter what we do, we are sacred monsters.' In her book, the things she writes about are basically true but she interprets them in her own fashion. For example, she says that Simenon sometimes drank and behaved most violently. Well, it's true. Simenon was sometimes drunk for days and weeks, and he could be violent. But it seems to come out differently in her book from what it really was like."

Nevertheless, it would be a masterpiece of understatement to say that neither was easy to live with. It was only a question of time before the inevitable explosion would come.

The Martinons had their forebodings from the start. Says Dr. Martinon: "They were both play-actors. This tag of being 'sacred monsters' allowed them all sorts of things. Georges had a strong sexual appetite and Denise would help him a lot on these lines. She would bring him girls and then she would ask him how it was and so on. There was a sort of complicity between them.

"On other occasions, when he had these outbursts of exaggerated admiration for her, we could see something in him which belied what he was saying.

"And that dates back to the very beginning of their time here in Cannes."

Whatever his other sexual adventures may have been, Simenon was still deeply involved sexually with his wife. He bought for her a little flat at Cagnes, a small hillside town along the coast, which he called *La Folie de Denise*. A tiny staircase led from the street to the door of the flat and he had a wrought-iron bannister, engraved "D. S.", made for it. All the linen in the place was also marked with her initials. It was supposed to be their little hideaway, but they only spent one night there. It was a whim, a fantasy.

But that did not prevent him taking his sexual pleasures elsewhere, whenever and wherever he could. There is this account in *Des traces de pas* ("Imprints of my Footsteps"), one of his volumes of dictated memoirs that have not been published in English, where he recounts a typically mechanical, anonymous exploit with a girl come to his house as temporary secretary:

> I see once again the great piece of furniture that served as my desk. Yet I see not at all the temporary secretary whom I engaged for a few weeks.
> Was she pretty? I don't think so. Ugly? That neither. Here was the commonplace and rather unsmiling face one sees so often in the streets.
> She typed the letters as I dictated because her shorthand was too inaccurate. I sat beside her to make sure that there were no mistakes. And, one day, her dress rode up. Continuing to dictate, I let my hand glide and was rather surprised, I swear to you, to find that her thighs parted almost automatically.
> I caressed her. She kept on typing. I kept on dictating. Then she gave me a look as if to ask me to stop dictating for a while. I did, but I went on

caressing her while she looked fixedly at the wall in front of her. Suddenly, I felt her belly tremble and an instant later she came abundantly.

Then, as if nothing had happened, she continued typing the phrase that I had already begun to dictate.

I think, in fact I am sure, that I never kissed her. I spoke no word of love or eroticism. Already, even at that very moment, I probably would not have recognised her in the street.

The next day, by her excited manner of typing, I understood that she was waiting for the same thing to happen. I caressed her again. She came. She went back to typing.

And that went on for nearly a month.

In the evening, he and Denise often went to the two striptease clubs that then existed in Cannes and, as he put it, he "became the friend of all the striptease girls." Often, Denise would say to him: "Aren't you going upstairs?" pointing to the narrow staircase that led to the girls' dressing rooms, and off he would go to where "quite simply, I made love with one or other of the girls." They told him their life stories, invited him home to their small furnished apartments. He even once played with the baby of one of them. If he were minded to find a hypocritical explanation for this form of activity (which for once, mercifully, he is not) he could claim that it was all valuable research in the field: in June 1957, while still living at the "Golden Gate" villa, he wrote a novel called *Striptease* (with the same title in English).

Denise denies that she ever pointed out other women to Simenon and suggested that he sleep with them. She says incredulously: "Why would I do that? That would be unbelievably foolish – to encourage my husband to go with other women!" When this remark is later reported to the Martinons, they both laugh. "We have seen her do it!" says Dr. Martinon. "All four of us were sitting on the terrace of the Carlton Hotel here in Cannes and Denise suddenly said to Georges: 'You see that women over there. Are you interested? I know she is.' And Georges left the table and went over to the other woman. Twenty minutes later, he returned to us with a broad grin on his face, looking very pleased with himself, and saying: 'That was very good!' . . . Georges has always been extremely kind to us and his fatherly love towards his children has blinded us to all the other shocking things he may have done."

Yet Simenon even brought his eldest son into his own sexual sphere of activity. On the evening of their arrival in Paris, on their way back from Lakeville, he and Marc, who was not yet sixteen, were having a drink in the bar of their hotel. A woman aged about thirty-five, elegant and attractive, was watching them and Simenon said to his son: "You see that woman looking at you so intensely? She used to be a former 'friend' of mine." Marc was feeling rather tired after the long journey and made only a non-committal reply.

Later that night there was a knock on his bedroom door. The same woman was standing there. Simenon had sent her. "I think he wanted to make sure I loved women and not men," says Marc. "I had been in boarding school where there was, of course, a lot of homosexuality and he wanted to make sure that I was 'all right'. This was his way of doing so. Unfortunately, I was so tired that I fear I did not properly do her justice."

Soon Marc was leaving his father in no doubt at all that he was "all right". Once he had passed his sixteenth birthday and Simenon was satisfactorily ensconced on the Riviera, Régine wrote her ex-husband a friendly letter from Nieul saying that the time had come when their son, as a growing young man, really needed more to be with his father and his young half-brother and sister than an ageing woman like her. Within a short while of his arrival, Marc was working as a beachboy on the golden sands of Cannes and having no shortage of adequate female companionship; without his father's help. Indeed, by now, the shoe was on the other foot and Simenon claims that they used to exchange phone numbers and addresses – although when this is recounted to Marc, he laughs and says: "I think that sometimes my father, whom I adore, gets things wrong!"

After nearly eighteen months at the "Golden Gate" villa, Simenon was visited by Sam White, one of the best informed foreign correspondents ever based in Paris. White found a man apparently at the plenitude of his powers. He was about to start work on a new novel the next day. A large table in his study was littered with maps, railway and bus timetables, and the telephone directories of half-a-dozen countries. Denise was on the telephone, busily cancelling all his appointments for the next eleven days, and a doctor was expected to arrive for his usual last-minute check-up "for Simenon is something of a hypochondriac and worried about his blood pressure."

Beside him as he consulted his maps and timetables was a tray full of some thirty pipes, and the inevitable manila envelope. On the back of the envelope, in his minute handwriting, was the name of the town in which the action was to take place (it was in Northern France, between Amiens and Boulogne), the names of the leading characters (to reduce

197

the danger of libel taken from the telephone directory of a town at the opposite end of France) and their families, histories and professions.

"I know nothing about the events which will occur in my book," Simenon told White, as he had told so many other interviewers before, "otherwise it would not be interesting for me. I write them chapter by chapter, usually a chapter a day. The problem is always the same – how to arrange matters so as to subject my characters to the utmost possible strain."

He intended writing that particular book in longhand (though over the years he has changed from typewriting to handwriting and back again – without, as far as one can see, any real difference in the value of the finished work). "I have to go on proving myself to myself," he said. "If I stay two months without writing, I begin to lose confidence."

He need not have worried – *yet*. Of the seven non-Maigrets and three Maigrets that he wrote in the little over two years that he lived in the South of France, two of the former group were among his finest novels ever: *Le Petit homme d'Arkangelsk*, the sad story of the Jew from Archangel who killed himself even though he could prove his innocence of murdering his non-Jewish wife; and *Le Fils*, the story of a father who, like Simenon with *Je me souviens*, tried to explain himself in writing a long letter to his son. The command of character and of style is as total as ever.

But soon a feeling of acute uneasiness was to creep into Simenon's writing. Temporarily, in his late fifties, his accustomed sureness of touch was to desert him. The well-spring of his imagination was to dry up. "I am finished! I am finished!" he was to cry out in despair when he came out of his study one day, almost in tears, unable to continue with a new novel he had started that very morning.

That was, however, in the future. In July 1957, soon after completing his novel, *Striptease*, he drove off with his family from the glamour of Cannes, once again to a new home. This was to be his last move of country in his search for a permanent base; for, despite Denise's pressing passion for France, he had decided to make Switzerland, that mecca of the wealthy and the tax-conscious, his final land of adoption. Nowadays, he talks rhapsodically about life with the Swiss; how they leave one alone and do not encroach upon one's privacy, as people do in the United States, in France or his native Belgium. He says he likes the calmness and the sense of stability. In *Mémoires intimes*, he writes:

"While we were still living in Cannes, I decided to take D. to Lausanne, with the hope of finding there, for her as well as for the children, a haven of peace." It was also a convenient location for a celebrated author who, at that stage, still needed to jet around all over Europe. But Dr. Martinon is perhaps nearer the mark when he says bluntly: "He went to Switzerland because of tax problems." (And why ever not? Alistair Maclean, Noel Coward, Charles Chaplin, William Holden, Sophia Loren and David Niven are just some of the famous names who have found the Swiss tax laws as conducive to a pleasant life within the country's borders as its other, less tangible, charms.)

Simenon elected, and understandably so, to live in the French-speaking part of the country, in the area around Lake Geneva. He took a six-year lease, renewable at the end of that period, on a sixteenth-century, twin-turreted château in the village of Echandens, in the hills seventeen kilometres from Lausanne. He would have bought the place outright, but it was not for sale. He set up his study in one of the turrets, in a magnificent room furnished with Sheraton antiques from eighteenth-century England, and accessible only by a spiral stone staircase.

But life got no better with Denise. Her "empire" as his business manager/agent/secretary grew out of all proportion. Soon *she* had three secretaries to assist her in her self-appointed task as Simenon's link with the outside world. She was a perfectionist and was genuinely doing her best for her husband, as she saw the need; but it was proving ever more exhausting to live with. And there was another factor: she was drinking more, he was drinking more. There were highlights: two visits to Brussels in the following year, when he presided over the Film Festival in May and delivered his speech on *Le Roman de l'Homme* ("The Novel of Man") at the World Fair in October; holidays in Holland, Florence and Venice, and frequent visits to Paris (where he left Denise at the George V to do her usual re-lining of the wardrobes and disinfecting of the bathroom while he visited the famous brothel of Mme. Claude). But Simenon was becoming increasingly aware that his marriage was slithering down the road to disaster.

"My father has incredible expectations of people," says John. "At the same time that he had all this love and tenderness for my mother – which he *did* have – he was very intolerant if things didn't work out. He would let her do a lot of things in connection with the running of the house and his business, but he expected an awful lot of her. I really think she could not bear the strain of it. He's exceptional. He is so demanding of himself. That pursuit of excellence.

199

"On a regular basis, things were really not going well in Echandens –
certainly, not towards the end of our time there."

In May 1959, Denise gave birth to their third child – a boy, Pierre.
Almost at once, he fell ill and it looked as if they were going to lose
him. He did not respond to treatment and, in *Un oiseau pour le chat*,
Denise graphically describes how her strenuous efforts, coupled with a
call for his aid to Dr. Martinon in Cannes, helped save her baby's life.
"That is typical of her!" he says. "We were on holiday at the time but
Denise phoned me and I advised a blood test. The results made me fear
a certain condition of the bone marrow. So I asked a consultant to take
a sample and Pierre was found to be suffering from an inability to
manufacture more cells in his body – but it was only transitory. He
responded to treatment here in France.

"Of course, Denise was very upset and did all she could for the
child – I don't deny that – but, if she hadn't been there, her husband
would have done the same. She tends to dramatise everything."

And it was getting very wearing for Simenon. In the whole of 1959,
he wrote just four novels – of which two were Maigrets and the other
two minor works, only one of which, *Le Veuf* ("The Widower"), has
been translated into English. Nineteen sixty was even less productive
with a total output of three novels, one a Maigret, to show for the
entire year. In May, he presided over the *Festival du Film* at Cannes
and the photographs show a highly successful dinner-suited author,
accompanied by his glamorous wife decked out with jewellery. But
there was one embarrassing incident when Simenon arrived to make a
very serious speech, full of stirring comments about the film industry,
oblivious of the fact that he had a woman's lipstick smeared on his
face.

After the Film Festival, Simenon had the idea for a new novel. It was
to be one full of sunshine and tenderness. He had the characters and the
background all mapped out. He sat down to write it – and only got as
far as the first three pages. Back at Lakeville, he had told an American
interviewer that if he fell ill for forty-eight hours during the writing of
a novel, he would throw away everything that he had written and
never again return to it. But now ideas were not so thick on the
ground. A short while later he *did* return to this basic theme but
transmuted it into the easier setting of a Maigret novel, in which the
same elements of tenderness and sunshine were present, but with the
characters now mainly in their seventies and eighties.

Despite this, the power of his natural genius came through and no
one reading *Maigret et les veillards* ("Maigret in Society") would suspect

the internal battle that it cost its author to produce. The opening sentences have a cadence and a serenity that totally belie the anguish which Simenon was living through:

> It was one of those exceptional months of May which one experiences only two or three times in one's life and which have the brilliance, the taste and the scent of childhood memories. Maigret called it a choral May, for it reminded him both of his first communion and of his first springtime in Paris, when everything seemed new and wonderful.
> In the street, in the bus, in his office, he would suddenly come to a halt, struck by a distant sound, by a gust of warm air, by the bright splash of colour of a blouse which took him back twenty or thirty years.
> The day before, just as they were setting out to have dinner with the Pardons, his wife had asked him almost blushing as she spoke:
> "You don't think I look too silly, at my age, in a floral dress?"

In his heart of hearts, Simenon must have longed to have had such a wife for himself. "At times, I lived almost on my own in my office at Echandens," he says, "because *she* wanted to be in hers. I was upstairs and she was on the ground floor. And do you know what? From time to time she asked somebody in the house to go up and make love to Monsieur! It was she who sent them to me!"

It was at about this time that Simenon took down a new set of notebooks (as he had done years before for *Je me souviens* after the Fontenay radiologist's false diagnosis) and began to write almost daily entries for his own solace, but not for publication. As he later wrote in the Preface when the notebooks appeared as *Quand j'étais vieux* ("When I Was Old"): "In 1960, 1961 and 1962, for personal reasons, or for reasons I don't know myself, I began feeling old, and I began keeping notebooks. I was nearing the age of sixty."

The entry for "Sunday noon", July 24, 1960 is significant: "I want to tell it simply, without comment. Yesterday, D. and I had an aperitif. We don't do this often. For several weeks she has been on edge, because of the secretary, then because of one of the maids, etc. She is capable of enormous energy and she can keep going for a certain length of time with two or three hours of sleep a night. Yesterday was the last straw, on the eve, almost, of leaving for vacation."

This is the first suggestion, in print, by Simenon of anything grievously awry in his personal life. What was it all about? " 'Because of the secretary'," explains Simenon, "refers to Aitken." (Joyce Aitken, an attractive blonde Scotswoman who was then Denise's personal secretary and does the same job for Simenon today.) "She had thrown her out, and she couldn't find her way through all the papers, etc. She was absolutely frantic. Then one day I telephoned Aitken at home and asked her to come back, saying that my wife was in a bad way and that it would have a significant effect on her condition, if only she would agree to return and help take the load off her shoulders.

"The reference to her 'enormous energy' is perfectly true, but I already knew that something was really wrong with her. At that time she was drinking an enormous amount . . . the number of times I found her drinking whisky, straight from the bottle! As for it being 'the last straw', well, I had to hire two planes to take us to Bügenstock by air, where we were due to start our vacation, because she couldn't go by car."

Life at Echandens was simply hell. Pierre, the baby, was far too small to know what was going on. John and Marie-Jo tried to keep out of the warring parents' way as much as they could. Marc had long since made his departure from his father's household and in April, at the age of twenty-one, had got married. Simenon and his wife saw the love that once existed between them festering into a running sore.

Appearances were still maintained. "Denise Simenon is as necessary to her husband as the beating of his own heart," gushed a writer in the ill-fated British newspaper *Woman's Mirror*, after a visit to Echandens in 1961. She quoted Denise as saying, "I am not a very independent woman. But then, I don't want to be. I am completely dependent on my husband." And Simenon is said to have enthused: "My wife is my collaborator. She has a specialised knowledge of international law concerning everything to do with publishing, cinema and TV." He told the gullible reporter that after the two of them had been at home together for several weeks working hard, "we take a holiday – and it is like another honeymoon."

In the magazine *Woman's Own*, in the same year, Denise allowed herself to be interviewed as "Mme. Maigret". "That is how she liked to consider herself," says Simenon. "The interviewer wanted to talk to me but I didn't have the time so I suggested that he might care to talk to my wife instead. And that is how it came out!"

As for his work, his "writer's block" still continued. Nineteen sixty-one saw only five books going off to Sven Nielsen's *Presses de la Cité*: two of them Maigrets and two of the other three, minor novels of little note. The only work of consequence of that year was *Le Train* ("The Train"), based upon his wartime experiences in La Rochelle when looking after the Belgian refugees who poured into that south-western corner of France after the Germans had overrun their country.

But even *Le Train* was, unlike the days of his full, rich genius when everything flowed easily from his pen in a minimum of days, a "worked at" book. He started it in November 1960, wrote just ten lines, then stopped and only picked it up again to process through onto the typewriter some five months later, in March 1961.

This then was the state of deep personal unhappiness and professional nadir into which Simenon was plunged, when shortly before Christmas 1961 he came face to face with an olive-skinned, black-haired woman of North Italian stock, twenty-three years younger than him, who, as soon as he saw her, he knew "was going to mean something important in my life."

Denise Ouimet, who had come into his life through passion, was about to leave it for the very same reason – only this time she was to be cast in the role that earlier Régine Renchon had played. Sadly for Denise, she was not to have Régine's strength of character.

CHAPTER 18

Death of a Marriage

No one except Simenon knows the surname of Teresa, the woman whom Denise engaged in December 1961 as her personal maid but who has long since taken her place, in all but name, as his wife. He keeps her background a deliberate mystery. Until the autumn of 1981, when it was necessary for the pre-publication publicity of *Mémoires intimes*, he would not allow any photographs of her to be taken for newspapers or magazines. As always, with women the closest to his heart, she had to be entirely for him; uniquely, his own.

Even today, no one knows the details of her birth or her parents, or where exactly in northern Italy she comes from. Her very strongly Italian-accented French would seem to indicate an origin in Piemonte, the region around Turin; but one could easily be wrong.

Denise, with her customary latter-day charm, has let drop in *Un oiseau pour le chat* the fact that before Teresa joined the Simenon household as a domestic, she had an illegitimate son. Nowadays this pleasant young man and his own small son visit Teresa and Simenon from time to time. Simenon refers to him as "my son-in-law", for that is how he regards him.

The voice of this last companion of Simenon is calm and assured. Her clothes have the simple elegance that only a great deal of money can buy. Her ascendancy over her much older lover is obvious even at the briefest meeting, and her aura of knowing serenity makes it difficult to believe she could ever have been someone's personal maid.

She seems today a typical *bourgeoise* woman of middle years and affluent circumstances who has kept her figure and knows how to look neat and attractive – with only a certain glint in the eye to betoken in the past a less comfortable existence than that which is now undeniably hers. One quality she has in abundance: *warmth*. She laughs a lot, she opens her arms wide in greeting, she looks at Simenon with affection, she guards his health with the care of a dedicated nurse; always with that same kind of knowing, slightly indulgent smile. One has seen that smile before: it is never far from the lips of Régine, his first wife.

But otherwise she is very different from Régine. There is a quality of sexual earthiness about Teresa even now that Régine could never claim to have had.

In his volumes of dictated memoirs, Simenon has gone on and on about his pure love for Teresa and how complete and intense is their union, including its physical side, to such an extent that some French critics have cried: "Enough! This is all very boring!" To be honest, it is; at least in print. In the flesh, it is rather touching; this spectacle of old age in apparent absolute contentment. *But it took him a long time to get there.* In one essential respect, the story of Simenon's love for Teresa is very different from that of his earlier love for Denise. Both were grounded on one initial act of passion, but in the case of Teresa there was no immediate supplanting of his lawful wife. It took eleven stormy and tormented years before their relationship blossomed into a total communion declared before the world.

Yet that has not prevented Simenon describing in print, in the most clinical detail, the first coupling of their bodies. The occasion did not have the spurious glamour, let alone comfort, of the luxurious hotel room in New York where he first took Denise in his arms. It happened swiftly, animal-like, virtually anonymously – as with the chambermaid in the Hôtel Bertha in Paris some forty years earlier, whom he possessed in the corridor while she went on polishing the guests' shoes.

Here is how Simenon, then nearly seventy-five years of age, told his readers in *A l'abri de notre arbre* ("In the Shadow of our Tree", but not published in English) of the first time that he had sex with Teresa:

> A month or so after she started work at Echandens, I unexpectedly walked into a room and found her bending over a table that she was polishing. The sight was too much for me. I advanced upon her, feverishly pulled down her knickers and penetrated her.
> I have already said that I have possessed, if one can use that word, thousands, if not tens of thousands, of women in my life. But never had I known such sexual joy, to which were added so many others that I still am unable to define.
> That experience has remained, for me, unique. Teresa did not play the coquette. She had an orgasm as violent as mine, still bent over the table, with a duster or a piece of chamois leather in her hand.
> I do not know if we kissed afterwards. I don't think so. We did not even look at each other. I just walked out of the room and locked myself in my office.
> It was a time when I was feeling very lonely. I thought or I tried to

make myself think that I was still in love with D., which still did not prevent me, with her entire consent, in having numerous other sexual experiences. How long did it go on? Almost every day thereafter, and without more ceremony, I took Teresa as I had taken so many others but already, on the days when she went down into the town, for example, I felt myself ill at ease, with a strange sensation in my heart.

According to Dr. Martinon, there has probably been only one maid in the Simenon household, in all the time that he has known him, who has not slept with her employer and, when he asked Simenon why not that particular one, he replied: "Because she said, 'No'!" It is impossible to judge when Denise first became aware that Teresa had joined this long, if not too illustrious, line but she does make quite a lot of the fact (in the only two pages of her book in which she deigns to mention Teresa) that very soon after starting work at Echandens she dismissed the maid on the spot for spying on her and Simenon talking through a keyhole. She was only prevailed upon to take her back when Boule (of all people) came to her, on behalf of the staff, saying that most of them threatened to leave unless Teresa was allowed to stay. Later during that same year of 1962, when, on a visit to London in connection with the Maigret television series, Teresa and Simenon made proper love to each other for the first time in a bed at the Savoy Hotel, and the following morning Teresa went straight to Denise and told her what had happened, Denise refused her offer to leave and said: "No. Stay as you are. Do what you like with my husband, but only one thing I ask of you – make sure you use the Pill."

Denise's view of this new intruder into her house, and her husband's bed, was in many ways much the same as Régine's had been of her some fifteen years earlier; she thought her marriage was inviolate. She could afford to humour this caprice of Simenon's. She was his wife, and she could not foresee that she could cease to be such either legally or practically. Unassailed (unlike Régine in the earlier years) by any feelings of physical jealousy, she could continue in her *grande dame* way and, if she did have moments of depression, well, there seems to have been the solace of the whisky bottle.

In any event her attention was soon taken up by an entirely new matter which appealed to the *arriviste* snobbery in her nature. It was announced that an autoroute was shortly to be built near the village of Echandens which would ruin the peaceful calm of the château. "So we'll build ourselves a new home entirely from scratch!" said Simenon. He bought a huge plot of land high in the hills above Lausanne near the village of Epalinges, and Denise took upon herself the task of planning, with her husband's help, their magnificent new home and overseeing its construction. "There were nights when I hardly slept," she says. "No one can know the amount of work that I put into the building of that house." "It became her life's work," says Dr. Martinon. "She was absolutely obsessed with it. What really triggered off the quarrels between her and Simenon was the building of that house. It brought out all her pathological perfectionism. She would not go to bed, she couldn't sleep any more. She became quite frankly unbearable. In the end, she had to be prevailed upon to find a doctor. I sent her eventually to a psychiatrist, whom Simenon knew and whom she liked at the beginning – although in her book she says the most terrible things about him, which I do not believe to be true."

During 1963, when construction work on the new villa, all gleaming white from the outside like a vast sanatorium, was going on at full pace, Denise had three times to go into the Swiss psychiatrist's clinic at Prangins on the banks of Lake Geneva to seek refuge from her ever-increasing torment. The house had twenty-six rooms, twenty-one telephones, eleven servants, a massive swimming pool with a unique form of water-cleansing that cost in itself one million Swiss francs. As always in Simenon's homes, each room was linked to his office and the matrimonial bedroom by an intercom so that they could listen to what was going on; allegedly, so that they could hear if any of the children wanted them in the night. "She had thought everything out," says Dr. Martinon. "She even designed a sitting room for her staff. There was a blue bathroom for the male staff and a pink bathroom for the female staff."

"I made myself ill over Epalinges," admits Denise. Their first night in their new home, in November 1963, she turned upon her husband and screamed at him: "I hate this house!" She was destined to remain there less than a year.

When asked why on earth he embarked on such a venture at such a precarious stage in his marriage, Simenon replies: "I really wanted to cure her. I genuinely thought she might live differently there. I had already met Teresa but at that stage I still hoped that things might yet somehow work out satisfactorily between us." "That is true," says Dr. Martinon. "He really did hope that all might yet be well. I know that he was already having relations with Teresa but he still did not give up his marriage easily. He was afraid, obsessed with the fact that Denise might be a schizophrenic – she isn't, incidentally – but his attitude was frankly ambiguous."

In fact, moving into Epalinges did nothing to solve Simenon's problems. It merely set the scene for the final break up of his marriage – and, perhaps more sadly, for the flickering out of his great talent as a storyteller.

Speaking of that period in his life, Simenon says: " 'The Lodger' did everything she could to stop me working." (Though this is not the image which he "sold" to his public at the time, praising Denise as his helpmate in countless contemporary interviews.) "When I was preparing a novel, for example, I warned the children that they were going to have to be particularly quiet for the next few days and I told Aitken, 'No more meetings after Monday' – and then the trouble would start! 'The Lodger' would make a great scene and really get on my nerves just when I needed to concentrate.

"There were all sorts of rows and sometimes I had to put off a new novel for a week and then another week before I could start working. She really hated my work. She would really have liked it to have been her that did the writing, her that was being interviewed."

The tension could not go on for much longer – especially in that large soulless clinic of a house at Epalinges. They were both drinking prodigious quantities. The scenes, the quarrels, the arguments, the mutual accusations were becoming a daily occurrence. "It was a horrible time," remembers John. Finally, came the day when her Swiss psychiatrist said that Denise should return to his clinic for an indefinite period of time. She did not want to go. She did not believe it was necessary. She had her work to do; she was in the middle of typing a contract for a remake of *Les Inconnus dans la maison* with James Mason starring in the old Raimu role in a Hollywood version of the story. She telephoned Dr. Martinon in Cannes for his advice. She wanted to remain in her home, at her post. She was adamant that her husband needed her and that her place was by his side. But the doctors said that her husband had developed "an allergy" to her.

In the end, one person persuaded her to leave the house for the clinic: her fifteen-year-old son, John. *"Maman*, you must do it . . . It's only for a few weeks . . . It's very difficult for me . . . But it's Dad you are saving . . . You are strong, you will come back." And so she left her dream house at Epalinges, her team of secretaries, her famous husband and the million-franc swimming pool. But it proved not to be "only for a few weeks." She never spent the night there again. The home, on which she had expended so much of herself, more prodigal of her nervous energy than her husband was of his millions, turned out to be both the culmination of her status as Georges Simenon's wife and the destruction of her place as his life's companion.

In *Un oiseau pour le chat*, she accuses her Swiss psychiatrist of being involved in an unscrupulous plot with her husband to get her out of Epalinges and away from her family. But the psychiatrist is one of the most respected medical men in Switzerland and Prangins itself has been in existence for a very long time as a highly reputable, and expensive, refuge for those who have everything in life except perhaps their reason or the will to live. It is where Nijinsky spent the final years of his life before dying after one last mad dance for Diaghilev.

How could John Simenon, still only a schoolboy, take upon himself so vital a role as making his mother leave his father in order to "save" him. Here is his thoughtful, troubled explanation nearly twenty years later: "Although I can't guarantee that this is how I felt at the time, I would say that it was founded on the realisation that, out of the two, the genius was my father. He was the man who meant most to us as a family unit. He was the pivot around which everything else revolved. I probably also dramatised things to myself a little, but on the basis that he still had many things to do and much to bring to the world in terms of writing – as well as to us as a family. You see, I am sure we would have lost Dad at that time, if my mother had not gone.

"I think we are extremely fortunate, given the very big crisis which he went through, that we did not lose him. There were several times when he could have died – I am convinced of it – simply because of his mental state. And if he *had* died, I think I would have been totally lost. I have no idea what I would have become. My sister, whatever happened to her afterwards, would never have been able to face his death either.

"I used to think of myself as being a fairly good diplomat and it's not impossible that by telling my mother that she was saving Dad, I was trying to give her the impression that she was doing something grand for someone, and it would therefore make it more acceptable to her. Did I think she was ill? I was never quite sure. But there is one thing I *was* sure of: things were not the way she was making me try to see them, with my father portrayed as a hopeless drunk. I was not sure they were the way my father said they were either.

"But at that time I needed something solid – when you are a child, you need that – and I made a choice. Who was the more solid of the two, my mother or my father? – I felt that even though he wasn't as solid as I wished, it was my father."

The arrangement was that Denise should visit Epalinges once a week and telephone there every day. She claims that on her first two weekly visits, she and Simenon made love after his siesta; but on the third week he made an excuse that he had slept badly the night before and that he felt an attack of aerophagia, his breathlessness from wartime days, coming on. She looked at her watch. It was 2.55 in the afternoon. At that precise moment, she says, she knew that their love for each other had died.

But her leaving the house had solved almost nothing. "The atmosphere was still terrible," says John. "Because then the problem started with Teresa!" To the outside world, she was still only a servant – and she was to continue as such for several years – but, in reality, she was slowly taking over her position as the mistress of the house. "I hated Teresa at that time," says John. "I had the feeling that she was adding more venom to an already unfortunate situation. She was telling my father everything that I was doing, and my father would come back at me yelling – like I was doing everything wrong all the time.

"Without Teresa, he was always on at me anyway. There was this tremendous contradiction in my father. He would not let me go down into the town by trolley bus like all the other kids in the village, but insisted on my always being taken in a car by the chauffeur; but then I had to make sure the chauffeur had other things to do in Lausanne anyway, otherwise he would yell at me, 'You're a rich kid. You are taking advantage of the chauffeur. You don't know how lucky you are!' It was very hard to cope.★

"And then there was his drinking. That did not stop either when my mother left. It went on for as long as he continued to live at Epalinges; big bouts of it. But when he was working on a book, he would never drink. So I loved it when he was writing. In fact, the legend [fostered

★This is probably the same chauffeur who assured Simenon's American publisher Helen Woolf, as he drove her up to the house on a visit in Simenon's gleaming Rolls Royce, that they would be eating in the servants' quarters exactly the same food as had been specially prepared for her. He told her that they always ate the same as the family and that after a meal Simenon would come in and ask if they had enjoyed it.

in many interviews by Denise and Simenon himself] that he was very difficult to live with when he was writing, was not true for me. For me, that was a good time! I wouldn't see much of him because he would be working and I would be at school, but what I did see of him, I found fantastic. I would really see a fantastic guy!"

Alas, there were not sufficient of those moments. In October 1967, having taken his *baccalauréat* at the age of eighteen, at the first moment that he could do so, John, the son that Simenon loved so much, followed the example of his older brother Marc and left home. In a sense, he was driven out. Driven out by his father's stifling love. "I had to get out of that house and forge my own personality so that I could come back and not worry about all those things that upset me so much." He went to Paris, to be near his brother for a while (blazing a trail that Marie-Jo, his younger sister, was later to follow at the same age), then on to the United States where he spent two years at Harvard Business School and then to London. "I phoned my father after I had been accepted at Harvard, which was quite a feat, and he said, 'Oh, that's great!' and that was it. That was all he said. That is probably the last time that he was able to affect me. If it had happened two years earlier and I had called him all that way to tell him such good news and got that kind of response, I would have felt it extremely strongly. But by then I had come to terms with my father within myself. What is it like nowadays?

"Gradually, my father has become different from the way he was; he no longer assumes the worst about me." (Sadly, it will be noticed that *that* is exactly what Simenon had always said his mother assumed about *him*!)

In October 1964, Simenon wrote to the good Dr. Martinon at Cannes: "Denise's aggressiveness has returned. The doctors forbid her to use the car. She is most of the time at the clinic. She is not allowed here on Sundays any more. They are continuing with the psychotherapy. She overworks the secretaries with cassettes which take hours to decipher. She phones all the time and for hours. Then she refuses to see me for days."

It was in that same month that Boule left Epalinges, never again to live under the same roof as her one-time *petit monsieur joli*. The exact circumstances of her leaving are a mystery. In *Mémoires intimes*, Simenon claims that it was because Denise had made it a condition of her possible return to Epalinges that this final link with his romantic past should be severed. "She never minded my liaisons that I made afresh, when I was actually living with her," he explains, "but she could not stand anyone with intimate associations from my past. It wasn't because Boule had slept with me but because she had lived longest with me and had known me through two eras. She detested Tigy for the same reason. Basically, she detested any woman that had known me before her, but those that I knew after we'd met didn't worry her."

For her part, Denise, although she does not mention Boule's departure in her book, says that Boule came to see her at Prangins to tell her that she was going of her own free will – to look after Marc's young children – before she was positively asked to go. She blamed it all on Teresa, and on the pressure building up in the house as the latter sought to increase her influence on Simenon.

Whichever version be the truth, Boule herself says nothing.

What is certainly true is that during the following year, there was still a chance that Denise might return to resume her place at Epalinges. No one, with any semblance of justice, can ever accuse Simenon of lightly jettisoning either of his two wives. He fought strongly to maintain his home; Teresa's position was still by no means assured. In a desperate attempt to see if there could be a reconciliation with Denise, Simenon took his whole family (including Teresa in her capacity as a maid) on a cruise up to the Bosphorous. One night, Denise came to him in his cabin. She wanted him to make love to her. He refused. Next morning, an embarrassed ship's captain told him that she had been on the telephone for two hours talking to her Swiss doctors. "I knew then it was the end," he says. "I could never again live with her as man and wife."

Soon after their return from the cruise, there was a formal meeting at Epalinges, at which were present Denise, Simenon, her Swiss doctors – and Dr. Martinon, come specially from Cannes. Denise said that she felt completely cured and ready to return to live normally with her husband. Simenon had been drinking: "I don't want to take her back," he said roundly. His voice was thick, his words slurred. "This is a whore, *messieurs!*" Denise claims that "whore" (*putain*) is what he always called her when he was drunk. (Annette de Bretagne does not believe this. "He always had a great admiration for whores," she says.) But did he call his wife this in front of the doctors? Dr. Martinon confirms that Denise's account of the interview is substantially correct.

Two days later, she left the clinic; but not to return to Epalinges. Instead, she went to a hotel at Divonne and eventually to one of the two comfortable homes that Simenon was to buy her. She claims that there was still some hope of a *rapprochement* between them until as late as December 1971. There may be some truth in this – up to a point. Simenon would deny it, but Dr. Martinon is compassionate to both of them: "At the present time, they explain the events of those years through their imagination. They are both very far from the reality and they have not enough self-control to judge what happened with complete clarity."

Henry James once began a short story: "Never say you know the last word about any human heart." It is almost impossible for anyone to know – Denise and Simenon included – what really went on inside their minds and hearts during those agonising years of the sixties when their marriage slowly bled to death. The contemporaneous record, in Simenon's letters to Jean Martinon, show at first only a troubled, anguished husband: "I am trying to follow your advice to surround Denise with affection which is not very difficult," he writes on November 27, 1965, "and to avoid irritating subjects. She is allowed to drive a car again and she came to lunch yesterday with friends. Her life is quite busy but I think it will take some months before she can come back home." "Denise is still at Divonne," he writes on October 1, 1969. "She leads a more and more personal life with friends and a busy timetable. She is very cheerful. She feels more and more strange in the house, and when she comes to visit us once a week she does not stay for long any more. It's a good sign."

But by the end of 1971, a sour note has crept in: "My wife, who shares her time between a flat in Avignon and a villa at Begnins, and whom I haven't seen for a year," he writes on December 9, "writes to me occasionally to ask for money and threatens to publish a book which will 'disclose' my true character.★ You see, her health has not improved. She is in the hands of a psychoanalyst in Avignon." Less than two weeks later, on December 20, he writes again: "Denise writes me extravagant letters. She asks for enormous sums of money. She threatens to sue me and so on."

In all this, it is difficult to believe that there was any real hope of a *rapprochement* for some years before 1971. In *Mémoires intimes*, Simenon recounts the many telephone calls and urgent messages that poured in

★Denise's version of the genesis of *Un oiseau pour le chat* is totally different. According to her, it had nothing to do with getting money from Simenon, but was instigated years later (1977) by the publishers of the book.

213

from his wife throughout the late sixties, souring his life and imposing a strain on him that was intolerable. She claims that, apart from two bouts at Echandens, she had no serious drinking problem until 1968. "I had never taken a drink alone before that year," she says, "and then I thought, 'After all, if I'm bound to live alone and I'd like a drink of whisky, why shouldn't I have it?' It's only in the late sixties, early seventies that I had my alcoholic bout when I drank to forget and I couldn't forget."

One cannot accept this. Nor can one accept the veracity of the incident that she claims, in *Un oiseau pour le chat*, occurred on the last occasion that she says she was alone with her husband. She says that it was on December 13, 1971, when she visited Epalinges to talk to Simenon about their children. He refused to discuss them with her. "It is I who occupy mysef with the children. You are only a whore!" He raised his hand to strike her and she seized a heavy stone ashtray to defend herself. "You see this ashtray, Jo? If you don't lower your arm and stop insulting me, you'll get it right in your face!" She claims that he lowered his arm and slumped into a chair in front of her. "On that day I knew that when you show yourself strong, Simenon abdicates," are the words with which she ends her book.

There is no mention of any such meeting, either before or after the event, in the two letters that Simenon wrote to Dr. Martinon of the 9th and 20th of that same month. Simenon maintains that he has not seen his estranged wife – apart from Marie-Joe's funeral in June 1978 – since 1970.

Why then have they not divorced? "Because it would cost me a fortune," says Simenon. "She does not want to divorce me because she wants to hang on for such inheritance she thinks she may be able to claim as my widow. I do not want to divorce her because it would mean calling doctors to give evidence about her condition and that they forbade her to live under my roof. I've no wish to do that. It's impossible. And besides, there is a jurisprudence here in Switzerland that says that, once a woman has been married to a man for a certain number of years, the husband has to guarantee her the same standard of living as when they were together. We last lived together at Epalinges, where we had eleven staff and the chef had a big white hat! It would cost me a very great deal of money – which would be money lost to the children."

So they remain man and wife – with a financial settlement that ensures her 15,000 Swiss francs (£1,875) a month, two comfortable homes and all her medical expenses paid for her. Even so, when she

...imenon (*née* Ouimet) Henriette Simenon, mother of G.S.

...ty house at Epalinges, 1979

G.S. with the young Marie-Jo

(*above*) a year or two before her
1978; and in 1968, aged 15

Some cinema 'Maigrets':
Pierre Renoir (*left*) in *La Nuit du carrefour*, 1932

Jean Gabin with Annie Girardot
in *Maigret tend un piège*, 1957

Michel Simon in the role in *Brelan d'as*, 1952

Charles Laughton as Maigret in
The Man on the Eiffel Tower, 1948

e Signoret and Jean Gabin in *Le Chat*, 1970

Unveiling the statue of Maigret at Delfzijl, September 1966
G.S. (*second from left*) with four TV 'Maigrets':
Rupert Davies (GB), Heinz Ruhmann (Germany), Jan Teuling
(Holland), Gino Cervi (Italy)

Maigret's 'home' at 130 Blvd. Richard-Lenoir, Paris;
he lived on the non-existent fourth floor

menon

Régine Simenon at La Richardière, 1980

photograph of Teresa taken in April 1979

G.S. at home in the 'little pink house' in Lausanne, April 1979

sent her stepson Marc a telegram for his birthday, it had to be paid for by the recipient. The marriage that was conceived with such frenzied passion in a hotel bedroom in New York survives in barren legality because it would be too expensive for either party to try and gain their freedom. The chains of lust have given way to the chains of monetary consideration.

There are three other events in the life of Simenon in the sixties that need to be chronicled.

The first is the visit, in November 1965, of his mother, then aged 85, to Epalinges. It has its own bitter-sweet quality, for, from the start, she showed that her doubting attitude to her only-surviving, famous son had not changed. Gazing around the frigid splendour of his magnificent new home, she asked him: "Why do you have so many servants in the house, Georges?"; and she anxiously enquired of a member of the staff: "Do you think the house is paid for?"; and again: "Don't you think my son has debts?"

She remained an indomitable matriarch. On her first day, she had lunch in her room because she was still tired from the journey (Simenon had thoughtfully sent Joyce Aitken, his secretary, to accompany her all the way from Liège) and she was supposed to take a little nap. However, when she had still not reappeared some time later, one of the maids went to see what was wrong. She found the old lady sitting, very shaken, on a chair, her face covered with blood, and clutching some tiny bags of gold coins in her hands. Beside her on the floor, lay a wardrobe fallen on its side. She had tried to climb up on the baseboard of the wardrobe to hide the bags on one of the upper shelves, but had missed her footing and the heavy piece of furniture had fallen on her. Luckily, her injuries were not too severe. But the bags of gold coins? Each bore the name of one of Simenon's four children. After working all her life "to provide for her old age," she had brought with her part of the fruits of her "scrimpings", to use her son's rather unpleasant expression, for her grandchildren. Each in its own little bag.

Nor was that all. Later that same day, her face wiped clean of blood and the colour somewhat returned to her pallid skin, she visited Simenon in his immaculate, ultra-modern office and handed him an envelope. It contained all the money he had sent her month after month over the past forty years, since the time that he had left her, newly widowed, waving goodbye to him on the station platform at Liège.

"You wanted to be poor, you wanted to make sure of ending your life in dignity, but you didn't want to be beholden to anyone for anything, not even, perhaps especially not, to your son," Simenon was to write in *Lettre à ma mère* after her death six years later.

The second event has little to do with dignity. It took place shortly after Mme. Simenon's visit to Epalinges, during the Christmas period. Marc and his young family were staying in the house. It was a convivial occasion. Marc had brought with him a video of his first film as a director to show his father. Simenon was much moved. He promptly gave Marc the film rights in one of his volumes of short stories, *Les dossiers de l'Agence O* ("The Files of the 'O' Agency"), published by Gaston Gallimard during the war (and which Marc was later to make into a television series). They had all had a fine dinner, with much drink, to celebrate. Everyone had dispersed to their own quarters in the vast house when Simenon was taken by an urgent need to go to the lavatory. He repaired to the small toilet that was *en suite* with his office and which he normally only used, as he says, "to make *pipi*". This time his need was more robust.

He accomplished his mission and then, in typical Continental style, felt the need to wash himself adequately in a *bidet*. Since the lavatory was not really intended for anything other than *pipi*, there was none. So, in his post-prandial condition, he tried to hoist his bare bottom onto the handbasin. Result: he slipped and fell heavily to the ground, breaking no less than seven ribs. He lay there for some time moaning until finally Teresa, alone of all the people in the house, came to his aid. At once she took command of the situation, called the doctor, got Simenon carried carefully upstairs to his bedroom, where she undressed him, put him to bed and then sat beside him all night.

For three weeks, he was in hospital – with Teresa sleeping on a camp bed beside him in his private room. When they returned to Epalinges, he installed a camp bed for her in his bedroom, for he still had need of her constant attention and nursing. For the past several months, his health had been in low ebb as a consequence of all the pressures and strains to which the situation with Denise had subjected him. Seven broken ribs on top of all that, plus (no doubt) the effect of his hypochondriac nature, served to ensure that his new-found nurse had a heavy responsibility on her shoulders. For Simenon, it was like a revelation of virtue: "From the camp bed, she passed into my bed," he says simply in *Un homme comme un autre*. "And so, little by little, our love was born. I am suspicious of this word 'love'. I use it less and less. I would prefer to say, 'Our union was born'."

It is said that Napoleon Bonaparte lost the Battle of Waterloo because of an attack of piles. Simenon found true love because he tried to wash his bottom, after going to the lavatory, in a handbasin. The ways of the Almighty really are strange.

The third event that needs to be related is of an altogether different nature.

By the mid-sixties, the character of Maigret had already achieved its paramount position in detective fiction. He was famous throughout the world and actors as varied as Charles Laughton – in a somewhat bizarre American film version of the early *La Tête d'un homme* (under the title "The Man on the Eiffel Tower", which does not figure at all in the original novel!) – Harry Baur, the great French-Jewish actor killed by the Germans during World War Two, and Jean Gabin had played the part on the cinema screen. The British actor, Rupert Davies, had virtually ruined his career for all other roles by being so exclusively identified with Maigret in no less than fifty-two films for BBC Television, and Jean Richard had made himself a household face in France through his performance (still continuing into the eighties) in the role on French television.

Despite the frequently quoted statement that he has never watched Maigret on either cinema or television screen, Simenon has his own very strong views on many of the actors who have played the part. "The three best Frenchmen have been Pierre Renoir, the very first one, because he understood that Maigret was a civil servant and made him behave like one; Michel Simon, who, although he played the part only once, was quite an extraordinary Maigret; and, of course, Jean Gabin, who I don't think ever saw a police *commissaire* such as Maigret in action and was really rather too sloppy in his personal appearance, with his tie not properly done up and that sort of thing, yet invested the role with his own singular authority.

"Jean Richard may be 'Maigret' for most French people because of all those television films, but for me he is quite honestly the worst. He is very bad. He acts as if he has seen too many American films with gangsters and gigolos. He will arrive at an old lady's or wherever wearing his hat and not take it off. He doesn't say, 'Good morning' but just 'Commissaire Maigret'. He goes on smoking and keeps his hat on all the time he's there – and he leaves in the same way. That shocked me. A Divisional Commissaire – that's equivalent to a Super-intendent at Scotland Yard – does have a certain amount of education.

He knows that you don't visit people with your hat on and smoking a pipe.

"Of the non-French 'Maigrets', Charles Laughton did his best but was really rather terrible. Gino Cervi, the Italian actor, was very good. But it was Rupert Davies, who was really the best. I would put him on a par with Michel Simon. I got to know him – and his wife and children – very well. He was a very nice man and he did his best to feel his way into the part. I remember him visiting me at Echandens before he began the series and asking me to explain how Maigret behaved with his pipe, and all that.

"One thing was rather amusing. I remember him saying to me: 'Madame Maigret, as soon as she hears Maigret's footsteps on the stairs coming home, opens the door to him. It's as if she felt he was coming and he never needs to use his key. But what does Maigret do when he sees her? Should he kiss her or what?' I got the young chambermaid to come over and did this . . ." he gives a practical demonstration of smacking her bottom – "and Rupert Davies, who was very English, blushed! 'That's what you must do,' I said, and that's how I showed him. It was only an affectionate gesture . . . nothing sexual . . . but all the same you could see that he had some difficulty in doing it. Yet he really was very good!

"The best 'Madame Maigret' in my opinion, even including the French ones, was the 'Madame Maigret' on Japanese television. She was exactly right."

In September 1966, Simenon received unique public acknowledgment of the universal fame of Maigret when he unveiled at Delfzijl, the small northern Dutch seaport where his character was "born", a massive bronze statue of the famous detective. Fourteen of his publishers from around the world and no less than five television "Maigrets" – Jean Richard, Rupert Davies, Gino Cervi, Heinz Ruhmann from Germany and Jan Teuling from Holland – stood by among the large crowd. Speeches were made, photographs were taken, homilies were uttered. Replicas of that impressive faceless statue are now to be seen at Régine's home at Nieul and on the bookshelves of John's London office, Marc's country home at Poigny-la-Forêt, and Denise's Swiss chalet at Begnins above Lausanne (although she was not present at the ceremony and it was Teresa who accompanied Simenon, discreetly in the background).

But as the plaudits rang out in the brisk Dutch air at Delfzijl, the superb talent that was being fêted was already, unknown to all those present – except perhaps to Simenon – grievously in decline.

DEATH OF A MARRIAGE

The time has now come to stand back for a while from the narrative and study the demise of a genius, not the physical death of a man but the slow attrition of his talent. Everything wears out in time and, although he has never brought himself fully to admit it, Simenon's creative imagination wore out in the sixties under attack from within and without.

CHAPTER 19

Death of a Talent

The slow death of Simenon's literary genius that occurred in the sixties has been masked outside France and his native Belgium by the inevitable time lag between the first appearance of his books in French and then – often many years later – in translation. Penguin Books, for instance, brought out in time for the Christmas trade in 1981 a new collection called "Maigret's Christmas", containing nine Maigret stories which had never before been published in Britain in paperback, but whose publication dates in France went back as far as 1947. Over the decades Simenon's output has been so vast that Roger Stephane, in his study *Le Dossier Simenon*★, could estimate in 1961 that a new Simenon book appeared somewhere in the world every third day. The figure would now not be so great but, even so, many, if not most, of the millions of people who read him in translation probably do not realise that he is no longer writing novels.

Even in France, the average reader, so used to seeing Simenon's quizzical face (photographed some years ago in late middle-age) staring out at him from behind the eternal pipe on the back of innumerable paperbacks in hundreds of bookshops and bookstalls, might find it hard to believe that his last non-Maigret novel was written in October 1971 and his last Maigret in February 1972.

He seems by now timeless, part of the literary fabric of the twentieth century. New films, whether for television or cinema, based on his novels are constantly being released in many parts of the world. Adaptations of his stories continue to be read on British radio and elsewhere. In France, his *Mémoires intimes*, published in the autumn of 1981, was a phenomenal success. Two book clubs competed for its distribution, it appeared in *L'Express* magazine's bestseller list for many weeks, and was selected by the literary review *Lire* as one of the "Twenty Best Books of the Year". Admittedly, as *Lire* says, "It is not

★("The Simenon File"), P. Laffont, 1961.

a literary work but an extraordinary document on the last 'sacred monster' of French literature" – nevertheless he remains *a name*.

Yet so far as his skills *as a novelist* are concerned – not his undoubted ability as a memoirist, telling the facts of his own life with apparently scathing honesty – his fame is solidly based on achievements that are long since past.

What is overlooked in most assessments of Simenon's work, at least outside France, is that the extinction of his great talent as a writer of fiction came comparatively early. Most informed French critics would agree with the view expressed by Maurice Dubourt* that his "last good novel" was *Le Chat* ("The Cat"), written in October 1966, when he was sixty-three. That is not old for a writer of fiction. It is true that Balzac, to whom the French most often compare Simenon (he has himself given interviews in which, separated by the passage of years, he has both said that he accepts and rejects the comparison), was dead at the age of fifty-one and, among the ranks of detective-story writers, although she lived on into her eighties, Agatha Christie's fame is almost exclusively based on books that she wrote in her forties and fifties. But Tolstoy wrote *Resurrection* at the age of seventy-two, Somerset Maugham wrote *Catalina* at seventy-four and Graham Greene is still a working novelist in his late seventies. It has not worked like that for Simenon. The nearest parallel that comes to mind is Ernest Hemingway, who also felt his inspiration running dry in his early sixties but who chose the route of despair with a bullet for his final exit. "Hemingway died yesterday," comments Simenon in *Quand j'étais vieux*. "I feel upset by it. I never met him. I read little of him. Nevertheless he was one of those with whom I felt a bond."

In *Le Chat*, there is not the slightest sign of a waning of powers. It is a magisterial novel, later brought tellingly to the screen by Pierre Granier-Deferre with Jean Gabin and Simone Signoret giving fine performances. It is the tale of two old people, a husband and wife, living alone together in a large house, locked into each other's existence by a bond of steely hatred. They no longer communicate with each other except in writing. They each prepare their own food, from their own larder locked with a key, and wait for the kitchen to be empty before they will eat. They fear the one is trying to poison the other, and when the husband suspects that his wife has killed his cat, he kills her parrot.

Finally, he escapes from the house and finds for a short while another woman who will give him solace and a home; but he is drawn

*In *Simenon*, published by L'Age d'Homme, Lausanne, in 1980.

back to the silent house of hatred. Then his wife dies and that very day he falls ill. He is taken to hospital and the last line of the novel is: "I was no longer anything."

It is a masterpiece. A review of the American version of the book in *Newsweek* described Simenon as "a master not only of the terse, paragraphic Parisian snapshot but also of the art of embellishing a single simple idea with the impedimenta of universality." In no way does it detract from Simenon's achievement but, unbeknown to everyone at the time, that "single simple idea" had a basis in fact: it was, in essence, the story of Simenon's mother's second marriage. Henriette, forever seeking the security of a pension, of which her uninsured first husband's death had deprived her, married again, years after Simenon had left Liège. He was a retired tram conductor on the North Belgian Railway, who had his own house and a State pension for his widow. He did not long survive before heart disease and old age took him off; but in the same house in which she used to have so many student lodgers, Henriette and Père André ("Father André", as he was known; André was his surname) were reduced to writing each other notes and guarding their own separate food in locked larders. For his greatest art, Simenon has always drawn more or less direct from life.

Of the eighteen more novels, equally divided between Maigrets and non-Maigrets, that Simenon was to write after *Le Chat*, none has anything like its stature. There are passages of felicity in the language and occasional flashes of the old intuitive genius, but for the most part they are no better or no worse than any other competent storywriter could have produced. Granted that his output would, as he grew older, inevitably have declined in quantity – by the late sixties he was down to two or three novels a year – why this sudden descent in terms of quality into the second-rate?

The decade had begun in good form. In October 1962, while still at Echandens, he had written one of the most acclaimed non-Maigret novels in the whole canon of his work: *Les Anneaux de Bicêtre* (published in Britain as "The Patient" and in the United States as "The Bells of Bicêtre"). It is a *tour de force*, worthy to set beside *La fuite de Monsieur Monde* which, in feel, it somewhat resembles. It tells the story of René Maugras, the editor-in-chief of a leading French newspaper, who suffers a stroke while at the peak of his career and is reduced to the state of a cabbage, lying paralysed and mute in a bed at the Bicêtre Hospital while his brain remains undimmed and he knows all that is going on around him.

His flight, in the style of Monsieur Monde, is into himself. As he lies immobile and helpless, his mind plunges into nostalgia. "Perhaps on account of the sunlight, glowing sumptuously red, which he could see from his bed, the two stories he told himself were brimful of light, warmth and well-being."

The first was of a delightful day out in the countryside with his first wife, Marcelle, the two of them slightly tipsy from a meal at a country inn. They had come upon a lonely stretch of the River Loire. They drank again from a bottle of wine they had brought with them. Then:

> Drowsy with the heat, they lay down on the sand, amidst the whispering reeds . . . His skin, burning hot, had the wholesome smell of country sweat. Everything smelt good, the reeds, the earth, the river. And the wine, once it was cooled, had a taste he had never met with again. He had chewed a blade of grass, lying on his back, his hands behind his neck, his gaze lost in the blue depths of the sky, where an occasional bird passed.
> . . . He remembered one gesture, his hand groping at his side, touching sand and then Marcelle's body. He felt so lazy that he took a long time to make up his mind and slide over on top of her . . . They stayed for a long time, almost motionless, like certain insects you see mating, and he felt the sun on his back, heard the lapping sound of the water, the shivering of the reeds . . .
> That was all. Afterwards, they finished the bottle. They tried to lie down again and recover the state of grace they had just experienced without seeking it.
> The spell was broken. The air had grown cooler.

The second incident occurred when he was on his own, crossing on "a boat with a yellow funnel" to the island of Porquerolles:

> When the boat slid away from its moorings he stood in the bows, leaning over the transparent water. For a long time he was able to see down to the bottom and for the space of half an hour he lived in music, as though at the heart of a symphony.
> That morning was like nothing he had ever experienced since. It was his great discovery of the world, of a boundless, radiant world of bright colours and thrilling sounds . . . He was drunk without the help of wine.
> . . . He had often been back to the Mediterranean seaboard. He had seen other seas equally blue, trees and flowers that were more extraordinary, but the magic had gone, and of all his discoveries, this was the only one to have left a trace.

Maugras reflects upon the fact that, on both occasions, water, sunshine, heat, fresh smells combined to work their wondrous effect – "and both times, too, irrational panic and a sullen homeward journey." The one word to sum up both experiences would be *innocence*

(Simenon's italics) and Maugras asks himself the question: "Was twice in a lifetime enough?"

During the eight days in hospital covered in the novel, Maugras changes from a dying man to someone who will return to a fuller life than he has ever known before. From his voyage into himself, he knows, as does Monsieur Monde, that there is no other meaning to life than life itself: "Even if he had not found any answers, he had asked himself questions, too many questions perhaps, and these would always dwell with him."

Yet even at this moment of triumph for Simenon, something was already wrong with his working mechanism. In a pre-publication interview in the French newspaper *Combat*, he speaks with all his accustomed braggadocio about the "concision and the precision" that went into the writing of the book and how he "cut, cut" so that, in the end, the five hundred pages announced by his publishers had become only three hundred and fifty. "The comma of the last phrase gave me the most trouble. It is a simple phrase: 'One day, he will go to see his father at Fécamp, with Lina.' If I leave the comma, Maugras remains alone and the novel finishes badly; if I delete it, Lina (his second wife) comes back to him, everything starts up again and the novel finishes well." "And what have you chosen?" asks the interviewer. "I deleted it," says Simenon. "But just a little flourish of the pencil and you would have had a different novel . . ."

It is a pleasing anecdote, but if one checks the text of the novel in both the French and English versions one sees that, in fact, the comma is there! Despite all that he says in the interview, the novel *does* finish badly.

Nineteen sixty-four saw the writing of the novel about which Simenon himself has said: "If I were allowed to keep only one of all my novels, I would choose this one." It is called *Le Petit Saint* ("The Little Saint") and is remarkable for containing no mystery, no dead body, no murder. It was written some months after Denise had finally been persuaded to leave Epalinges. A tremendous feeling of relief swept over Simenon. He wrote only two novels that year: a run-of-the-mill Maigret and this one, on completion of which he exulted, "At long last I have done it! With each successive novel for at least twenty years I have been trying to exteriorise a certain optimism that is in me, a *joie de vivre*, a delight in the immediate and simple communion with all that

224

surrounds me, and to attain, in order to describe such a state, to some
kind of serenity. However, after the first third or half my earlier novels
invariably turned into tragedy. For the first time, I was able to create,
in *Le Petit Saint*, a perfectly serene character, in immediate contact
with nature and life."

It is undoutedly an idealised self-portrait, although he says that in
many ways the painter Marc Chagall was the real-life model. "The
Little Saint" is the nickname given to the book's hero, Louis Heurteau,
by his schoolmates because of the serenity with which, even as a child,
he accepts the buffetings of life. "That's what his classmates call him,"
says his mother. "Because he lets himself get knocked around without
defending himself. All he does is put up his arms to protect himself,
and then he refuses to tell the teacher who hit him." Why did he not hit
back? This is Louis' explanation: "The blows didn't hurt much. After
a few seconds, he didn't feel anything and there was no point getting
involved in a fight. Someday they would tire of always picking on the
same one and would let him daydream in his corner. He didn't like
people to bother about him, didn't like to be asked questions, to be
torn from his thoughts of the moment."

And so he continues throughout his life. One of his brothers is killed
in the First World War, his sister becomes fat and callous, another
brother dies in prison, a third lives with his wife in South America and
spends his time hunting butterflies and birds of paradise. His mother,
who has brought him up by her own efforts because he is illegitimate
and his father soon de-camped, enjoys "what is good in life, contenting
herself uncomplainingly with what is less good, and ignoring the rest
as if it did not exist." He lives through all of this, and by the end of the
book has become a famous painter – at which stage, he asks himself,
"Had he not taken something from everything and everyone? Had he
not used their substance?"

> He didn't know, he mustn't know, otherwise he would be unable to
> carry on to the end.
> He continued to walk with little steps, to smile.
> "May I ask you, Maître, how you see yourself?"
> He did not reflect very long. His face lit up for a moment as he said
> joyously and modestly:
> "As a small boy."

And so the book ends on a note that to some will seem mawkishly
sentimental, as indeed will the book as a whole. Yet it was a considerable success both in France and abroad, and at least one British

critic (John Raymond) commented that although it was "a novel of sentiment", it was "too briskly told and too crisply written" to be sentimental.

There was only one other novel of consequence before *Le Chat* ran down the shutter on his brilliance, and that was *La Mort d'Auguste* ("The Old Man Dies"), written in March 1965, seven months before *Le Chat*. The *Auguste* of the title is 78-year-old Auguste Mature, who opened a restaurant in the Les Halles district of Paris, near the old fruit and vegetable market, in the days before the First World War when, as a young man, he arrived in the capital from his native Auvergne. Called "Chez l'Auvergnat" and specialising in the cuisine of Auguste's native region, it has become one of the celebrated "little restaurants" of Paris, with a varied and discerning clientele.

The novel opens on a night when the restaurant, as usual, is crowded and the British Ambassador is dining with a party. Auguste has long since handed over the day-to-day running of the business to Antoine, one of his three sons; but he is still there every night, strolling from table to table, like the classical old restaurateur he is. But on this night, as he is talking to two young customers, he collapses at their table, dragging with him to the floor the red and white checked tablecloth to which he is clinging.

He is carried upstairs to his large old double bed in his apartment above the restaurant, in which his wife, one year older than him, is already sleeping. Senile and "no longer in her right mind", she hardly stirs as her husband, still barely breathing, is undressed and put into bed beside her. With her still unknowing, he dies during the night and the drama of the novel unfolds.

Antoine and his brothers can find no will. The old man, with a peasant's cunning, had always kept the true extent of his finances from them, but the restaurant was highly successful and they believed him to have amassed quite a fortune. But how to get access to it?

Antoine discovers that Auguste had had a "business adviser", whom he had trusted implicitly because, like him, he had come from the Auvergne. But he is disturbed because he also discovers that this man had died in prison, where he had been sent for fraud.

The only clue to the whereabouts of their father's "fortune" is the key to a safe deposit box that they find in his wallet. They go through various legal formalities and finally manage to open the box – to discover that the "business adviser" had indeed cheated the old man. The stocks that the box contains are valueless.

Antoine, who (unlike his brothers) has gained in stature throughout

226

the novel, realises that his father, when he discovered the truth, had not lodged a complaint against the man who had betrayed him because that would have been to admit his naivety and to have lost face with his sons who would then have known that he was not leaving them the inheritance that they expected.

"He had worked all his life, ever since the age of twelve, to accumulate a fortune, counting every sou, and all that remained of it was the restaurant, which was really run by Antoine. He had lived for months with a sense of shame, knowing that when he was gone he would leave behind him bitterness instead of regret.

"Antoine had the feeling that he had never understood his father so well, his peasant character, his humbleness and pride."

The elegiac note has much in common with that with which Simenon was nine years later to end his *Lettre à ma mère*: "What stood between you and me was the merest nothing. That nothing was your ferocious need to be good, in the eyes of others, but most of all perhaps in your own."

Back in Lakeville, Simenon had told American literary editor Carvell Collins that entering into the skin of his characters and living their lives with them, while he was writing his books, became "almost unbearable after five or six days. That is one of the reasons my novels are so short; after eleven days I can't go on – it's impossible. It's physical. I am too tired." But that was when he was in his early fifties, when he was in rigorous good health, with everything seemingly going well in his life. How much more must his writing have taken out of him ten years later, when his personal life was in tatters, his drinking had become a problem and the whole physical framework of his body was beginning to give way under the strain – not to mention the added hazard of seven broken ribs that had not mended too well?

He could still put on a good performance, when necessary. Writing to him in June 1965 after a "wonderful afternoon you gave the family and me at your beautiful house and swimming pool, not forgetting the superb lunch and the superb wine," Charles Chaplin paid tribute to "the stimulation of your 'magical self'." Signing himself "With admiration and affection, Charlie", he wrote: "In spite of your misfortune, nothing has dimmed your amazing vitality. We can all be happy and grateful that you are your usual self and that you have recovered from your accident."

But the truth was more sombre. By 1966, Simenon was suffering from increasingly frequent fits of giddiness, caused by Meunier's disease, and from pains in the chest produced by a recurrence of his aerophagia, which was itself nervous in origin. In the following year, his doctors diagnosed that he was suffering from an abdominal hernia, which he had almost certainly had from childhood and accounted for the habitual bouts of vomiting with which he had been plagued, at moments of creation, throughout his writing career. That too was nervous in origin and the symptoms became more acute as he found himself in his middle sixties.

He began to feel less assured than in the past. In June 1967, in a rare preface to one of his novels, a perfunctory work called *Le Déménagement* ("The Neighbours"), he actually felt the need to explain why the book was so short:

> Certain critics, rare it is true, certain foreign publishers used to fine big books, really thick ones, have reproached me for only writing short novels.
> This one is particularly short. I could have spun out its length. I would have considered myself, if I acted in that way, guilty of cheating my readers and myself.

One wonders if that is completely true. He was by now losing nearly two pounds in weight a day through the expenditure of nervous and physical energy that writing a book cost him. When the Swiss psychiatrists came to visit him at Epalinges in 1968 for *Simenon sur le gril*, he found himself at the end of the day as exhausted as if he had written the chapter of a new book, his clothing drenched with sweat. In that same year, he decided to make no more long journeys abroad; he had lost his appetite for travel, finding it too strenuous. On October 1, 1969, he wrote to Jean Martinon at Cannes: "I have the impression that I am not ageing quickly but nevertheless I find it more tiring to write my novels. Perhaps that is because they are becoming more difficult."

The simple truth is that he *was* tired. He was becoming written out – which in itself is hardly surprising, although he is unlikely ever to admit it. His personal life was still unhappy. Teresa remained officially a servant until he left Epalinges, which was not until the autumn of 1972; although in *Mémoires intimes* he describes her all-important role in his life at that time as if she were already his third "wife". His health was not good. Denise was still a perpetual source of sadness and anguish. Even his beloved Maigret had lost his sparkle for him; the last

Maigret novels are clockwork, automatic things with sloppiness in the plotting and a palpable disenchantment on Simenon's part for all the new "gadgetry" of forensic science with which a modern policeman would have to work. When Maigret talks, in *Maigret et l'affaire Nahour* ("Maigret and the Nahour Case"), written in February 1966, about a "paraffin test that can reveal crusts of powder on the skin up to five days after a shot has been fired", it just does not sound convincing.

Professor Jean Fabre of Montpellier University makes the point that the very titles of some of the post-war Maigrets suggest that the detective, and maybe also his creator, are engaged more and more in a confrontation with new methods and new techniques that are not to the liking of either of them. *Maigret a peur* ("Maigret Afraid") and *Maigret se trompe* ("Maigret's Mistake") date back to Lakeville days, but *Un echec de Maigret* ("Maigret's Failure") came from Cannes and the very first novel that Simenon wrote upon moving into the wonder house at Epalinges was *Maigret se défend* ("Maigret on the Defensive") – a title not without significance if Maigret *is* Simenon's *alter ego*. In January 1968, the year that Simenon gave up all substantial foreign travel, he wrote *Maigret hésite* ("Maigret Hesitates").

"If he were still in the police force today, Maigret would at once resign," Simenon told an interviewer in the late seventies. And that is undoubtedly true. "There are no Maigrets today," says M. Marcel Leclerc, who in 1981 was *Chef du Brigade Criminelle de Paris* (Chief of the Paris C.I.D.), the last rank that Maigret held. "Maigret's method of investigation is very 'individualised', so to speak. One gets the impression that only Maigret pulls the strings, like a *deus ex machina*. While in fact today the *Brigade Criminelle* works as a group. Its *chef* co-ordinates the work of all his collaborators but he doesn't play a major part. I have got 110 civil servants working with me.

"The police have changed at the same pace as society. Maigret does not exist any longer because he works like a craftsman, while the modern policeman takes advantage of all sorts of means, materially speaking, which require the contribution of several people."

By the early seventies, although some literary critics remained loyal to the old detective, there were increasingly those who, from their own stance, shared this senior policeman's view. "One must have the courage to say it, and so much the worse for the faithful who will complain," wrote a reviewer in *L'Actualité* magazine in December 1970 about one of the last Maigret novels, *La Folle de Maigret* ("Maigret and the Madwoman"), "but Commissaire Maigret does not exist any more. Georges Simenon, worn out by so many books, and today's society, which, like the police itself, functions by computer, has killed him." "The new book by Simenon is not to be classed among his best," wrote Jacques de Ricaumont in the influential *Nouvelles Littéraires* in October 1972 about *Maigret et M. Charles* ("Maigret and Monsieur Charles"), which turned out to be the last Maigret – and the last novel – that Simenon ever wrote. "One has the impression that the author is out of breath and that his hero is fading away . . . This is really a third-rate Maigret." Noelle Loriot in *L'Express* was no more complimentary. "Here is Simenon's latest book, *Maigret et M. Charles*, a police thriller so alarmingly bad that one wonders what would have happened to it, if it had been the manuscript of some unknown 'Mr. Smith' who has sent it in to the publishers? Refused for mediocrity, lack of action and feebleness of style? Probably."

It was not only the Maigrets that were receiving an unsympathetic Press. (*Quand j'étais vieux* was well received when it came out in 1970, but of course it was not a work of fiction.) His other novels did still get some good reviews but more and more were like that written by François Lourbet in *L'Actualité* in April 1971. Its subject was *La Disparition d'Odile* ("The Disappearance of Odile"), a sadly prophetic book about a young girl who runs away from home, just as Simenon's beloved daughter Marie-Jo was to do only five months later. "You are, they say, very rich," wrote Lourbet. "You are, most certainly, famous. Nothing could possibly add to your fortune or your glory. And I have the impression – from reading *Quand j'étais vieux* – that you have from time to time been afraid: has Simenon disappeared? Let me remove from you this doubt which torments you. Georges Simenon has truly disappeared. So, Monsieur, for mercy's sake, find him again for our pleasure and for your inner peace. Or cease to write . . ."

In January 1971, Simenon's mother died in Liège and, with Teresa waiting patiently for him back at their hotel, he had sat beside Henriette in her last long week of agony. At that time, the pressures building up on Simenon were horrendous; and when nine months later Marie-Jo ran away from Prangins, the same psychiatric clinic where her mother had for so long been a patient – for she had, alas, inherited some of Denise's mental instability – it must really have seemed to the ageing writer as if his whole world was crashing in on him.

Following exactly the same path as John four years earlier, Marie-Jo went to Paris to seek the protection of Marc. "I shall never forget her phone call from the clinic," he says. " 'Marc, I am going to make an escape', she said. Why did she not go to her father at Epalinges instead of to me in Paris? Because it was from *Epalinges* that she was escaping, not so much from the clinic! She could have walked out of there at any time. She adored her father, but her mother had by then said so many horrible things to her about him, blackening him, saying what a horrible man he was, that Marie-Jo really did not know what the truth was any more. She had to get away." Some months later, Simenon wrote to Jean Martinon: "The doctors advised me to let her do what she wants. She came back a fortnight later for a few days. She wants to join the Paris Drama School and now she lives in a studio flat on the Boulevard de la Madeleine. She lives with a young actor. She phones me every four days. She sounds happy, more sensible and balanced than a few months ago.

"Obviously, I would have preferred another sort of cure. But she is determined to fight for her freedom. She is 18 years old now. You would not recognise her."

The patriarch who loved his children with an intensity they could not bear was left alone in the vast mansion at Epalinges with only the twelve-year-old Pierre and Teresa for company.

After this letter to Dr. Martinon in December 1971, Simenon wrote only one more novel: the mauled *Maigret et M. Charles*, which he completed the following February. Seven months then passed without his even attempting to write another book. His bouts of giddiness were troubling him. He and Teresa spent most of the summer at Valmont, a luxurious hotel-clinic in the tree-covered hills above Montreux where he was often wont to take refuge – that is his word – from the world. "One could say that all of a sudden my cares of those past years weighed upon me with a burden that was both painful and heavy," he was to write later in *Mémoires intimes*.

Then on September 18, 1972, a national holiday in Switzerland when no one else was at work, he went into his office at Epalinges at nine o'clock in the morning, three hours later than his usual time, and wrote on a brand new manila envelope the one word "Victor". That was the title he had decided on for his new book (at least, that is what he says in *Mémoires intimes*. In *Un homme comme un autre*, dictated seven years earlier, he says that the name of this projected novel was to have been "Oscar". As so often, wittingly or otherwise, he creates a mystery in his life.

He sat there and looked at the word – whichever it was – and nothing else came. No visions of the characters, not even the glint of a possible start to a storyline; the cupboard of his imagination was almost bare. He made one or two notes – but, despite the usual routine, the "Do Not Disturb" sign, the sharpened pencils and the rest, he knew it was not going well. Later, he rejoined Teresa in one of the sitting rooms. She looked up at him anxiously. "*Tout va bien*" ("Everything is all right"), he said, and they had lunch.

Next morning, he tried again and endeavoured to dredge up from his sub-conscious some kind of "turning point" for the book that would allow the narrative to flow. But there was still a blockage. Nothing came. The telephone rang and it was his bank telling him of some new demand from Denise, requesting information about receipts and expenses on their former joint account. He called his lawyer and asked him to deal with it; by now "Victor/Oscar" seemed even further away. He told Teresa: "Tomorrow, if I think then as I do today, I will tell you, yes or no, whether I shall continue to write."

And the next day, he told her: "No. I am not going to write any more. I have written my last novel." Shortly afterwards, he informed her: "We are leaving Epalinges." The two decisions were almost two sides of the same coin; but for the moment only the decision to leave Epalinges was made known to the world. In a long interview in October 1972 with Victor Franco of the Parisian newspaper *France-Soir*, in which not one word about Teresa appears, he said that he was leaving his vast house, selling all his furniture and his paintings, getting rid of his five cars "without regret".* "I look around me now with curiosity," he said in one of the large sitting rooms of Epalinges, drenched in the autumnal sun, "and it is already as if none of this belongs to me any more." He had already chosen his new home: two modern flats, comprising in all seven rooms, that he was having converted into one apartment on the eighth floor of a tower block on the Avenue de la Cour about a mile from the centre of Lausanne, with a magnificent view of Lake Geneva from each room. "I am renewing myself!" he said, with perhaps more exaltation than he was in fact feeling.

Within a month – as always, moving fast, even in his low state, once a decision to change homes had been taken – he had installed himself with Teresa, Pierre and Yole, their Italian maid, in the new apartment. Contrary to his original intention, he did not put Epalinges on the market. For the time being his secretariat would remain there until it too could move down into Lausanne, to a modern apartment converted

*The decision was later changed to put most of the more valuable paintings into store.

into offices. Then, the house would stand empty (as it has done to this day) waiting for his children to decide what to do with it, once he is dead.

In early February 1973, shortly before Simenon's seventieth birthday, a local journalist whom he particularly trusted received a telephone call to visit him at Valmont, where he was staying for a few weeks. "Why? What's it all about?" Henri-Charles Tauxe asked Joyce Aitken, Simenon's secretary, who had made the call. "M. Simenon himself will tell you," she said.

"From now on," Simenon announced to the startled M. Tauxe, who had a world exclusive on his hands, "my passport will bear the words 'without profession' instead of 'novelist'. *Maigret et M. Charles* will be my last novel." He gave as his reason his bouts of giddiness that over the last two years had become intolerable. "To write my novels I must be in 100 per cent good form," he said. "This is for me a deliverance. For the last fifty-five years, I have lived in the skin of my characters. Now I want to live my own life. I have put myself at liberty. I feel myself happy, with a perfect serenity."

The younger Simenon would have known that there is no such thing as perfection and that serenity is a will-o'-the-wisp.

CHAPTER 20

The Key to the Mystery

There he was, under a lowering springtime sky of dark rain-filled clouds, living in the strangely anonymous setting of a modern purpose-built apartment in a block of uninspired architecture looking out over the snow-covered mountains on the other side of Lake Geneva. Even though only four people lived in the apartment, Teresa was still not his openly avowed "wife". Officially, it was father and young son and the two women who looked after them.

What did the future hold for Simenon as he embarked upon his seventies, divested of his large house, many servants and luxurious limousines?

Undoubtedly, there *was* considerable happiness: the happiness of relief, of a burden lifted from his shoulders, of the knowledge that he no longer had to try and measure up to past achievement. "I didn't want to write a false novel and I don't want to kill myself trying to write a true one," he said in September 1973. There was sadness at leaving Maigret. "I feel myself full of remorse for having completely dropped Maigret after 'Maigret and Monsieur Charles'. It is rather as if one has left a friend without shaking his hand."

There was also a nagging emptiness; a feeling that he must, at all costs, fill the void that now existed in the centre of his life. On February 13, 1973, his seventieth birthday, he bought himself a tape recorder. All right! – he was not going to write any more. But he was still going to work. He was still going to continue his search after the truth that had been eluding him all his working life: the truth about himself. Practically every day for the next seven years, he was to sit down and dictate a ragbag collection of memories, reflections on his work and thoughts about day-to-day events, both in his life and in the world at large. The ever-loyal Joyce Aitken would duly transcribe the cassettes; he would revise the draft and, in all, twenty-one volumes of his *Dictées* ("Dictations") were to appear – all during his so-called retirement. In reality, it proved more of a change of direction than an end to a journey.

234

In *Un homme comme un autre*, the first *Dictée*, appear these significant words: "All of my life I have been occupied with others and trying to understand them. Now I struggle to discover the truth about myself, a truth that I thought I knew but I have lost along the way." Sadly for Simenon, it would seem to have proved a profitless search, as sterile as all his previous attempts to solve his own mystery. Back in 1968, he had told the Swiss psychiatrists that he was like his old friend, Charles Chaplin, who once said to him: "When I don't feel right beneath my skin, I write a book or make a film. That takes the place of psychoanalysis and, instead of paying out money, they pay me." Even in his "retirement", Simenon still tried the same public form of profitable self-analysis, first with his *Dictées*, and then with the 617 pages, laboriously written by hand, of his massive *Mémoires intimes*. But it has not worked.

With eight decades of existence behind him, he is still as far from knowing the truth about himself as ever he was. As Edward Behr wrote in a review of *Mémoires intimes* in *Newsweek*: "Nowhere is there an answer to the question that less prolific – and less gifted – writers will be asking themselves for generations to come: how on earth did he do it?"

As for the *Dictées*, apart from the marvellously structured and deeply felt *Lettre à ma mère*, which is not really part of the series but an attempt to delineate once and for all his relationship with his mother, and is the only volume to be published in English, they have received an overwhelmingly bad press:

> A few pleasant aphorisms worth putting down on paper, notably about the education of his children, but not a few useless dilutions, notably the eternal paeans of praise about his third "wife". This becomes frankly fatiguing. *Vers l'Avenir*

> Simenon seized by banality . . . One would believe that Simenon, the novelist, and Simenon, the writer of the intimate journal, are two totally different men. *Tribune de Genève*

> It is necessary to speak frankly about this ninth volume of his dictated memoirs. One hopes it will be the last. *Le Pèlerin*

> There is nothing more dreadful than this false calm of Simenon, this bill-posting of his "non-work", this atrocious attitude of someone withdrawn from inventive life. His narrative of day-to-day events, his family anecdotes, his good jovial tone of a man who "does not get worked up about anything", it is all for me a trick. *Le Parisien*

THE MYSTERY OF GEORGES SIMENON

Despite his exclamations of joy and of gratitude thrown off for Teresa,
his children and the serenity of the beautiful Swiss scenery in which he
walks and lives, Georges Simenon at 76 does not seem a happy man.
L'Echo de la Bourse

But perhaps one of the most hurtful reviews was that which appeared
in *L'Express* in June 1979, dealing with the twelfth volume of dictated
works, *Je suis resté un enfant de chœur* ("I have remained a choir-boy"). It
was written by a long-time admirer of his novels, Angelo Rinaldi, and
its message is poignant: "There have already been eleven volumes of
these *Dictées* and here is the twelfth. They are so many stairs down
which we descend to find the zero level of thought . . . There is nothing
of music, of theatre, of cinema: literature appears only in the form of
some compliment that Gide once paid him . . . The intellectual void is
almost total . . . Simenon has understood everything, except himself."

Marc defends his father. "I think that lots of people did not properly
understand the *Dictées*. They thought he was rather pretentious and
many reviewers said he was saying trivial things. But I think that he
wanted to make people understand that he *is* simple. That he is not a
thinker or a philosopher. And he showed that. As soon as he started
writing philosophy, it became commonplace." Marc is a loyal son,
but that seems almost as specious a claim as some of Simenon's own
explanations for his conduct in the past. The title of the first volume –
Un homme comme un autre ("A man like any other") – sets off this whole
exploration into himself on a false note. As his publisher Claude
Nielsen says: "He is not 'a man like any other'. Perhaps he thinks that
the life he is living now is the life of a man like any other but it is not,
and he can only live as he does now because he has lived another style
of life before. It is false modesty on his part, but he is convinced of
it. Perhaps he is trying to prove that what he did before was only an
artefact in his life as an author and that only now has he found the true
happiness, serenity, stability of life."

In the last decade, Simenon has been as boastful of his total happiness
as he was to Brendan Gill, back in 1952, of his complete contentment
and serenity at Lakeville – three years before abruptly, literally overnight, he decided to leave.

It has been a period of almost complete rejection of the material
attributes of great wealth. In February 1974, only fourteen months
after moving into the large eighth-floor apartment on the Avenue de la
Cour, he moved again – to his thirty-third and, he swears now, his last
home. It is a small house dating back to the eighteenth century with an
enormous 250-year-old cedar tree standing in its garden, in a narrow

mews-type street within a hundred yards of his tower block flat. He still keeps up the apartment but only visits it twice a year, to make the change of his winter and summer clothing, still stored there in the dust-wrapped emptiness. Even when his children or grandchildren visit him, they do not use the apartment but stay in a nearby hotel.

He calls his home "our little pink house" and lives there a life of apparent simplicity and total dependence on Teresa, who, from the moment they moved in, was at last made clear to the world as his wife in all but name. No more subterfuges, no more need for her to call him *Monsieur* and address him in the respectful second person plural *vous* instead of *tu* in front of other people.

The ground floor is almost entirely taken up by one large room that serves as a bedroom/living room for the two of them, with the largest single piece of furniture, his old double bed from Epalinges, placed in a corner. Pierre, his third son and in his early twenties, lives alone (when home from Geneva University) in virtually a self-contained flat on the one upper floor. He seems to have gone through none of the trauma of his older brothers and sister in his relationship with Simenon; like John, he does not visit his mother and his attitude to his aged father is almost like that of a young man to a dearly loved grandfather.

All Simenon's manuscripts★, working papers and professional memorabilia have gone to the Simenon Centre of Studies, set up at Liège University in 1976 through the resourceful efforts of Professor Maurice Piron. He reads no books except for biographies or the occasional technical journal. He does not go to the theatre, the cinema or the concert hall. He turns on the television set only to watch the news or current events programmes. Every day he feeds the three hundred birds that settle in the branches of his cedar tree – although, unless there is a photographer present, he never sits on the bench under the tree as he is continually shown doing in the press (and on the cover of *Mémoires intimes*). That is one more falsehood. He eats only the simplest food; the days of his Belgian trencherman tastes are past.

He and Teresa are in bed every evening by 9.30. She goes everywhere with him and even waits for him when he goes to have his hair cut. His recreation is for the two of them to go for long walks together, tightly arm in arm. "I long ago told him that I did not mind if he went with other women," she says. But he is, at this late stage of his life, and for the first time, totally faithful to one woman.

Denise, although she has never visited the "little pink house" and herself now occasionally practises as a psychiatrist from her second

★ From 1945 onwards (see page 146).

home at Avignon (by a quirk of French law, if someone has been the patient of a psychiatrist long enough, they can take on patients themselves) says: "Do not tell me that Simenon still does not feel something for me. Why then does he still go to bed every night with Teresa in the same bed *we* used to share? I not only think I am the woman he loved the most, but I think I am the only woman he ever really loved. He doesn't love Teresa as a woman. He loves himself, and Teresa hasn't got either the personality or the intelligence to offer him anything but a pool to look into and see his face. *She's a mirror, not a woman.*"

For his part, Simenon, in a typical *Dictée* effusion, says: "For me, an old man who has had the time to think and reflect, love is silence first of all. It is the ability to stay together in the same room without speaking, each one conscious of the other's thoughts . . . it is a hand that unconsciously seeks the other's body in sleep, not for sexual reasons, but only for contact . . . [it is] complete spiritual and physical contact. It is thinking of the same things together, experiencing the same reactions, the same emotions, and seeking the reflection of these emotions in the other's eyes." That is what he claims to have found – at last – with Teresa.

But it is in the reality of his sexual encounters – not in the chimera of his dreams nor the wish fulfilment of his old age – that we must seek the answer to his personal mystery. Within his time at "the little pink house" two events have occurred which stand like signposts along the way. The first is his boast to the world, in 1977, that he had slept with 10,000 women (a claim later extended in one of the *Dictées* to "tens of thousands of women") and the second is the suicide in the following year of his daughter, Marie-Jo. The old storyteller kept back almost to the end the two most revealing incidents in his own personal story.

The legend of the 10,000 women is both amusing and revelatory. In fact, Simenon made the claim twice, both shortly before and shortly after his seventy-fourth birthday, an age when most men have either forgotten, or would prefer to forget, their experiences of the flesh. The first time, in January 1977, was during a discussion that took place between him and Federico Fellini, the Italian film director, in connection with the imminent first public showing of Fellini's latest film, based on the life of Casanova. *L'Express* magazine had the promotable idea that Simenon, the old newspaper man, should interview Fellini on the subject; and the Italian director, who in any event new Simenon well, was happy to travel to Lausanne and talk to him. John Simenon, recently returned from the United States, was in charge of recording their conversation.

The result was a cover story for *L'Express* under the banner headline: "*Fellini-Simenon*. Casanova, our brother . . . An important dialogue on the mystery of artistic creation." It is on the last page of the thirteen–page article that this passage appears:

> *G. Simenon*: You know, Fellini, I believe that, in my life, I have been more Casanova than you! I made the calculation a year or so ago that I have had 10,000 women since the age of thirteen and a half. It wasn't at all a vice. I have not the slightest sexual vice, but I have the need to communicate. And even the 8,000 prostitutes that are to be counted among those 10,000 were human beings, female human beings. I would have liked to know all women. Unfortunately, because of my marriages, I was not able to have true adventures. You wouldn't believe how many times in my life I had to make love "between two doors", in the time between one door closing and the other opening!

What is incredible, in contrast with what happened later, is that the world's press did not pick this up at the time. Even John, watching over the spools of his tape recorder, was not all that impressed. He thought his father "might be bragging a bit", but that was about all.

The "world scoop" that flashed across the international telephone lines and cables and earned Simenon his unique place in the record books for sexual prowess occurred four months later when, in April, Simenon repeated the claim in the course of an otherwise uneventful interview with a reporter from the Zurich German-language newspaper *Die Tat*. He used almost the same words. He said that he had made love to 10,000 women since he was a boy of thirteen "because I wanted to learn the truth. I needed them physically and I also had a need for communication. You only know a woman when you have slept with her.

"If I saw a beautiful woman, my first reaction was: 'How is the expression on your face during orgasm?'

"I chased after that all my life to know which one is the true woman, the one who is all dressed up and wears diamonds or the one who cries out at a certain moment without knowing it. That is the key to a woman. And there I contend that one knows a woman only after one has slept with her. I wanted to know women, I wanted to learn the truth.

"I do not know these women any longer, I have forgotten them . . . but with these 10,000 women I am beginning to know 'the' woman."

Journalist reaction on both sides of the Atlantic was immediate. Associated Press picked up the story and the *Die Tat* interview became an overnight sensation. Simenon had claimed in the course of it that he had checked his amorous career before granting the interview and found the figure of 10,000 was correct. So a journalist from London telephoned Joyce Aitken, his secretary, to ask about it. "He may well have had his tongue in his cheek," she said. "I am sure he wasn't working with a computer."

But Simenon insists that he did *not* have his tongue in his cheek, at the same time dismissing the whole matter as an irrelevance. In *Mémoires intimes*, he says magisterially: "To reply, in passing, to the legends that make of me someone obsessed with sex, I permit myself to comment that I have very normal tastes and I am not the only one to be moved, since my tender adolescence, and still today, by imperious sexual needs." Even so, in one of the later *Dictées* he claims that the real figure for his women is "tens of thousands" and, when questioned as to why he has sought so many sexual experiences, says: "I wrote about women in my novels. I had to know them in order to write about them. Yes, the prostitutes as well. The only way to know a woman is to sleep with her – and it does not matter for how short a time it is."

But he also wrote about men. Has he slept with 10,000 men? "No," he says with a smile, tapping his pipe on the ashtray beside him. "I was never tempted."

That may well be just a flippant answer to a seemingly flippant question, but it may also be a road in to the truth. Oscar Wilde was caught out in cross-examination because, in answer to the question, "Did you ever kiss Walter Grainger?" (one of the young men he was accused of having relations with), he replied: "Oh, no! He was far too ugly!" Simenon's reply that he was never tempted to sleep with men and that is why he did not do it, could be said to expose the hypocrisy, or at best the self-deception, of the reason he gives for sleeping with so many women: that he had to do so "for his art." He slept with a great number of women because he wanted to. That is all. Provided that one is stunted emotionally at around the age of eighteen (although some might well put the age considerably later), promiscuous sexuality can be very enjoyable; there is no need to wrap up one's natural predilection for this pleasurable form of activity with high-sounding phrases. *Unless one is masking from oneself the real reason for doing so.*

For it is, with all respect to Simenon, demonstrably nonsense to claim that to write about women one must know vast numbers of them in circumstances of sexual intimacy. How does it help to "know" a woman – or a man for that matter – to discover whether or not they shout out in the course of sexual intercourse? Are historians doomed never to understand the characters of, say, Elizabeth I (assuming she

240

really was not a virgin), Catherine de Medici or Mary Queen of Scots because they do not know, and never can know, whether they exclaimed in moments of sex? There again, some of the most perceptive observers of women have been homosexuals: Proust and Henry James come immediately to mind. (Beverley Baxter, doyen of London theatre critics in the fifties, once started a review of Terence Rattigan's play, *The Browning Version*, by asking, tongue in cheek, how was it that a "bachelor playwright" could know so much of the mainsprings of a woman's character.)

And there is one other vital circumstance: the women in Simenon's novels are nearly all the same; with the notable exception of Madame Maigret. Apart from that idealised mother-wife of his *alter ego*, Jules Maigret, most of the women he has created are either unimportant or wicked, scheming creatures. Says Annette de Bretagne: "In his books, it's the men who have the primary position; it's not really women at all. But if there are women in the foreground, they are mistresses, wicked women. Let's say they are not very savoury women. He's not very generous to women in his books."

Apart from Madame Maigret, the wife in *Le Chat* and one or two others, he has not created an outstanding female character in all his hundreds of books. As Professor Lucille Becker writes in her study of Simenon: "Women, in [most] of Simenon's novels, serve merely as catalysts, provoking the reactions of the males, since, for the author, it is the destiny of the male that is paramount." Says Annette de Bretagne again: "Women are often rather *bourgeoise* in his writing. Rather wooden characters." So why the need for all that specialised research in the field to ensure his knowledge of women is so varied and complete? As ever, Regine has her own pungent comment: "In his books you find only two kinds of women, the prostitutes and the very good-hearted women who are probably widows, somebody like his mother. Simenon may have known thousands of women, as he says, but I do not think he knows 'a' woman. I think he was very influenced by his mother and for him women are represented by her – when it is not by a prostitute!"

This reference to his mother goes to the root of the real reason for Simenon's womanising; for that is surely what it is, stripped bare of the literary smokescreen that he has built around it. It is not glib amateur psychology to go to his relationship with his mother as a starting-point for an enquiry into his sexuality, for this is the woman who lived so long, while denying him love, and said to him those devastating words: "What a pity, Georges, that it's Christian who had to die." His sexuality has remained stunted, preserved for ever as it was in his teens. For that was when his rebellion against his mother coincided with his own sexual awakening. A psychic crisis occurred then, says André Parinaud, the French critic, as a result of which woman became "both the enemy and the desired object. In order to be possessed, she must also be humiliated to be brought down to the level of the man. Therefore, he wants a woman who has been soiled." That is why, writes Professor Becker, "there are so many men in Simenon's work who are impotent other than with whores, many who even marry whores, and others who become infatuated with fallen women. Sexuality in Simenon's work is always described with the pitiless crudity of this adolescent vision."

But it is not only the vision that is adolescent, it is the sex itself. In all of his writing, whether describing his own love making or that of his characters, there is hardly an instance of a delicate, tender act of communion between two loving human beings. Women, for Simenon, are almost an emetic, a way of achieving quick release. "At heart, I have always had a thirst for tenderness, for giving and receiving," he says in *Un homme comme un autre*; but in reality the sexual acts that he describes are always swift, clinical and completely self-assured in their teenage aggression. It is instant sex, instant ejaculation; never a failure. He has remained for ever the adolescent rejected by his mother, endlessly seeking elsewhere the solace that he can never find. (On rare occasions, he *has* described his sexual encounters in other than swift, animalistic terms. For example, the "little countess" on the transatlantic liner coming back to Europe for his visit to Liège in 1952 who "has an orgasm once, twice . . ." before "at the moment when she senses I am going to ejaculate", gently pushes him back, points to Denise and says, "No! for her . . ." Or his claim to writer John Mortimer that he "always let prostitutes have their pleasure first. And of course I was enough of a connoisseur to know if their pleasure was faked." But is not this boasting itself adolescent – and, indeed, like many juvenile claims of sexual prowess, not entirely to be believed?)

The comment of a professional psychiatrist is of value. Says Dr. Pierre Rentchnick: "His is a very primitive sexuality. He sees a little maid walking past – he pulls up her skirt, and there we are! He is a sexual machine. One erection, one woman; but it could be anyone. He doesn't give a damn for his partner. I remember once going to the Motor Show here in Geneva and Simenon was there with Denise. I said to myself, I know how he is going to choose his cars. It'll be exactly how he makes love – no preparation, no romance. And I was right! The whole thing took five minutes; he bought three cars in five minutes. 'I'll buy this one!', it was a Rolls-Royce; and then Denise said, 'I'll buy that one!', and it was a Mercedes; and then they saw another one and they bought it for the chauffeur. No normal car lover would have proceeded that way. It was just like three orgasms."

Simenon was at that time a car lover; his autobiographical writings abound with talk about cars and their makes. He bought his cars as he made love to his women – and as he wrote his novels – in quick, thrusting bursts.

The claim to have made love to 10,000 women fits into the picture of this perpetual adolescence. "Certainly in this story of 10,000 women there is an exhibitionism," says Dr. Rentchnick. "The *alter ego* disputes with him and says that he has also known a lot of women – more than *him*! These are the sort of exploits that young men of fifteen and sixteen brag about between themselves."

On a factual basis, the figure of 10,000 does stand up to examination; provided one takes as the basic statistic three different women a week. (Simenon has also claimed that it was three women a day but this would mean that, starting at the age of thirteen, he would have reached the 10,000 mark by the time he was twenty-two – which really does seem too far fetched.) Three women a week makes 156 a year, which would give him sixty-four years to reach his total. Starting in 1916, that would take him to 1980; and he made his proud claim in 1977, some three years earlier. Knocking off three years for the time he was out of action owing to the Fontenay-le-Comte radiologist's mistaken diagnosis, that would be approximately correct.* That is clearly what Simenon meant when, in the second interview (in *Die Tat*), he said that he had checked the record and found his original calculation right.

Yet the question remains: why, at the venerable age of seventy-four make the claim at all? What has it got to do with anyone else? Why embarrass one's family?

Clearly, as Dr. Rentchnick says, part of the explanation is sheer exhibitionism on a teenage scale, and there is certainly nothing new about Simenon broadcasting the facts of his private life – and that of those close to him – from the rooftops. And you could say that it is a very Anglo-Saxon, and therefore irrelevant, reaction to be disturbed about the age at which such a claim is put forward. Annette de

*This is not so remarkable as it may seem. Simenon has said that he once had sex with four prostitutes in one afternoon while his wife was packing the bags for a trip to New York.

Bretagne, for example, with a typically Gallic shrug, can see nothing wrong with it from that point of view and most of her countryfolk would probably agree.

Nevertheless, there would seem to be a sadder, more sombre explanation for Simenon's twice-repeated, almost desperate outburst. No longer anything like the man he once was, buffeted by life, in far from robust health, all too aware of his waning physical powers (of which sex is only one manifestation) and of the irrevocable loss of his creative genius, he makes a platform from which to cry out his defiance at old age and to present himself still as the rampant, dynamic figure of his earlier years. The claim itself may sound like a boastful schoolboy but the circumstances in which it is made are worthy of King Lear.

In the end, the two most significant relationships that Simenon has had in his long life – and an understanding of which are essential to the unlocking of his mystery – have not been with any of his 10,000 women. Nor have they been with either of his two wives or with Teresa, his third and ultimate companion. They have been with his mother and his daughter: the only two women closely tied to him in a blood bond.

His tragedy is that the one rejected him – and he *had* to reject the other.

The frustrated search for his mother's love blighted, in his inner being, the triumphant years of his success. The sadness of his daughter's love has embittered the final years of his so-called "serenity". In both, there is an element of guilt. Simenon has never really been able to purge himself entirely of his sense of shame and selfishness in leaving behind the recently widowed, pensionless Henriette – "a woman in mourning, in long black veils", as he evocatively described her in *Lettre à ma mère* – when he left Liège. And he still carries a tremendous burden of guilt for not having realised earlier the true, warped nature of his daughter's love for him; for not having done far more than he ever did to help her, to guide her, to lead her away from the path towards self-destruction. "He can only love his children for himself and not for them," says Denise, not without bitterness; and for once her judgment is right.

As early as the age of eight, Marie-Jo showed that her love for her father bore within itself the seeds of something more than the pure devotion of a child for her parent. She insisted that he buy her, not an ordinary ring or a little girl's bauble, but a miniature wedding ring:

THE KEY TO THE MYSTERY

a true facsimile of the ring that a man puts on a woman's finger when he takes her as his wife. Thereafter, as she grew older, she had the ring made larger so that she could continue to wear it and, when finally she took a shotgun and put a bullet through her heart, she left a message for her father that he should have her cremated with the ring still on her finger.

He chose her dresses for her until she was in her early teens. In the photographs, she looks up at him with her child's eyes full of a love and hero-worship that disturb by their sense of complicity. She fell ill and had to follow her mother to the psychiatric clinic at Prangins. She runs away from there to Paris at the age of eighteen, but in her subsequent letters he remains *Mon bon vieux Dad* and she continues to write to him only in terms of the greatest affection. It is not from *him* that she is seeking to escape. In *Mémoires intimes*, Simenon admits that as far back as when she was only sixteen, he felt himself more and more worried by Marie-Jo, who at that stage he already regarded as "the weak link of the family", throwing herself into so many different activities with a "disturbing frenzy".

But he gives her no effective help. He has always preached (perhaps as a reaction against his own childhood) that children should be allowed to grow up in absolute freedom, with no guidelines laid down by their parents. So he indulges his daughter, with whom he is besotted and who, in his eyes, can do nothing wrong. "I have always been concerned for her," he told a reporter of the French magazine, *Le Nouvel Observateur*, shortly after the publication of *Mémoires intimes*. "I offered her everything that she wanted. She wanted to do painting; so I gave her an art teacher. She wanted to do classical dancing; so I gave her a classical dancing instructor and I had installed in her playroom a ballet dancer's *barre* and a mirror two metres by three. Afterwards, she wanted to do modern dancing. Above all, she wanted to write, and at the end of *Mémoires intimes* I have published just a small part of the hundreds of letters that she has sent me. She classified them herself, year by year, for me to publish them. She asked me to do that in 1973."

Indeed, his memoirs bear on the cover the words: "Followed by the Book of Marie-Jo", and his selection of her letters and cassettes makes up the last 136 pages of the book. The memoirs begin *"Ma toute petite fille"* ("My dear little child") and take the form of a letter, primarily to her (although also to his other children), seeking to explain himself to them, just as earlier he had written *Je me souviens* as a letter to the infant Marc. "Dad felt he had to write that book," says John. "At one time, he told me that he thought he might never live to finish it."

245

Why this deep feeling of obligation to the child who killed herself? *He* did not pull the trigger and the strong view of Simenon and Marc, and to a lesser extent John, is that if any human being other than the tragic Marie-Jo herself is to blame, it is Denise – whose book, *Un oiseau pour le chat*, came out only two months earlier and had caused a tremendous scandal with its "exposure" of Simenon. "One discovers a man who is pretentious, egoist, a drinker, literally unlivable with," wrote, for instance, the reviewer in the newspaper *Le Soir*. Marc himself found a copy of the book, with passages describing Simenon's alleged failings underlined by Marie-Jo, lying beside her dead body. "I was very close to my sister," he says. "She lived here [in his house at Poigny-la-Forêt] for twelve years before she moved to her little studio over the *Lido* on the Champs Elysées where she died. She was looking for the father that she remembered from her childhood – but he no longer existed. Too many things had happened to change him. So in a way I had to become her father. The tragedy is that in the last few weeks before she died, she had been on the way to recovery. My stepmother's book caused her final collapse . . . Denise really demolished her father to Marie-Jo. To a large extent, she was the real culprit.

"I saw Marie-Jo three days before her death and I would never have thought she would go as far as that. She had already made five or six attempts to kill herself, with pills and that sort of thing, but they had all been cries for help. This was premeditated. The police inspector told me it is very rare that a woman shoots herself in the chest. That is a man's way of committing suicide. She must have been very brave."

As might be expected, Denise denies that her book had anything to do with the suicide of her daughter. She says that she saw her in Paris the week that she killed herself and that Marie-Jo told her how much she liked the book. She speaks with tears in her eyes of her love for her daughter and of the two large photographs of her that she keeps, one in each of her two homes, so that she is never without her. She says that she does not believe Simenon's version of Marie-Jo's last wish that she should be cremated, wearing her "wedding ring", and her ashes scattered in the garden of his "little pink house". "I believe she wanted her ashes scattered at Epalinges," she insists.

In *Mémoires intimes*, Simenon discloses for the first time the full circumstances of an incident that occurred in February 1974, four years before his daughter's death, and one which opened his eyes fully to the true nature of Marie-Jo's feelings for him.

It was on the very day that Teresa and he moved into their small mews house in Lausanne. Marie-Jo, who was in town, came to visit them and, after a while, Teresa left the two of them alone. Marie-Jo looked at her father in a way that he says he was "frightened to understand". "Why her and not me?" she demanded, as if stifling her anger. "You don't understand, my little child," he replied. "Understand what?" He pointed to the double bed that stood in the corner of the room – "Teresa shares *all* my life."

"So what?" replied his daughter, then nearly twenty-one years of age. She showed him the gold wedding ring that he had given her as a child. "All that she can do for you, I can – can't I?"

His entry for that date – February 8, 1974 – in the current volume of his dictated memoirs, *Des traces de pas*, merely contains the statement that he has received at his daughter's hands "one of the hardest shocks of my life". He gives no details. He says it is "a purely family matter". But he goes on to say that all that was between them is "now broken. Perhaps it was her fault, perhaps mine. It's rather as if, on the eve of her twenty-first birthday, relations have been brutally broken off between us. I feel completely crushed. I suddenly had the impression of a stranger standing before me, not even a stranger, but an enemy."

Des traces de pas was published in the following year and Marie-Jo, a dedicated reader of her father's works, would certainly have read it. It is difficult to see any possible reason for branding his daughter to the world as "an enemy" and for causing such pain to her in the process. Nor can one readily understand the sudden sense of horror that he proclaims. Was it vanity, lack of interest or deliberate blindness that had veiled his eyes all those years? He knew full well of her terrible feelings of guilt, of her continually washing her hands, like Lady Macbeth, in vain search of cleanliness, of her pitiable attempts to escape from the phantom in her head that she called "Madame Anxiety" and of her desperate, idolatrous love for him.

In *Mémoires intimes*, after giving the full version of what Marie-Jo had said to him, he quietly adds the comment: "I had always feared what suddenly I then discovered." But he *still* publishes *Des traces de pas* a year later with the reference to his daughter as "not even a stranger but an enemy" intact!

The incestuous link that bound Marie-Jo to her father continued up to the last hours of her life. At eleven o'clock on the morning of Friday, May 16, 1978, she telephoned him at home. "I love you, Dad . . . Tell me that you love me also," she said. "I love you infinitely, my dearest," he replied. "No, I want you to tell me, without any more, simply: 'I love you'." Simenon, relating this conversation in *Mémoires intimes*, says that he felt troubled by her insistence: "*Tell me, 'I love you'*." Tenderly, he pronounced the words: "I love you." He wanted to say more – but she put down the receiver. He tried to call her back, but there was no reply.

Later that day, having bought herself a shotgun (as one can do legally in France, without a licence), Marie-Jo tidied up her flat, put everything in order and sat down to write her father two brief dis-jointed letters. "Take care of yourself, for me, for all that I was not able to be," she told him. Then she took the shotgun and shot herself through the heart.

When next day Marc, worried because he had not heard from her for twenty-four hours, let himself into the flat with his key, he found her lying dead. Near the body was a second bullet she had bought in case the first one failed. But it had not been necessary. Her hand had been steady.

For the rest of his life, Simenon will mourn the death of his daughter, but it is a grief tinged with guilt. The guilt may be shared with Denise, but it is one of which he is all too conscious. *Mémoires intimes* is not written for Marie-Jo, as he would have his readers and his remaining children believe. It is written for himself. It is a work of expiation – although, even several months after it had been published, he still could not be one hundred per cent honest about it: "Everyone else was writing about me. I thought it was time to tell the truth," he told John Mortimer in the London *Sunday Times* interview of May 1982. Vanity – and self-centredness – can go no further.

The relevance of Marie-Jo's tragic story to Simenon's own life and to an understanding of his character is that it exposes, alas, his funda-mental weakness as a person. It bears out Denise's remark that he loves his children for himself and not for them.

It is his first wife, the robust Régine, who gives the vital clue to unlocking his personal mystery: "Throughout all his writings," she says, "he seeks himself. *He* is 'the naked man' whom he is searching to describe in his novels."

Sadly, the "naked man" that he seeks so hard to find is, in his own case, exactly that, naked – or, to vary the metaphor and, indeed, to make it more accurate, *empty*. Simenon is a magnificent receptacle, an inner world manufactured by nature for the creatures of his subconscious to inhabit. In his lecture at the World Fair in Brussels that was quoted in the first chapter of this book, he defined the novel as "a passion that completely possesses and enslaves the writer and permits him to exorcise his demons by giving them a form and casting them out into the world." In the very core of his being, Georges Simenon does not exist. In his *L'Express* interview with Fellini, there is this vitally significant passage: "It isn't because one searches for human contact that one finds it. One finds more often emptiness, doesn't one?"

His search all his life has been an impossible one: the emptiness of a man searching for over half a century for the love of a mother who never loved him. It has been a quest into the hollow centre of someone who functions as an automaton, whose body and mind are taken over by his "demons", the creatures of his subconscious.

He seeks for human contact because in his very heart he feels himself lacking in humanity. He *is* a phenomenon, although he hates the word. He creates, therefore he exists. And when he can no longer create new images and fresh personalities in his later, failing years, he turns back on himself and his family and makes out of them the *dramatis personae* of his final and greatest novel: the story of his own life. The man who nearly forty years earlier had written *Pedigree* partly to free himself from the real-life characters of his childhood so that he had space in his imagination to create new ones, now has, in his barren years, only the raw material of his own intimate experience to draw upon. He has lost little of his ability as a storyteller, so that the result is still fascinating and a considerable commercial success; but it is all very far from the calm worldliness of the books about Maigret.

In nothing does Simenon more clearly exhibit his capacity for selfishness and cruelty than in one crucial passage of *Mémoires intimes* in which he cites, from a cassette left behind by Marie-Jo, the tortured young woman's description of an incident which she said occurred when she was eleven years of age and which made her "never able in my life to be a real woman in front of men." It is a most painful account of how she claims that at that tender age, her mother, with her legs stretched wide in front of her, masturbated herself before the child's eyes.

Denise, in *Un oiseau pour le chat*, freely admits that, as early as the age of six, she had happily practised masturbation and "confessed" it to her priest. It became her "besetting sin", to which she tried to return for solace in the anguished months after marriage with Simenon failed – only to find that it no longer gave her any pleasure. "My childhood had disappeared."

Simenon further claims, in *Mémoires intimes*, that Denise has admitted to her doctor at Prangins that Marie-Jo's account is true.

Even so, how can that justify Simenon wishing to print it, and emblazon it to the world? In November 1981, after only 30,000 copies of his book had been printed, Denise succeeded in obtaining from the French High Court in Paris, despite Simenon's objections, an order deleting the passage and allied extracts from all later editions (there are just blank spaces to bewilder the reader in the subsequently printed text) as "an extremely grave violation of her private life".

Simenon palpably believes Marie-Jo's account to be true. He calls it his dead child's "secret". He would seem to regard it as the thing that ruined most her hopes of happiness and led almost inevitably to her death. But even if this is so, Simenon himself, as we have seen, must share some of the responsibility for his daughter's fate.

Nothing can bring the dead girl back to life. There can be no satisfactory explanation, therefore, for imposing such heart-ache upon Denise as to make public this sort of material – unless it be to assuage Simenon's *own* sense of guilt. What has happened to this great man's sense of compassion? Counsel for Denise branded his conduct before the Parisian court as "unspeakable" putting her, as it did, in the position of being unable to defend herself or free herself from the crushing weight "of an insupportable moral responsibility". There is much force in this contention. However deep and sincere is Simenon's grief for his lost child, this hardly seems the same person whose noble motto once was: "Understand and do not judge."

"I have said everything," Simenon told an Associated Press reporter towards the end of 1981, when commenting on *Mémoires intimes*. "It will be my last book to be published during my lifetime. There will not be another one." One hopes that is so. He has suffered much. He has also caused much suffering. Yet he deserves his peace. One can only hope that his demons are at last exorcised.

He is in excellent health, for a man of his age. Three times a week a physiotherapist visits him for exercise sessions. There are occasional sorties to Valmont, the luxurious clinic-hotel high in the hills just a few miles along the banks of Lake Geneva. Teresa watches over him with a care that would do credit to a mother – or a nurse. "How I love that music!" she exclaims with ecstasy, when he taps out his pipe against an ashtray.

Contrary to all his previous demands for "lack of artifice" in a woman's appearance, with cosmetics and painted fingernails banished from his gaze, the latest photographs show a man who has started to dye his own hair: a youthful dark brown, worn somewhat long, has taken the place of the white head of hair trimmed neatly at the neck. "I adore life but I don't fear death," he tells the Associated Press reporter. "I prefer to die as late as possible."

The final mystery is Teresa. Despite her twenty years or more with Simenon, she remains an enigmatic figure; always by his side but rarely sharing the limelight. Indeed Simenon has gone out of his way to protect her from publicity and prying eyes. Nevertheless one thing is certain: Teresa has brought Simenon a large measure of happiness in his last years. At whatever moment it may come, the old newspaperman can await, without too great a sense of urgency, his last great deadline.

Index

NOTE: Simenon's works are listed together under the English title where there is one, otherwise in French, as Works

INDEX

Casanova, 238–9
censorship, wartime, 124–5
Cervi, Gino, 218
Chagall, Marc, 225
Chaigneau, Pierre, 135, 153–4
Chandler, Raymond, 1
Chanel, Coco, 126
Chaplin, Charles, 227, 235
characterisation, 68, 80–1, 227, 233
Château de la Cour-Dieu, 112
Château de Terre-Neuve, Fontenay, 134–7, 143–4
Chevalier, Maurice, 125, 187
children, attitude to, 6–7, 45, 46, 47, 117–21, 136, 173–4, 177–8, 188, 196–7, 210–11, 230–1, 237, 244–8
Christie, Agatha, 8, 88, 221
Clair, René, 126
Clouzot, Henri-Georges, 127
Cocteau, Jean, 126, 149, 187
Colette, 54, 146
Colin, Paul, 51, 76
collaboration, wartime, 125–6, 153–4
Collins, Carvell, 227
Colombia, visits, 102
Comédie Française, 125
Conan Doyle, Sir Arthur, 83, 87
Continental Film Company, 127
Cortot, Alfred, 125
country life, 93–5, 112, 117, 131–2, 134–136, 145–56, 178–9
Cowley, Malcolm, 41
critical response to, 2, 91, 103, 110, 115, 123, 156, 164, 181–2, 220–1, 222, 226, 229–30, 235–6, 241–2
Czechoslovakia, visits, 101

Damia, singer, 92
danger, love of, 31, 34, 55–6, 98
Darrieux, Danielle, 125
Davies, Rupert, 217, 218
death, attitude to, 22, 37–8, 250, 251
Deauville, France, 77
decline, literary, 220–1, 222, 224, 226, 227, 228–33, 234
Delfzijl, Holland, 64–6, 70, 71, 72, 77, 116, 218
Demarteau, Joseph, 29–30, 33
Demengeot, Mylene, 58, 138

Detective magazine, 65, 71–2, 74
Dindurand, Jim, 135, 136
Dissane, Odile (pseud.), 159
divorce, 173–5, 184, 214–15
dreams, 28
Duboart, Maurice, 221
Duvivier, Julian, 92

early writing, 26, 32–3, 47–8, 50, 52–4
East Indies, visits, 102
Egine, Jean-Louis, 2
Egypt, visits, 96–7
Einhorn, Maurice, 142
Embourg, Belgium, 24
Epalinges villa, 5–6, 16, 206–7, 208, 209, 210, 211, 213, 214, 215, 216, 228, 229, 232
Eriau, Doctor, 147, 148, 151, 152
Echandens, Swit., 199–200, 202, 218, 222
Etretat, France, 57
exotic novels, 103–8

Fabre, Jean, 229
Fallois, Bernard de, 110
fantasy, GS's, 3–4, 28, 66, 83, 103, 154, 188
Faulkner, William, 3, 19
Fayard, Arthème, 70–1, 73, 74–6, 82, 95–6, 108, 109, 111, 182
Fayard, Jean, 182
Fécamp, France, 61, 64, 68, 77, 80, 224
Fellini, Federico, 238–9, 249
films, 77, 83, 90–2, 119, 123, 126–7, 135, 162, 208, 217–18, 220
Fischer, Doctor, 27, 28
Flanner, Janet, 77–8
'flashback' technique, 53–4
Foch, Marshal, 30
Fontenay-le-Comte, France, 132, 134–7, 143–4, 153, 179, 243
food, love of, 22, 41, 42, 237
Forces Français de l'Interieur (F.F.I.), 153–4
Franco, Victor, 232
French Foreign Legion, 171, 172
Fresnay, Pierre, 126

Gabin, Jean, 51, 126, 187, 217, 221
Galapagos Islands, visits, 102, 103
Gallimard, Claude, 138–9

INDEX

prolific output, 1–2, 52–3, 74–5, 77, 83, 90, 95, 117, 164, 180, 181, 200, 220
prostitutes, 5, 23, 32, 39, 43, 55, 98–9, 212, 242
Pryce-Jones, David, 124, 126
pseudonyms, 52, 53, 73
publishers, 110, 124–5, 157, 164, 182

Quadi-Halfa, Belgian Congo, 97

Raimu, 119, 126, 208
Rattigan, Terence, 241
Raymond, John, 226
Réalités, 162
reality, flight from, 115–16, 127
Reggiani, Serge, 126
Reichstag, burning, 100
religious belief, 21–2, 23, 25, 28
Renchon, Régine, *see* Simenon, Régine
Renchon, Yvan, 120
Renaud, Madeleine, 125
Renoir, Jean, 77, 90–1, 126, 187
Renoir, Pierre, 77, 91, 217
Rentchnick, Pierre, 4, 86–7, 154, 194, 242, 243
restlessness, 7, 51, 55, 59, 65, 89–90, 114, 234
revues, 47–8
Ricaumont, Jacques, 230
Richard, Jean, 217, 218
Richardson, Maurice, 40, 78, 104, 126, 156
Rinaldi, Angelo, 236
Riviera, life on, 78, 90, 190–1
Robinson, Cap, 176, 179, 189
Robinson, Orpha, 185
"Roches Grises" villa, 90
Romance, Vivienne, 125
Ronet, Maurice, 162
Ruhmann, Heinz, 218
Rumania, visits, 101
Russian literature, 19–20

Sachs, Maurice, 41
'sacred monsters', 127–8, 195, 221
St Mesmin-le-Vieux, France, 144, 145–156, 163, 176
Sartre, Jean-Paul, 125
Schneider, Romy, 123

self-knowledge, 3–4, 25, 127, 234–5, 236, 248–9
sex life, 3, 5, 39, 43–4, 55–8, 87, 90, 98–9, 101, 108, 118–19, 136–7, 149–50, 160, 168–9, 182–3, 185–6, 195–6, 205–6, 239–44; "10,000 women", 4–5, 23, 238–40, 243–4; early, 20, 23–5, 30–2, 242
Shadow Rock Farm, Lakeville, 176–80, 183
Sigaux, Gilbert, 110, 164, 181
Signoret, Simone, 221
Sim, Georges (pseud.), 26, 30, 33, 52, 73
Simenon, Chrétien (grandfather), 10
Simenon, Christian (brother), 17, 19, 20–1, 97–8, 101, 170–2
Simenon, Denise (wife), 127, 157–60, 162–3, 168–70, 237–8, 249–50; alcohol problems, 192–4, 199, 202, 206, 214; business affairs, 184–5, 193, 197, 199, 206–7; and fame, 185, 187; hatred of, 4, 158, 208, 249–50; illness, 186–9, 199, 202, 207–13; love, 169, 170, 205, 238; marriage, 4, 159, 173, 174, 182–4, 184–91, 195–6, 201–3, 206–8, 212–13; *Oiseau pour le Chat, Un*, 158–9, 169, 182, 200, 204, 209, 246; *Phallus d'Or, Le*, 159–60; separation, 208–9, 213–15, 224
Simenon, Désiré (father), 9–10, 12–13, 14, 15, 17, 18, 27–8, 31, 34, 36, 37–8, 45, 68
Simenon, Georges: childhood, 13–17, 18–22; divorce, 173–5, 184, 214–15; family background, 9–17; jobs, 28–37, 41–2, 48–9; marriage, 4, 37, 44–7, 57, 148, 149–50, 160, 174–5, 184–91, 199–200, 201–3, 204–8, 209–10; retirement, 6, 233, 234–5, 236–8, 250–1; schooldays, 18–22, 25, 26, 27; works, *see under* Works
Simenon, Henriette (mother), 36, 44, 45, 185; background, 10–11, 15–17; marriage, 10, 12–13, 18, 222; personality, 17, 18–19, 26, 183–4, 215–16; and GS, 26–7, 30–1, 140, 141, 170, 184, 230, 241–2

257